The Dollar Paradox

The Dollar Paradox

Why America Must Borrow to Stay Rich

The Ultimate Answer to Why the U.S. Must Pay Interest on Money it Could Print for Free.

by

BOSCO MUTARAMBIRWA

DARWIN BOOKS

AN IMPRINT OF STERLING ANALYTICS MEDIA

NEW YORK

Published by:

Darwin Books, an Imprint of **Sterling Analytics Media**

New York | London | Kinshasa

For permission requests, contact:

Email: contact@darwinpublications.com

Website: www.darwinpublications.com

Paperback ISBN: 979-8-9936653-6-8

eBook ISBN: 979-8-9936653-7-5

Cover Design and Interior Layout by **Darwin Books Studio**

Printed in the United States of America

10 9 8 7 6 5 4 3 2 1

Dedication

To my family, who patiently endured countless hours of late-night research, lived through my constant debates on hyperinflation, and provided the unshakeable foundation that made this work possible.

A Note to Christopher and Aiden

As you stand on the brink of adulthood, you will be told many things about money, success, and the world. Forget the noise and remember this one simple truth about systems, just like the one detailed in this book:

The greatest asset you will ever own is your institutional credibility.

Financial systems, political systems, and personal relationships all run on trust. Learn the difference between **debt** (which is merely a tool) and **solvency** (which is having more value than you owe). Don't focus on *how much* money you make; focus on **how valuable** you are. Value is built through skill, consistency, and showing up when you said you would.

Be honest, be dependable, and choose growth over complacency. That is the only true currency that can never be printed away.

ACKNOWLEDGMENTS

This book, by its nature, is a synthesis of complex ideas drawn from history, academia, and the high-stakes world of global finance. It would not have been possible without the wisdom, generosity, and critical insight of many people.

I owe a debt of gratitude to the academic economists and central banking historians whose foundational work—particularly on the 1951 Accord and the nature of sovereign debt—formed the bedrock of Part I. To the professional market participants who shared their insights into the mechanics of the repo market, the Treasury auction process, and the quiet truth of "collateral scarcity," thank you for shedding light into the dark plumbing of finance.

A special thank you to my early readers and anonymous peer reviewers, whose sharp questions forced me to clarify the most counterintuitive points of the paradox, ensuring the final narrative was as accessible as it was accurate. Your critique was invaluable.

Finally, and most importantly, thank you to my family and friends, who believed in this project from the moment the title was conceived. Your support is the most precious resource of all.

Table of Contents

GLOSSARY

A quick-reference guide to the book's central concepts, institutions, and technical terms.

Access Risk — The risk that a holder of an asset may be prevented from using, transferring, or realizing it even if the issuer performs flawlessly. The 2022 immobilization of Russian central-bank reserves made access risk far more prominent in global reserve management.

Bretton Woods System — The post-World War II international monetary order created in 1944, under which the U.S. dollar was convertible into gold for foreign official holders and other major currencies were pegged to the dollar. Its breakdown in the early 1970s marked the transition to the modern fiat-dollar era.

CBDC (Central Bank Digital Currency) — A digital form of central-bank money denominated in a country's national currency. Depending on its design, a CBDC may be used by financial institutions, the general public, or both, and may incorporate varying degrees of privacy, traceability, or programmability. It differs from decentralized cryptocurrencies such as Bitcoin.

CIPS (Cross-Border Interbank Payment System) — China's cross-border payment, clearing, and settlement infrastructure for renminbi transactions. CIPS supports the international use of the yuan and can reduce reliance on traditional correspondent-banking channels, although it is not a one-for-one replacement for SWIFT.

Collateral — An asset pledged to secure a loan or other financial obligation. U.S. Treasury securities are among the world's preferred forms of collateral because of their credit quality, market depth, liquidity, and transparency.

De-dollarization — The process by which countries, institutions, or market participants reduce their reliance on the U.S. dollar for trade invoicing, reserves, borrowing, or settlement. It may be driven by economic diversification, geopolitical concerns, sanctions risk, or a desire for greater monetary autonomy.

Debt Service Cost-to-GDP Ratio — Government interest costs expressed as a share of Gross Domestic Product. It is an important measure of how burdensome debt service is relative to the size of the economy and is more informative than the absolute dollar amount of debt alone.

Exorbitant Privilege — A phrase associated with French finance minister Valéry Giscard d'Estaing in the 1960s describing the advantages the United States enjoys as issuer of the world's primary reserve currency, including deep demand for dollar assets, comparatively favorable financing conditions, and the ability to borrow in its own currency.

g > r — The fiscal relationship in which the economy's growth rate (g) exceeds the effective interest rate on government debt (r). When g exceeds r, the debt-to-GDP ratio is easier to stabilize or reduce, all else equal. When r exceeds g, fiscal arithmetic becomes less forgiving.

Geopolitical Default — A term used in this book for a financial rupture in which a sovereign is prevented from accessing assets because of political decisions by the jurisdictions or institutions that hold them, rather than because the asset issuer cannot pay.

Golden Guardrail — The central metaphor of this book: the web of laws, institutions, market practices, and political constraints that keeps the fiscal Spender from controlling the monetary Printer. The Guardrail imposes visible costs and market discipline on borrowing so that direct monetary financing does not become the easy political option.

Hyperinflation — An extreme and accelerating loss of a currency's purchasing power, usually associated with severe fiscal and monetary breakdown and a collapse in public confidence. Historical examples discussed in this book include Weimar Germany, Zimbabwe, and Venezuela.

Interest Rate Parity — A no-arbitrage relationship linking interest rates and foreign-exchange prices. Under covered interest parity, the forward exchange rate should offset the interest-rate differential so that comparable, currency-hedged returns are closely aligned across currencies.

Iron Law of Separation — The term used in this book for the institutional separation between the government's fiscal authority and the Federal Reserve's monetary authority. Legal restrictions, including the Federal Reserve Act's open-market framework, prevent the Treasury from simply ordering the central bank to finance its spending directly.

Liquidity — The ability to buy or sell an asset quickly, at scale, and with limited effect on its price. The U.S. Treasury market is among the deepest and most liquid securities markets in the world, helping make Treasuries benchmark safe assets and collateral.

Petrodollar System — The practice of pricing and settling much of the world's oil trade in U.S. dollars, reinforced by network effects, financial infrastructure, and the recycling of oil-exporting countries' surpluses into dollar-denominated assets.

Policy Trap — The term used in this book for the danger of responding to fiscal stress with policies that undermine either growth or monetary credibility, especially excessive austerity on one side or direct monetary financing on the other.

Primary Dealers — A select group of financial institutions that serve as trading counterparties of the Federal Reserve Bank of New York. They are expected to bid on a pro-rata basis in Treasury auctions at reasonably competitive prices, make markets in government securities, report market activity, and participate consistently in relevant Federal Reserve market operations.

Programmable Money — Digital money designed so that specified rules or conditions can be attached to its use, such as where, when, or for what it may be spent. Some digital-currency systems can support programmable features, but programmability is not inherent to every CBDC.

Quantitative Easing (QE) — A monetary-policy tool in which a central bank purchases large quantities of longer-term securities, such as Treasury securities or agency mortgage-backed securities, to put downward pressure on longer-term interest rates, support market functioning, and ease broader financial conditions when conventional policy tools are constrained.

Repo Market (Repurchase Agreement Market) — The short-term secured funding market in which institutions borrow and lend cash against securities, especially U.S. Treasuries. Many repos are overnight, although longer terms are also common. The repo market is a critical part of the plumbing of global finance.

Reserve Currency — A currency held by central banks, governments, and other institutions as part of their foreign-exchange reserves and used widely in international trade and finance. The U.S. dollar is the world's primary reserve currency.

Reserve Neutrality — The term used in this book for the expectation that official reserve assets should remain broadly insulated from political interference. Earlier precedents existed, but the scale and coordination of the 2022 immobilization of Russian central-bank reserves sharply challenged that assumption.

Spender and Printer — The book's shorthand for the fiscal and monetary sides of the U.S. system. The Spender encompasses Congress, which authorizes federal spending, and the Treasury, which executes payments and finances deficits. The Printer is the Federal Reserve, which manages monetary conditions and creates central-bank money. The Iron Law of Separation keeps the two functions institutionally distinct.

Stealth Tax — The book's metaphor for the additional financial pressure that dollar dominance can transmit abroad through borrowing costs, exchange rates, capital flows, and exposure to U.S. monetary policy. It is not a literal tax collected by the U.S. government.

SWIFT (Society for Worldwide Interbank Financial Telecommunication) — The Belgium-based global financial messaging network used by banks and other institutions to transmit standardized payment and securities instructions. SWIFT does not itself hold or transfer funds, but access to its network is critical to international finance and can become consequential in financial sanctions.

Treasury General Account (TGA) — The federal government's primary operating account at the Federal Reserve. Tax receipts and borrowing proceeds flow into it, and federal payments flow out of it. The account cannot be overdrawn, so Treasury must maintain sufficient cash to meet authorized obligations.

Treasury Securities — Debt instruments issued by the U.S. Department of the Treasury, including bills, notes, bonds, Treasury Inflation-Protected Securities (TIPS), and floating-rate notes. They finance federal borrowing and serve as benchmark safe assets and collateral throughout the global financial system.

Weighted Average Maturity (WAM) — The average remaining maturity of outstanding marketable Treasury debt, weighted by the amount of each security. At the end of fiscal year 2025, WAM was about 71 months, or roughly six years. Managing WAM helps Treasury balance refinancing risk against borrowing cost.

INTRODUCTION

The Question That Kills Common Sense

It is the most frustrating, common-sense financial question in the world, and it is the single greatest reason that American finance feels like a deliberate political conspiracy to the average citizen: **Why does the wealthiest nation on Earth borrow money it can simply print?**

Every taxpayer, investor, and casual observer knows three simple, undeniable truths:

1. **The King Dollar:** The U.S. dollar is the undisputed reserve currency that fuels international trade, diplomacy, and stability.
2. **The Mountain of Debt:** The federal government is buried under a staggering accumulation of trillions that grows every second.
3. **The Printer:** The Federal Reserve—the powerful, independent central bank—has the exclusive, digital authority to create more dollars with the stroke of a key.

When these three facts collide, the result is the massive, infuriating contradiction that defines modern finance: **The Dollar Paradox.**

Why do we send billions of dollars in interest payments to foreign competitors like China when we have an unlimited digital source of that same currency sitting in Washington? Why does the government beg for cash in global markets, paying a premium to store its liabilities, when it could simply fund its own infrastructure, education, and medical programs with fresh dollars, cutting out the middleman entirely?

The common perception is that this is either a deliberate act of sabotage, a catastrophic failure of intelligence, or a sign of impending national bankruptcy. It certainly *feels* insane. The costs associated with this borrowing ritual are tangible and corrosive: money spent on interest is money not spent on fixing failing infrastructure, money not supporting local schools, and money not funding relief for the burdened middle-class taxpayer. It traps the American worker on a **Taxpayer Treadmill**, watching dollars disappear into a debt vortex while vital domestic needs go unmet.

The Counterintuitive Truth

This book will reveal the counterintuitive truth: The reason the U.S. borrows dollars is not because it is broke, not because it is stupid, and not because it is desperate. It is because of a single, non-negotiable economic imperative: **the preservation of institutional credibility, and the fear of inflation.**

The entire ritual of borrowing is a sophisticated, self-imposed restraint designed to protect the very value of the dollar that the world depends on. The moment the government chooses to print money to pay its bills, the dollar commits suicide, and the world—and the U.S. economy—collapses into financial ruin, a lesson learned tragically from historical failures like the Weimar Republic (Chapter 2).

The paradox is maintained by the absolute separation of two critical functions, enshrined in the **Iron Law of Separation** (Chapter 3):

1. **The Spender:** The political body that determines spending and receives money (The Treasury Department).
2. **The Printer:** The independent economic body responsible for maintaining the value of that money (The Federal Reserve).

The debt is not a liability; it is the **Golden Guardrail** that prevents the Spender from ever controlling the Printer. The borrowing ritual is the institutional handshake that allows the political spending to occur without immediately destroying the currency. The **Mountain of Debt** is the world's safest, most liquid collateral—the ultimate form of savings—and the interest payment is the **rent paid for global power.**

What This Book Reveals

The Dollar Paradox is a comprehensive journey into the mechanics, history, threats, and future of this essential financial ritual.

Part I: The Foundation establishes the two houses of finance and the history of why borrowing became mandatory, culminating in the pivotal 1951 Accord (Chapter 7) that institutionalized the Fed's independence.

Part II: The Mechanics of the Ritual dives into the plumbing of the system, detailing the roles of the Treasury (the debt product manufacturer), the Federal Reserve (the central broker), and the massive global **Repo Market Engine** (Chapter 8). We examine how foreign buyers accumulate this debt and the resulting geopolitical leverage (Chapter 9).

Part III: The New War addresses the contemporary challenges to the dollar's supremacy, including the **De-Dollarization Narrative** (Chapter 11), the rise of **Central Bank Digital Currencies (CBDCs)** (Chapter 12), and the risk of **Geopolitical Default** explored in Chapter 10.

Part IV: The Policy Choice moves from analysis to prescription, dismantling the myth of austerity and advocating for the **True Policy Path** (Chapter 15): a relentless focus on maximizing productive national **Growth** to outpace the debt, while examining how to sustain the Golden Guardrail in a multi-polar future (Chapter 16) and manage the conflict between trade deficits and tariffs (Chapter 17).

This is a story of power, fear, and discipline. To understand the debt is to understand American power, and to understand the paradox is to understand why, even with a digital printing press, the world's most powerful nation must remain perpetually subject to the painful, transparent judgment of the global market.

PART I

The Foundation of the Paradox: Why Borrowing is Mandatory

Chapter 1

The $30 Trillion Question

The Mountain and the Myth

The United States' national debt is not a sterile accounting entry tucked inside a government spreadsheet; it is a living symbol that shapes public emotion and political imagination. It stands before the citizenry like a colossal mountain—its summit obscured by clouds of rhetoric, its slopes etched with the anxieties of generations. Every day that mountain grows, measured in billions of new dollars, and every day it provokes the same visceral response: *How can this be sustainable?*

To the average American, the figure—thirty-something trillion—feels like a mortgage on the nation's future. It conjures a grim picture: their children forever laboring under a debt they never chose. Each paycheck garnished by invisible interest, each tax season a treadmill of frustration. The metaphor is powerful because it borrows from personal experience. Households know the fear of debt; they live it. And so they imagine the nation as a reckless household scaled to the size of an empire.

But this metaphor—so emotionally satisfying, so morally convenient—is also catastrophically wrong. It confuses the fear of a family with the function of a superpower. A government that issues its own currency plays by different rules entirely, yet the emotional imprint of the household remains. The result is a permanent sense of national exhaustion: taxpayers feel they are running harder just to stay in place, feeding an insatiable system that never sleeps. Welcome to the Taxpayer Treadmill.

The Mythology of Scale

Numbers this large lose meaning. To restore perspective, try converting time into money:

A million seconds equals eleven days.

A billion seconds equals thirty-two years.

A trillion seconds reaches back thirty-one thousand years—before the first cities were built.

Now multiply that by thirty. That is the debt.

Once numbers exceed the human capacity to visualize, they stop being information and become mythology. "Trillion" ceases to describe a quantity and begins to evoke a mood—alarm, confusion, moral panic. Politicians understand this instinctively. The figure's very incomprehensibility makes it the perfect weapon. Hold up a red-ink chart, shake your head gravely, and you can win an argument without evidence. Scale itself becomes persuasion.

The irony is that the panic such theatrics induce rarely leads to restraint. It breeds cynicism instead. Citizens tune out, convinced that no reform can matter at those magnitudes. The number, meant to awaken responsibility, anesthetizes it.

The Cost of Trust

Yet behind the mythology lies a real cost—the interest payment that never sleeps. That annual bill, measured in hundreds of billions, is not optional. It arrives before Congress funds soldiers, schools, or science. Economists call it "debt service." Ordinary people call it robbery of the future. In truth, it is the toll a democracy pays to remain credible.

Interest is not a moral punishment but a market price—a constant public referendum on America's reliability. When investors buy Treasury bonds, they lend faith, not charity. The interest rate is what faith costs. As that price rises, taxpayers feel the incline steepen beneath their feet. They are running harder—paying more—simply to stay where they are.

Projections now show the cost of interest soon overtaking national defense. For a country that equates strength with firepower, this is an unsettling inversion: the greatest superpower on earth will spend more defending its reputation in markets than defending its borders. The line item called "net interest" is not just an expense; it is the mirror of trust.

The Treadmill Effect

Every dollar of tax revenue has a first destination. Before it repairs a road or funds a hospital, it is legally earmarked for mandatory obligations—Social Security, Medicare, interest on existing debt. Only what remains can be debated in the halls of Congress. That inversion of priorities explains the unease that colors public life. Citizens feel the drag of yesterday's promises on today's possibilities.

The treadmill accelerates whenever rates rise. Politicians call it a "fiscal squeeze," but to the citizen it feels like gravity itself—an invisible pull that makes progress harder. The paradox deepens: cutting spending can slow growth, while borrowing more risks higher rates that demand even more spending later. The treadmill has no finish line because the finish line is the motion itself.

The Moral Shadow of Debt

Debt provokes a deeper discomfort than arithmetic can explain. It challenges the nation's self-image of virtue. From Puritan ledgers to modern credit scores, Americans have equated solvency with moral worth. "Neither a borrower nor a lender be," said Shakespeare, and the advice survived the Atlantic crossing. Fiscal prudence became civic religion.

This is why debt debates sound like sermons. Politicians invoke grandchildren as prophets of future reckoning. Pundits speak of discipline, repentance, and sin. The Mountain of Debt becomes a mountain of guilt. Yet the same nation that preaches thrift also worships growth, innovation, and risk—all impossible without borrowing. The contradiction is not hypocrisy; it is civilization's engine: ambition pulling against restraint, fear against faith.

To understand why the United States deliberately subjects itself to this exhausting ritual—why it insists on borrowing instead of printing, why it treats interest as sacrament rather than waste—we must descend into the architecture of the system itself. The treadmill is not chaos; it is choreography. The next section unpacks the mythology of household finance that misleads the public and reveals the five fallacies that separate the debtor family from the sovereign nation.

The Mythology of Scale and the Cost of Interest

When the national debt passes thirty-trillion, the number itself stops functioning as information. It becomes theater—large enough to silence reason, vivid enough to feed outrage. Politicians use it the way magicians use distraction. "Look how huge it is!" they cry, while the real story happens in the smaller print—the interest cost, the structure of borrowing, the mechanism of discipline.

The true burden of debt isn't the principal; it's the *rent* America pays on trust. Interest is the price of remaining credible to the world. Every year that rent grows, quietly eroding the space in which new dreams fit. It is the nation's mortgage payment on confidence itself.

In 2025, the annual interest bill is projected to exceed the entire defense budget. That means the United States will spend more protecting the dollar's reputation than protecting its territory. It's a stunning image: aircraft carriers and missiles on one side, Treasury coupons on the other—and the coupons win.

To most citizens, this is infuriating. They imagine interest as waste, money that vanishes into the ether. But interest is also income: pension checks, insurance reserves, mutual-fund dividends. The treadmill that exhausts the taxpayer feeds the retiree. The system recycles pain into stability.

Why the Interest Bill Exists

Every federal budget begins the same way: before Congress debates a single discretionary dollar, the Treasury must meet its mandatory payments—entitlements, contractual obligations, and, above all, interest. Only what remains can be negotiated. That legal hierarchy makes debt service the first claimant on every taxpayer's dollar. It's why voters feel perpetually shortchanged; their taxes arrive, but the money seems to vanish into yesterday's promises.

If rates rise, that first claim grows louder. Politicians then face the cruel arithmetic of trade-offs: cut benefits, raise taxes, or borrow more. Each choice breeds another round of public anger, another headline about fiscal insanity. Yet beneath the noise, the logic holds: paying interest keeps the system honest. It is the reminder that power still costs something.

The Illusion of the Household

To the average voter, debt feels personal. They imagine Washington as a family that refuses to tighten its belt. "If I can't live beyond my means, why can they?" It's a moral question disguised as an economic one—and it's wrong in every meaningful way.

A family borrows in a currency it cannot issue; the U.S. borrows in a currency it prints. A family must earn income before it spends; the U.S. spends to create income. A family can go bankrupt; a currency-issuing government cannot—at least not in its own money.

The household metaphor survives because it comforts. It turns the infinite complexities of macroeconomics into the familiar drama of parental discipline. But what works at the kitchen table collapses in the Capitol. The nation's balance sheet isn't a morality tale; it's an operating system.

Breaking the Illusion: The Five Fallacies

1. The Currency Constraint

A household is a *currency user*; it must find dollars before it can spend them. The U.S. government is a *currency issuer*; it creates dollars when it spends. The difference is not semantic—it is structural. A family's solvency depends on income; a sovereign's depends on credibility. The danger for a family is default; for a nation, it is debasement. The United States could always print its way out of nominal debt, but doing so would shred the very trust that makes its money valuable. Hence the paradox: it can print, yet it chooses to borrow.

2. Taxation as Demand, Not Funding
For households, taxes are an expense. For the sovereign, taxation is a design feature. Taxes create permanent demand for the currency: citizens must acquire dollars to pay them, ensuring the dollar's universal acceptance. The government does not tax to get money—it taxes to give money value. This single insight turns the moral story upside down. Paying taxes isn't merely civic duty; it's participation in a monetary ecosystem. The IRS is not the collector of solvency; it's the engineer of legitimacy.

3. Bankruptcy vs. Inflationary Default
A family that cannot pay its mortgage loses its home. A nation that over-prints loses its purchasing power. The courtroom equivalent is the grocery store: where the price of bread becomes the judge. Hyperinflation is the sovereign's bankruptcy—a default not in law but in trust. Germany's wheelbarrows in 1923, Zimbabwe's trillion-dollar notes, Venezuela's empty shelves—all tell the same story. Printing solves the short-term pain but kills the long-term promise. The U.S. avoids this fate by making debt expensive on purpose; the pain of interest is its inoculation against panic.

4. Debt as Global Collateral
For households, debt is a burden; for the U.S., it is export merchandise. Treasury securities are the world's preferred form of collateral—the foundation of the global credit market. Banks, hedge funds, and central banks all use Treasuries as the risk-free asset that makes modern finance possible. Remove that supply and the global system would seize up like an engine starved of oil. Far from signaling weakness, America's debt is proof of confidence: the world's demand for safety manifests as a craving for U.S. IOUs.

5. Perpetual Debt as Stability
Families dream of zero balance; nations require rollover. The government's debt never truly "ends." Maturing bonds are replaced by new ones, ensuring a continuous supply of safe assets. Stability, not elimination, is the goal. Attempts to extinguish the debt would

yank the foundation out from under global finance—exactly what happened after World War I when nations rushed to pay down obligations and instead collapsed growth. The debt, paradoxically, is what keeps capitalism liquid.

The Moral of the Fallacies

Each fallacy survives because it flatters common sense. It makes economics moral, politics simple, and complexity ignorable. But nations are not families, and money is not virtue. The borrowing ritual—the auctions, the ceilings, the endless noise—is not evidence of failure; it is evidence of restraint. The United States pays for credibility in cash so that it never has to pay for chaos in kind.

These fallacies explain why the U.S. submits itself to a painful process it could technically bypass. Borrowing imposes discipline; printing would destroy it.

The Origin of the Paradox: The Institutional Discipline

The U.S. financial system is not an accident of paperwork; it is an intentional act of self-restraint. It was built not to maximize freedom, but to contain it. After centuries of empires that ruined themselves by merging political will with monetary power, America chose separation as its form of wisdom.

This separation—between the power to spend and the power to print—is the foundation of everything that follows. It is not a bureaucratic quirk but a civilizational choice: to protect prosperity from politics. The system is designed to make borrowing painful, so that printing never becomes easy.

Pain, in this context, is not punishment; it is discipline encoded in law. The architects of the modern dollar understood that without friction, democracy would devour itself through generosity. They made sure the government could never fund its promises by simply turning on the presses. Instead, every dollar spent must be raised in public, under the gaze of markets that judge, price, and penalize excess. That is the ritual Americans mistake for dysfunction. It is, in fact, the performance of restraint.

The Spender vs. The Printer: A Battle of Incentives

The paradox lives within two machines that must cooperate without touching—the Spender and the Printer. Together they power the economy; apart they preserve its sanity.

The Spender—Treasury and Congress.
This is the political organism, driven by emotion, ideology, and ambition. It writes budgets, funds wars, promises pensions, and cuts taxes. Its nature is centrifugal—it spends outward, pleasing voters and deferring consequence. The Spender lives on applause. Every election reaffirms its appetite.

The Printer—The Federal Reserve.
This is the economic organism, insulated by design from the noise of democracy. It sets interest rates, regulates banks, and guards the dollar's purchasing power. Its nature is centripetal—it pulls inward, restraining euphoria, cooling inflation, and defending value. The Printer lives on credibility.

Between them lies tension as old as civilization: the temptation of power to create money versus the necessity of trust to preserve it. If the Spender ever controls the Printer, the result is disaster. History has no gentler word for it—hyperinflation. The collapse is not slow; it is instant. The printing press, once politicized, burns the currency it produces.

That is why the U.S. made the most radical decision in monetary history: to divorce its political will from its monetary muscle. It created a system where the government must beg for the very money it has the authority to create. The begging is the point.

The Golden Guardrail: Pain as Credibility

The separation between the Spender and the Printer is maintained by a web of laws and rituals collectively known as the *Golden Guardrail.* It is the invisible barrier that keeps the Republic from the easy road to ruin. The Guardrail doesn't stop spending; it makes spending expensive, converting political desire into financial consequence.

It operates through four stages of discipline—each one deliberately inefficient, each one essential to trust.

1. The Decision to Spend — Where Politics Becomes Debt

Every act of spending begins with Congress and the President authorizing programs that outstrip tax revenue. The moment a budget passes, a legal obligation is born. The Treasury now owes payments it cannot fund with existing cash. The decision is political, but the debt it creates is real. At this point, the nation's promises exceed its purse, and the cycle begins.

Here lies the first truth of American finance: *spending creates the need for borrowing, not the other way around.* The deficit is not an accident; it is the footprint of democracy's ambition.

2. The Forced Borrowing — The Iron Law of Separation

Unlike many nations in crisis, the U.S. Treasury cannot ask the Federal Reserve to print money to cover its bills. By law, it must raise funds from the market. This is the Iron Law—the literal separation of the Spender and the Printer. The Treasury must sell bonds, in public view, to investors willing to buy them at market-determined interest rates. It must endure scrutiny before spending a dime.

Even the *debt ceiling,* so often mocked as political theater, plays a moral role. It forces Congress to face the consequences of its past votes, to publicly acknowledge the cost of its own promises. The limit may always rise in the end, but the debate itself is democracy's stress test—a reminder that every dollar borrowed is borrowed in the open.

3. The Market's Judgment — The Price of Faith

Once the Treasury issues bonds, the global market delivers its verdict. Every auction is a trial. Banks, pension funds, foreign governments—all submit bids. The result is a yield, the precise numerical expression of global confidence in America's word. When that yield rises, it is not punishment; it is correction. The market is telling the Spender, *we believe you less than yesterday.*

Unlike kings of old, who ruled by decree, the United States rules by consent—by the daily consent of investors who trust it enough to lend. The yield curve is democracy's report card written in numbers instead of words.

4. The Penalty — Interest as the Price of Supremacy

The final step of the Guardrail is the penalty itself: the mandatory interest bill. Every year, the Treasury must pay hundreds of billions in interest to those who financed its past decisions. This payment cannot be postponed or ignored; it ranks higher than almost every other expense. It is the inescapable cost of the promise.

To the citizen, this looks like waste. To the world, it looks like integrity. Those interest payments are the rent the United States pays to maintain the world's trust. They are the receipts of credibility. The moment they disappear—if the Treasury ever simply printed instead—the rent would vanish, and so would the empire built upon it.

The Pain That Saves

Every part of this ritual hurts. The debt ceiling scares markets. Bond auctions raise costs. Interest payments drain budgets. Yet each pain is a proof of health. The U.S. built a system where suffering is feedback—where the ache of interest replaces the agony of inflation. Nations that avoid pain die of indulgence. America institutionalized discomfort and, in doing so, achieved endurance.

The Golden Guardrail is not elegant. It is noisy, inefficient, and politically exhausting. But that noise is civilization's heartbeat. It is the sound of temptation being denied.

The Guardrail keeps the Spender and the Printer apart—but not idle. Between them lies a marketplace that transforms government promises into global currency.

Chapter 2

The King Dollar's Global Mandate

The King's Temptation

Every civilization that mastered money has eventually faced the same seduction: the belief that the printing press can outwit pain. Rome diluted its silver denarius to pay legions it could no longer afford. Revolutionary France printed *assignats* backed by confiscated church lands until bread cost millions. Each generation rediscovers the same mirage—the idea that wealth can be created faster than work, that governments can spend without consequence.

For the United States, the **Golden Guardrail** described in the previous chapter is the vaccine against that temptation. America borrows, suffers, and pays precisely because it remembers what happens when others didn't. To grasp why that pain is worth trillions, one must walk through history's monetary graveyards. Hyperinflation is not a technical glitch; it is the political unification of the Spender and the Printer—the moment the king seizes the mint.

The Original Sin: The Political Temptation of the Printing Press

Every episode of hyperinflation begins with an emergency and ends with an excuse. The emergency can be war, drought, collapse, or populist promise. The excuse is always the same: *we had no choice.*

Printing appears painless—no debt-ceiling spectacle, no market auctions, no foreign creditors to placate. It delivers cash without conflict, votes without taxation, applause without delay.

Three illusions drive this behavior:

1. **Zero-Cost Illusion** – Borrowing demands interest; printing feels free. The sovereign convinces itself that creating currency is cheaper than earning credibility.
2. **Frictionless Politics** – Debate vanishes. The treasury becomes its own ATM, and accountability dissolves.

3. **Infinite-Supply Illusion** – Numbers can rise forever, therefore wealth must too. But reality—labor, raw materials, productivity—cannot be printed.

The flaw is ancient: confusing *money* with *wealth*. Money is a claim; wealth is what the claim buys. Creating more claims without producing more goods simply divides the same pie among more plates. The first slice tastes generous; the meal soon disappears.

The Mechanism of Collapse

Hyperinflation obeys a brutal psychology: confidence dies, velocity rises, and money becomes memory.

Stage 1 – The Inflationary Tax

It starts quietly. The government prints to cover a shortfall—often after war or recession. Liquidity feels like relief. Then prices drift upward; savings buy less. Citizens sense a stealth tax—purchasing power stolen by policy.

Stage 2 – The Velocity Shock

Fear replaces patience. Holding cash becomes self-harm. Money accelerates through the economy: *buy now, before it costs more tomorrow.* Shops change prices hourly. Payrolls shorten from monthly to daily. Economists record velocity; families experience chaos.

Stage 3 – Currency Rejection

Eventually citizens refuse their own money. Wages arrive in wheelbarrows and leave in baskets of bread. Barter returns. Taxes go unpaid because no one wants the legal tender required to pay them. Once trust evaporates, no decree can recall it.

CASE STUDY:
The Weimar Republic (1921–1923)

Germany's collapse after World War I remains the definitive lesson in monetary hubris. The Treaty of Versailles demanded reparations of roughly **132 billion gold marks**—payable in gold or foreign currency, not paper. The defeated nation faced three choices: raise taxes and risk revolt, borrow abroad and accept humiliation, or print. It printed.

At first, printing worked. By 1922 factories hummed again; unemployment fell. Politicians called it stimulus. But each new mark devalued the last, forcing ever more printing to buy the same foreign currency. The loop tightened: print → devalue → print again.

German statistics tell the scale of ruin:

- January 1922 – 160 marks bought a loaf of bread.
- January 1923 – 250 marks.
- November 1923 – 200 billion marks.

Prices rose **29,500 percent per month**. The currency's half-life was four days. Families burned banknotes for heat; children flew them as kites. Teachers and civil servants saw lifetime savings vanish.

The disaster was moral as much as monetary. The social contract—work, save, prosper—disintegrated. Humiliation bred extremism; extremism, dictatorship. Every modern central banker studies Weimar as scripture: *Thou shalt never let the Printer obey the King.*

Why Weimar Still Matters

Today's economists dismiss wheelbarrows as relics, yet Weimar did not begin with madness—it began with compassion. Each small act of printing was justified, rational, humane. Only in hindsight did the sum reveal catastrophe. Hyperinflation is never declared; it is discovered.

For the United States, the memory endures not as guilt but as guidance. Every Federal Reserve chair—Volcker, Greenspan, Bernanke, Yellen, Powell—has invoked Weimar's lesson before Congress: *credibility once lost is almost impossible to regain.* The cost of borrowing, however high, is cheaper than the cost of disbelief.

Modern Echoes of Collapse

Weimar's ghosts did not stay in Europe. They crossed oceans, resurfacing whenever politics drowned out prudence. The pattern—crisis, printing, collapse—repeats perfectly: a government faces shortage, convinces itself that ink can substitute for production, and discovers again that faith cannot be fabricated.

Zimbabwe: Printing for Power

At independence in 1980, Zimbabwe was southern Africa's breadbasket. By 2000, after mass land seizures that expelled farmers producing 40 percent of export revenue, output halved within three years.

President Robert Mugabe's government ordered the central bank to "provide liquidity"—bureaucratic code for *print money*. By 2007, inflation exceeded **1,000 percent**; by mid-2008 it hit **231 million percent**. Prices doubled daily. Workers carried backpacks of cash; shops repriced goods twice a day. The Reserve Bank eventually issued a **100-trillion-dollar note**, worth less than US $1.

By 2009 the currency was abandoned for U.S. dollars and South African rand. Savings, pensions, and trust vanished. The mechanism was simple: production fell, the Spender captured the Printer, and faith died.

Venezuela: The Oil Mirage

Venezuela began its downfall not in poverty but in prosperity. Oil provided over 90 percent of export revenue and financed vast subsidies. When prices collapsed in 2014, so did the treasury. Barred from borrowing abroad, President Nicolás Maduro turned to the printing press.

Between 2016 and 2019 the money supply grew **one million percent**. Inflation surpassed **10 million percent** according to the IMF. By 2019, a monthly wage bought a carton of eggs. Hospitals ran out of medicine; seven million people fled the country.

As in Zimbabwe, politics met arithmetic and lost. The tragedy was not ideological; it was mathematical.

The Universal Law of Hyperinflation

These collapses look spectacular because they end in ashes. Yet behind the spectacle lies a universal principle: when the political authority erases the cost of spending, money erases its meaning.

Hyperinflation respects no ideology. It has struck monarchies and Marxists alike. Printing is not finance; it is confiscation by stealth—transferring wealth from savers to the state, from the cautious to the connected. In the end, it devours the legitimacy it sought to sustain.

And yet, not every violation of the Guardrail ends in instant currency death. Some nations bleed slowly. Two modern democracies show what chronic disobedience looks like.

The Chronic Cases: Argentina and Turkey

If Weimar, Zimbabwe, and Venezuela represent the spectacular implosion of trust, Argentina and Turkey embody its slower decay. Their currencies have not yet died, but neither do they live fully. They limp forward—kept alive by habit, not faith.

Argentina: The Habit of Inflation

A century ago, Argentina ranked among the world's richest nations. In 1913, its GDP per capita rivaled France and Germany. Buenos Aires was known as *the Paris of the South*. Then came the steady corrosion of institutions. Fiscal populism became the national rhythm: overspend in prosperity, monetize in decline.

Since 1950, Argentina has **defaulted nine times** and entered **22 IMF programs**. The 1980s brought inflation averaging over **200 percent**; by 1989, prices doubled every few weeks. A reform in the early 1990s, the Convertibility Plan, pegged the peso one-to-one with the U.S. dollar, and for a decade stability returned. But politics cracked the peg. By 2001, the government borrowed heavily to maintain parity, defaulted, and devalued.

In the 2010s, deficits again widened. The central bank financed the treasury directly. Inflation passed **100 percent in 2023**, according to Argentina's national statistics agency. Citizens now measure time by prices: wages arrive on Friday and vanish by Monday.

Cash dollars serve as the true store of value. Real estate is priced in greenbacks; landlords quote rent in U.S. currency even though contracts must nominally list pesos. Argentine economists joke grimly that their currency has "nine lives, none of them stable." A peso can circulate, but it cannot convince.

Turkey: The Politics of Denial

Turkey's story is the mirror opposite—a fast-growing emerging market that chose ideology over arithmetic. For years it was an economic success: strong exports, modern infrastructure, and moderate inflation. Then, beginning in 2018, President **Recep Tayyip Erdoğan** announced a new creed: *"Interest rates cause inflation."*

From that moment, monetary policy became theater. The president fired every central-bank governor who raised rates against his wishes—four in less than four years. Between 2019 and 2023 the lira lost more than **80 percent** of its value. Official inflation peaked near **85 percent** in late 2022; independent estimates placed it above **100 percent**.

Stores re-tagged goods daily. Savers fled to dollars and gold. The government imposed price caps and accused grocers of "economic sabotage." Yet factories still ran, airports still gleamed, tourists still arrived. Turkey had not collapsed; it had adapted—an economy functioning in permanent distrust.

Each month of high inflation shifted wealth from workers to the well-connected: those who could borrow cheap lira and repay in cheaper lira profited; the salaried majority paid the invisible tax. Chronic inflation became not an error but a political model—an instrument of power that rewards speed over stability.

Chronic vs. Terminal: The Spectrum of Decay

Argentina and Turkey prove that collapse is not binary. Some nations explode; others erode. In both, the central bank exists in form but not in freedom. The treasury dictates policy, and interest rates obey elections, not economics. Economists call it **fiscal dominance**—when politics controls the cost of money.

Weimar burned its currency to ashes in two years. Argentina has smoldered for decades. Turkey may smolder for decades more. The tempo differs; the melody is the same: the loss of separation between the one who spends and the one who prints.

The Lesson for the Dollar

For the United States, these stories are not curiosities; they are warnings. Every congressional hearing that scolds the Federal Reserve, every headline about rising rates, every televised debt-ceiling fight is proof that the Guardrail still stands. Noise is health. Conflict means distance. Distance means independence.

If markets ever sense that the Federal Reserve has become an arm of the Treasury, they will treat the dollar as they treat the peso or the lira—still useful, no longer sacred. Credibility cannot be declared; it must be suffered for. America's pain—its deficits, debates, and interest costs—is the receipt of restraint.

The Architecture of Restraint

The Guardrail's genius is its universality: it does not depend on virtue, only on structure. It assumes politicians will always overspend and central bankers will always overtighten. By separating their powers, it converts human weakness into systemic strength.

The borrowing ritual, with all its inefficiency and theater, is the price of immunity. It is the insurance policy against the fate of every nation in this chapter. The rule is simple but absolute: **the Spender must fear the Printer, and the Printer must fear the People.** Between those fears lies stability. Break that triangle, and history repeats itself.

The Iron Law of Separation: The American Firewall

The United States built its financial constitution on memory. Every catastrophe in this chapter—Weimar, Zimbabwe, Venezuela, Argentina, Turkey—serves as a ghost in its design. The Founders separated powers in politics; modern policymakers separated powers in money. The **Iron Law of Separation**—dividing the Spender from the Printer—isn't an administrative convenience. It is survival made legal.

The idea is brutally simple: the Treasury may promise, but it cannot print; the Federal Reserve may print, but it cannot promise.

Between them lies a moat of law that no crisis may cross. The pain of borrowing replaces the poison of inflation.

Section 14(b) of the Federal Reserve Act enshrines this moat. The Fed may purchase Treasury securities **only "in the open market," never directly from the Treasury.** That single clause—the most consequential comma in American finance—prevents the union of political appetite and monetary muscle that doomed every nation described earlier. Every federal dollar must pass through a market auction, face investors, and bear a price. *Pain first, stability later.*

The Federal Reserve: Designed to Say No

The Federal Reserve's independence is not decorum; it is discipline. Its governors serve staggered fourteen-year terms precisely to outlast presidents. Its dual mandate—**price stability** and **maximum employment**—forces it to disappoint everyone at least half the time.

When inflation rises, the Fed tightens. Politicians call it sabotage; markets call it sanity. In 1981, Chairman **Paul Volcker** raised rates above 20 percent, triggering the worst recession since the Depression but ending a decade of runaway prices. His unpopularity was the measure of his success.

Modern chairs inherit that creed. They testify before Congress not to please it but to warn it. Their weapon is credibility; their enemy is expedience. In every crisis—from the 2008 financial meltdown to the pandemic— the Fed has expanded its balance sheet but kept to the Guardrail: buying Treasuries **only after** markets set their price, and pledging eventual reversal. That ritual tells investors what Weimar forgot: *pain is temporary, trust is forever.*

Why Independence Matters

If the Fed were ever folded into the Treasury—if the Spender commanded the Printer—the dollar would instantly lose its status as the world's "risk-free" asset. Investors would demand inflation insurance; yields would surge; borrowing costs would skyrocket. The global system—built on U.S. collateral—would quiver. The entire purpose of the borrowing ritual is to make that scenario unthinkable.

The debt, therefore, is not a symptom of dysfunction but the receipt of discipline. America borrows publicly to prove it will never print privately. The interest bill is the invoice of credibility—the annual fee for belonging to the world's trust club.

From Kings to Congress

From kings who ruled by decree to democracies that rule by consent, every government faces the same question: *Who commands the money?* The United States answered not with rhetoric but with architecture. The Iron Law of Separation ensures that even the most powerful democracy must still kneel before the market.

We have walked through the ruins of paper empires and the slow bleed of modern economies. Each failure whispers the same warning: money dies when it becomes politics.

Chapter 3

The Two Financial Giants

The Wall That Saves the Dollar

The distinction between the **Spender** (the U.S. Treasury—the political arm) and the **Printer** (the Federal Reserve—the monetary arm) is not etiquette. It is law, machinery, and survival. The Iron Law of Separation is the quiet engineering that keeps the world's reserve currency from self-destruction.

Every morning, in the subterranean data rooms of the Federal Reserve Bank of New York, servers execute millions of transfers through a single ledger—the Treasury General Account. The screens look ordinary; the stakes are civilizational. If the Treasury could spend without limit, the United States would become the next chapter in the history you just read. The wall between the Spender and the Printer is the firewall between order and inflationary anarchy.

The Legal Framework: How the Wall Was Built

The Iron Law's legal foundation emerged from crisis. After the Great Depression, Congress realized that money could not serve two masters. The **Banking Act of 1935** completed a process begun in 1913: it created a central bank strong enough to act, yet distant enough to refuse.

Before 1935, the Treasury routinely leaned on the Fed to keep interest rates low and to finance deficits—especially during World War I and the 1930s recovery. The arrangement blurred fiscal and monetary authority. Inflation followed. Lawmakers concluded that political will and monetary power must never share a desk.

The result was an institutional divorce written in the most consequential paragraph of American finance: **Section 14(b) of the Federal Reserve Act.**

Section 14(b): The Forbidden Shortcut

Section 14(b) allows the Federal Reserve to buy and sell U.S. Treasury securities—*but only in the open market.*
It **forbids** the Fed from purchasing new government debt directly

from the Treasury. In plain language: the Printer may never hand the Spender a blank check.

Why it matters:

1. **Market Price Discovery** – The Treasury must sell its bonds to private investors first. Only after the market sets the interest rate may the Fed intervene. Every auction subjects government promises to a real-time vote of confidence.
2. **No Direct Funding** – If the Fed could buy directly, Congress could spend at will, setting its own interest rate of zero. Money would lose meaning overnight. The Iron Law forces humility: every dollar spent must first survive public scrutiny.
3. **The Historical Exception** – Beginning in 1942, Congress temporarily authorized limited direct purchases of Treasury obligations by Federal Reserve Banks, subject to a statutory cap. Congress renewed that authority for decades, but it was allowed to expire in 1981. Today, Federal Reserve purchases of Treasury securities are conducted in the open market.

That single legal barrier is why America's debt is still considered safe. It ensures that every borrowing decision carries visible cost. Pain replaces temptation.

The Operational Barrier: Where Law Meets Wires

The Iron Law is not only legal; it is physical. The Treasury and the Federal Reserve inhabit the same marble buildings but operate on different ledgers. The **Treasury General Account (TGA)** at the New York Fed is the government's one and only checkbook. It cannot overdraft.

The Treasury General Account (TGA)

Every federal payment—Social Security checks, military payrolls, Medicare reimbursements—flows through the TGA. Its funding sources are strictly limited to three:

1. **Taxes** – Cash drawn from the productive economy.
2. **Borrowing** – Proceeds from Treasury securities sold to investors.
3. **Existing Balances** – Surplus cash left from previous cycles.

Printing money is not on the menu.

When Congress passes a spending bill, Treasury accountants verify that the TGA contains sufficient funds. If not, the Treasury must choose: raise taxes or issue more debt. It cannot simply summon dollars from the ether. This mechanical dependency is the Iron Law rendered in code.

The Flow of Funds

Consider a stimulus payment sent to a household in Ohio:

1. Congress authorizes the expenditure.
2. The Treasury initiates the payment.
3. Funds are drawn from the TGA.
4. The Fed—acting only as banker—transfers those dollars to a private bank account.

At no point does the Fed "print" money for the Treasury. It merely moves existing balances. The Treasury is an enormous, politically noisy customer—nothing more. If the TGA ever hit zero and Congress failed to raise the debt ceiling, the government's ability to pay bills would stop cold. The screens would flash red, and the nation that prints the global currency would discover that it cannot print for itself.

The Debt Ceiling: Politics as Ritual

The Debt Ceiling is Washington's most misunderstood drama. It does not authorize new spending; it exposes old promises. It is the political expression of the Iron Law—the moment when Congress confronts the cost of its own past generosity.

When the ceiling is reached, the Treasury cannot issue new debt. Payments continue only as long as cash remains in the TGA. The spectacle terrifies markets, yet it forces an essential truth into daylight: even the United States must publicly debate its addiction to credit.

The debate's value lies not in its outcome—Congress always raises the limit—but in its visibility. Democracies maintain discipline through embarrassment. The Debt Ceiling ensures that borrowing remains painful, visible, and argued over in front of cameras.

Without it, deficits would expand quietly, invisible to voters. The Iron Law would erode in silence.

Why the Pain Is Necessary

Economists often describe this architecture as inefficient. It is. But inefficiency is the point. The friction—the auctions, the debates, the ceilings—is the cost of integrity. Each barrier reminds the Spender that the Printer does not obey. The visible pain of borrowing is the invisible anchor of trust.

The Political Theater of Restraint

Each time Congress nears the debt ceiling, the world watches in disbelief. News anchors warn of default; markets tremble; foreign investors question American sanity. Yet behind the noise lies a strange genius. The ritual proves that even the issuer of the world's reserve currency must still bow to law.

The Treasury mails warning letters to Congress. The Fed counts down the remaining balance in the Treasury General Account. Cable networks broadcast tickers: *Days Until Default.* The anxiety is real, but so is the message to creditors: America is not indifferent to its debts. It may quarrel, but it will not quietly monetize. The shouting is the sound of the Iron Law holding.

To outsiders, this looks inefficient. To historians, it looks deliberate. Democracies institutionalize tension so that power never becomes silent. The debt-ceiling ritual is not a flaw; it is a scheduled confession.

When the Guardrail Seems to Bend: Quantitative Easing

If there is one policy that confuses the public—and fuels conspiracy theories—it is **Quantitative Easing (QE)**. To the casual observer, QE looks indistinguishable from money printing. The Fed creates reserves out of nothing and buys Treasury bonds by the trillions. How, then, is this not the Spender commanding the Printer?

The answer lies in **sequence and intent**.

1. **Sequence:** The Treasury issues bonds to private investors in a competitive auction. The Fed enters later, buying some of those bonds *from banks*, not from the Treasury. The market has already priced the debt. The Treasury has already received its money. No shortcut has occurred.
2. **Intent:** The Fed's goal is not to fund Congress but to stabilize interest rates and liquidity. When credit markets freeze—as in 2008 or 2020—the Fed buys assets to inject confidence and keep lending alive. Its action is *monetary policy*, not *fiscal rescue*. The difference is not semantic; it is legal.
3. **Reversibility:** QE is temporary. The Fed can later sell the bonds back, shrinking the money supply in a process called **Quantitative Tightening (QT)**. Direct funding, by contrast, is permanent and irreversible.

Every round of QE blurs the optics of separation but not the substance. The Iron Law survives because each transaction passes through the crucible of the market. The Treasury suffers the pain of price discovery before the Fed enters the scene.

A Moment of Global Confusion

During the COVID-19 pandemic, that distinction nearly vanished in the public mind. The federal deficit soared above **$3 trillion** in 2020;

the Fed bought similar amounts of Treasuries within months. Commentators called it "monetization by stealth." Yet the legal firewall held. Every bond still passed through an auction. Every rate was still set by competitive bidding.

The result was paradoxical: record spending without hyperinflation. Prices rose later—from supply shocks, not from the mechanics of QE. The system had stretched but not broken. The reason was structure, not luck. The Fed had acted as lender of last resort to markets, not as paymaster to the state.

This episode reinforced a hard truth: *form protects function.* The architecture mattered more than the rhetoric surrounding it. The Iron Law endured not because politicians respected it, but because they couldn't reach across it.

The Reversibility Principle

The reversibility of central-bank actions is the modern definition of integrity. When a policy can be unwound, trust survives. When it cannot, trust dies. QE expands the Fed's balance sheet temporarily; **direct monetization** would expand it permanently.

The difference is invisible to the public but obvious to the market. Investors know that QE creates reserves, not consumer cash; it affects bank liquidity, not grocery prices. That knowledge keeps yields low and panic contained.

Reversibility also grants accountability. Every bond the Fed holds can, in theory, be sold back. Each sale is a reminder that money creation is a lease, not a gift. The United States rents liquidity; it does not seize it.

The Shadow Critics

Hard-money purists and modern-monetary advocates both claim victory in this confusion. The former warn that QE is slow-motion debasement; the latter insist that since inflation remained tame, direct financing would be harmless. Both miss the core lesson of Chapter 2: *trust decays faster than data.*

Confidence in a currency is not an equation; it is an emotion. Once the public believes that money is political, no model can restore faith. The Iron Law is thus not only legal or mechanical; it is psychological. Its very visibility—the auctions, the ceilings, the public acrimony—keeps faith alive by showing restraint at work.

The Three Pillars of the Iron Law

Every safeguard described so far—Section 14(b), the TGA, and the Debt Ceiling—forms one pillar of the same structure.

1. **Law:** Prevents direct financing.
2. **Mechanics:** Forces spending to pass through real balances in the TGA.
3. **Politics:** Ensures the pain of debt is public, not hidden.

Together, they create redundancy. If one layer fails, another absorbs the shock. The law stops shortcuts; the mechanics expose deficits; the politics shame excess. The United States endures because it tolerates embarrassment better than inflation.

Why Other Nations Copy the Model

Since the 1990s, dozens of emerging markets have amended their constitutions or central-bank charters to mimic this structure. Brazil, Mexico, Indonesia, and South Africa all rewrote monetary laws to forbid direct government borrowing from their central banks. Each reform cited the American precedent.

Some have faltered under political pressure, but the design principle holds: independence is the only cheap insurance against national humiliation. It is easier to survive scandal than hyperinflation.

When the Guardrail Breaks

History's graveyard of currencies reminds us that the Iron Law is not self-enforcing. It survives only as long as governments fear to touch it. When that fear fades, law becomes suggestion and suggestion becomes inflation.

Japan is often cited as proof that a nation can blur the line safely: its central bank has bought more than **45 percent** of outstanding government bonds, and yet prices barely move. But Japan's miracle rests on context—deflationary demographics, domestic savers, and cultural tolerance for low returns. It is the exception that proves the rule. Its structure is still formally intact: the Ministry of Finance spends, the Bank of Japan buys in the market, and every purchase remains reversible. The day that separation is ignored in law rather than blurred in practice, the yen will learn the lesson of Weimar in a modern key.

The Hypothetical American Breach

Imagine a moment when Congress, paralyzed by gridlock, abolishes the debt ceiling "to avoid future crises." The Treasury, no longer constrained, issues debt at will. A populist administration, frustrated by rising rates, orders the Fed to buy the new bonds directly "for the good of the people." The Fed complies once—just once.

Within hours, yields plunge artificially; markets cheer. Within weeks, the dollar weakens. Foreign creditors whisper the word *monetization*. Investors demand higher yields on future debt. The Treasury pays more to borrow, not less. Inflation edges upward as confidence edges down. What began as efficiency ends as erosion. The firewall of credibility—built over a century—crumbles in a single press conference.

No tanks, no riots, no wheelbarrows; only screens flickering red as algorithms re-price American trust. That is how modern hyperinflation would begin—not with printing presses, but with policy slides.

The Cost of Credibility

Pain, in America's design, is not punishment; it is maintenance. Each interest payment is a receipt of trust purchased anew. The borrowing ritual is democracy's confession that it cannot be trusted with unlimited power. The moment borrowing becomes painless, the confession ends—and faith with it.

Every rule of the Iron Law serves one moral purpose: to make government live within visible limits. Section 14(b) makes printing illegal; the Treasury General Account makes overspending operationally impossible; the Debt Ceiling makes denial politically impossible. Together they force the world's most powerful nation to prove, over and over, that it still believes in consequence.

The Invisible Dividend

The reward for this discipline is invisible yet immense. Because investors believe the Fed will never print for politics, they lend to the U.S. at lower rates than to any other nation. That "trust discount" saves taxpayers **hundreds of billions** each year. It also anchors global finance: from Tokyo pension funds to Nairobi banks, all rely on Treasury securities as the benchmark of safety. The Iron Law keeps not just the dollar stable but the world liquid.

If credibility is the currency of civilization, the Iron Law is its mint.

The Human Angle

This architecture might feel abstract—clauses and ledgers, not people—but its consequences touch every household. The rate on a mortgage in Kansas City, the yield on a 401(k) in Atlanta, the price of food in Lagos—all are by-products of whether the U.S. obeys its own financial commandments. The citizen who complains about interest payments is unknowingly paying for the world's insurance policy. The cost is high; the alternative is chaos.

The Moral of the Machine

The Iron Law works because it humbles everyone. Congress must face voters; the Treasury must face markets; the Fed must face math. No participant gets what it wants. That mutual dissatisfaction is equilibrium. The absence of pleasure is the presence of order.

In the long run, stability is not built on efficiency but on friction well distributed. America engineered that friction into its bloodstream so that no single heartbeat could race ahead of the rest.

The wall between the Spender and the Printer is only half the system. Between them lies the marketplace—the silent jury that prices every promise. Chapter 4 enters that arena: the bond auctions where the world decides, minute by minute, how much faith it still has in the United States. There, pain becomes price, and credibility becomes yield.

Chapter 4

The Treasury: The Checkbook and the Mint

The Room Where Trust Is Sold

At exactly 1:00 p.m. in Lower Manhattan, a hush falls over a windowless room inside the Federal Reserve Bank of New York. On a bank of curved screens, figures stream faster than thought: trillions of dollars in bids, each flashing with a fraction of a basis point.
Every few seconds, a new order blinks into existence—from London, Tokyo, Frankfurt, São Paulo.
Within eight minutes, the world has decided what price the United States must pay to borrow money.

The ritual is unremarkable to the public and sacred to the markets.
This is the **Treasury auction**, the recurring moment when democracy's promises meet capitalism's calculus.
When the stop-out yield appears on the screen, a silent exhale ripples through global finance. The result determines everything from the cost of a Brooklyn mortgage to the yield on a Japanese pension.
It is here—not in Congress—that the world measures America's credibility.

The Beating Heart of the Dollar System

To the average citizen, the **U.S. Treasury** is a bureaucratic address that sends refund checks in April and warnings about the debt ceiling in October.
In truth, it is the **largest manufacturing operation on earth**, producing not cars or phones but the single most demanded product in human commerce: **U.S. Treasury debt.**

Its mission is existential.
The Treasury must ensure the federal government never runs out of cash to meet a lawful obligation—Social Security payments, military salaries, Medicare reimbursements, interest on prior debt—ever.
It fulfills this duty by continuously **designing, pricing, and distributing** securities that the world cannot live without.

Unlike a corporation that borrows for growth, the Treasury borrows for discipline.
Each auction is a public confession of need and a test of faith.
By submitting itself to the market's judgment, the Treasury transforms political will into financial consequence—the essence of the Golden Guardrail.

From Hamilton to High-Frequency Bidding

The ritual traces back to **Alexander Hamilton**, who in 1790 proposed consolidating Revolutionary-War debts into a single federal obligation.
That audacious move created both a bond market and a nation.
Through the Civil War, World War I, the Depression, and Vietnam, the mechanism evolved from handwritten ledgers to instantaneous digital clearing, but the principle never changed: every dollar the Republic spends must first face the public's price of belief.

When inflation ravaged the 1970s, Treasury Secretary **Michael Blumenthal** and Fed Chair **Paul Volcker** refined modern issuance calendars to restore confidence.
In 1992, the adoption of the **single-price (Dutch) auction** permanently democratized bidding, preventing favoritism and stabilizing participation.
Today, the same core idea Hamilton sold to skeptical congressmen still holds: trust is America's only irreplaceable export.

The Debt Product Line

The Treasury's catalogue is a masterpiece of financial engineering, built to match every conceivable time horizon and risk appetite.

1. Treasury Bills (T-Bills)

- **Maturity:** from a few days to 52 weeks.
- **Design:** sold at a discount, pay no coupon.
- **Function:** the purest cash equivalent in existence.

For global corporations, money-market funds, and central banks, the T-Bill is oxygen—risk-free, infinitely liquid, and instantly pledgeable.
Every dawn in finance begins with its yield; every crisis begins when that yield spikes.

2. Treasury Notes (T-Notes)

- **Maturity:** 2 to 10 years.
- **Coupon:** paid semi-annually.
- **Function:** the global yardstick for credit.

The 10-year Note is the world's reference rate for the price of time.
When it rises, mortgage costs climb, corporate valuations fall, and currencies realign.
A change of ten basis points can add $25 per month to a typical U.S. mortgage or erase billions in stock-market capitalization.

3. Treasury Bonds (T-Bonds)

- **Maturity:** 20 and 30 years.
- **Coupon:** semi-annual.
- **Function:** the ultimate promise.

Each long bond is a 30-year declaration that the United States will honor its debts through multiple presidencies, recessions, and wars.
Their buyers—pension funds, insurers, sovereign wealth funds—are the custodians of generational money.
Every successful 30-year auction is a global vote of confidence in the American future.

Debt Management as Art and Science

Inside the **Office of Debt Management**, a handful of economists balance three imperatives:

raise the cash the government requires, minimize long-term cost to taxpayers, and never surprise the market.

Their key metric, **Weighted Average Maturity (WAM)**, represents the average lifespan of all outstanding debt—currently around seven years.
Too short, and refinancing risk explodes: trillions must be rolled over constantly at whatever rates investors demand.
Too long, and taxpayers are shackled to high coupons for decades.

Managing WAM is less like budgeting and more like conducting an orchestra: thousands of instruments, one missed beat, and the harmony collapses.
Predictability itself is policy; a calm issuance rhythm is worth billions in reduced interest costs.

The Auction Ritual

Every Treasury auction is public theater staged with mathematical precision.
Dates are pre-announced months ahead; settlement occurs like clockwork.
At the appointed hour, bids stream into the **Fed's Automated Auction System**, encrypted and time-stamped.

The participants fall into two groups:

- **Competitive bidders**—large institutions specifying yield and quantity.
- **Non-competitive bidders**—smaller investors agreeing to accept whatever yield clears.

The system ranks bids from lowest yield (highest price) upward until the total amount offered equals the government's borrowing need.
The highest accepted yield becomes the **stop-out yield**, and every winner—big or small—pays the same price.

This **single-price rule** aligns honesty with advantage.
If investors sense higher risk, they demand higher yield; the cost to the Treasury rises immediately.
The market, not politics, decides what America's promises are worth.

A History Written in Auctions

After the terrorist attacks of September 11, 2001, investors fled to Treasuries, sending yields to record lows—proof that fear anywhere converts instantly into demand for U.S. debt.
During the 2008 crisis, when confidence in every private asset evaporated, only Treasury auctions still cleared with ease.
And in March 2020, when pandemic panic froze the world, the Treasury again met the market—and the market responded, proving that trust in the U.S. government outlasts trust in almost anything else on earth.

Each successful auction is a line in the nation's invisible constitution: credibility is renewed not by speech but by sale.

The Global Echo

Every Treasury result is a planetary signal.
A weak auction rattles currencies; a strong one steadies them.
Central banks recalibrate reserves, hedge-fund models update risk premiums, mortgage lenders adjust rates within hours.
The yield on a ten-year U.S. Note quietly dictates borrowing costs in dozens of countries that never voted in an American election.

In this way, the Treasury is both a national institution and a global utility.
Its auctions are not domestic finance events; they are the world's recurring referendum on American reliability.

The Gatekeepers of Trust: Primary Dealers

The Treasury may design the debt, but it cannot sell it alone.
Between the Spender and the global investor stands a select guild of financial intermediaries: the **Primary Dealers**—roughly two dozen

powerful institutions that serve as the market's permanent underwriters.
JPMorgan, Citigroup, Goldman Sachs, Morgan Stanley, Bank of America, Barclays, and a handful of foreign banks form this exclusive circle.

Their role is not optional.
Each is expected, as a condition of primary-dealer status, to **bid at every Treasury auction**, ensuring that the United States never fails to raise the cash it needs.
In exchange, they earn prestige, access, and the privilege of dealing directly with the **Federal Reserve**.

When the auction clock strikes 1:00 p.m., the Primary Dealers are the first responders.
They enter billions in bids, balancing their own balance sheets against client demand and global conditions.
Their bids shape the *stop-out yield*—the moment when supply meets demand, and the Treasury learns what its promises are worth today.

The system works because every participant has skin in the game:

- The **Treasury** needs money.
- The **Dealers** need to perform to keep their status.
- The **Fed** needs the system itself to function.

This tripartite relationship keeps democracy's finances from collapsing under its own weight.

The Dealers' Burden and Reward

The Dealers' obligations are heavy.
They must:

1. **Participate Meaningfully in Treasury Auctions** across market conditions.

2. **Make Markets**—continuously quoting buy and sell prices to other investors, ensuring constant liquidity.
3. **Report Activity**—providing the New York Fed with detailed data on their trades and inventory.

Their reward is privileged market access: Primary Dealers are regular counterparties in the Fed's open-market operations and play a central role in Treasury-market liquidity. That access is important, but it is not unique to every Fed liquidity facility; eligible banks and other approved counterparties can participate in certain facilities as well.

It is this closed circuit that enforces the **Iron Law of Separation** operationally: the Treasury cannot ask the Fed for cash; it must sell debt to Dealers.
The Fed cannot buy directly from Treasury; it trades later, in the open market, with those same Dealers.
The circle is closed, the barrier intact.

The Irony of Enforcement

There is a poetic irony buried in the arrangement.
Many of these same institutions nearly collapsed during the **2008 financial crisis**, surviving only because the government—the Spender—bailed them out.
And yet, in the decade since, those rescued institutions have become the very agents enforcing fiscal discipline on their savior.

At every auction, they remind Washington that even the most powerful nation must still earn its financing through market pricing. Their bids—or their hesitation—set the cost of America's debt. They are both subordinates and masters, symbols of a system that transforms self-interest into global order.

As one former Treasury official put it, "They keep us honest because they're paid to."

Liquidity as Law

The beauty of this architecture lies in its self-correcting logic.
No political body dictates the interest rate on U.S. debt.
It is discovered in real time by millions of decisions—each driven by profit, fear, and faith.

In effect, the **bond market functions as an unelected Senate,** voting continuously on the nation's fiscal credibility.
Its chambers are trading floors; its quorum is liquidity.
When investors sense risk, yields rise.
When confidence returns, yields fall.
This invisible feedback loop disciplines Congress more effectively than any statutory limit ever could.

Every investor, from a Chinese central banker to a Kansas retiree, participates in the same global referendum: *What is a promise from the United States worth today?*

The Global Demand Machine

The reach of Treasury debt is staggering.
Foreign central banks hold roughly **$8 trillion** in U.S. securities, led by Japan and China.
Oil exporters in the Gulf recycle petrodollars into Treasuries; European banks hold them as collateral for repo transactions; global corporations use them as the base layer of cash management.

For emerging economies, Treasuries are not just investments—they are insurance policies.
Holding them stabilizes exchange rates and signals solvency.
For the United States, this foreign hunger for safety creates a privilege economists call the **exorbitant advantage**: the ability to borrow in its own currency, at lower rates, indefinitely.

Every auction, therefore, is not just a domestic event—it's a planetary one.
A Tokyo pension fund's demand for 10-year notes affects mortgage rates in Texas.

A central bank's decision to roll maturing bills reverberates through the Chicago futures market within minutes.
The Treasury's machinery is global gravity—its pull subtle but inescapable.

The 2020 "Dash for Cash"

March 2020 tested this system to its limits.
As the pandemic exploded, investors everywhere sold everything—even Treasuries—to raise dollars.
Liquidity evaporated.
Bid-ask spreads—the tiny gap between buying and selling prices—widened tenfold.
For a few chaotic days, the world's safest market began to wobble.

In Washington, the Treasury still had to fund a $2 trillion relief package.
Auctions loomed.
Would buyers show up when everyone was selling?

They did—but barely.
The **Primary Dealers** shouldered enormous inventory, straining balance sheets already under stress.
To prevent total gridlock, the **Federal Reserve** intervened—not to fund the government, but to restore market plumbing.
It began purchasing Treasuries from Dealers at scale, re-injecting liquidity and unclogging the system.
Within days, yields stabilized, and the market began functioning again.

The architecture had bent, not broken.
The Iron Law remained intact because even in crisis, the Fed bought from intermediaries—not directly from the Treasury.
The wall held.

The Market's Memory

That episode became a quiet legend in Washington and Wall Street alike.

It proved that the Treasury market—the spine of global finance—could survive a once-in-a-century stress because its design distributed risk through private channels instead of concentrating it in the state.

The lesson was simple and profound: **America's greatest strength is not control but constraint.**
Its financial system works because no single entity—neither Congress, nor the Treasury, nor the Fed—can dictate the price of trust.
That price must always be discovered, never declared.

The Global Web of Consequence

Every component of the system—the Dealers, the Fed, the foreign buyers, the domestic savers—is bound by one mutual dependency: the continued credibility of the United States.
If that credibility ever faltered, the consequences would be immediate and global.
Treasury yields would spike, foreign currencies would convulse, and the cost of money would rise everywhere at once.

In this sense, **U.S. fiscal discipline is a global public good.**
The world benefits from America's self-imposed pain.
Its debt, paradoxically, is everyone's stability.

The Moment of Sale

Every Treasury auction ends not with applause but with a number.
At 1:08 p.m. Eastern, the stop-out yield flashes across trading terminals worldwide.
For an instant, global attention narrows to a single decimal—3.976 percent, perhaps, on a ten-year note.

Within seconds, screens in Tokyo, London, and New York update.
Currencies twitch. Mortgage rates tick. A million algorithms rewrite their expectations.

In that quiet eight-minute interval, democracy's finances have been repriced by the planet.

No speech from Congress, no executive order, no press release carries greater consequence.
The stop-out yield is the price of trust, expressed to three decimal places.
If the number is higher than expected, it means investors demanded more compensation to lend.
If lower, it means they believe—still—that the United States remains the safest debtor alive.

The ceremony is bloodless, but its verdict is moral.

Debt as Discipline

To most nations, debt is a burden.
To the United States, it is a **ritual of accountability**—a mechanism that transforms promises into prices.
Every auction forces politicians to confront the cost of their decisions.
The market's judgment cannot be filibustered, delayed, or spun.

When the Treasury sells bonds, it is not merely borrowing; it is confessing.
The interest rate it pays is the tangible measure of national credibility.
The higher the rate, the greater the penance.

This process—expensive, public, and constant—is how the Republic enforces financial morality on itself.
The pain of interest is not a flaw of the system but its proof of virtue.
Each coupon payment is a reaffirmation that America still believes in consequences.

The Treasury as Manufacturer of Stability

Inside the Bureau of the Fiscal Service, the language of production dominates: *issuance, rollovers, maturities, coupon schedules.*
Officials speak of **maintaining product integrity**, as if describing

precision machinery.
And in a sense, they are.

Every bond, note, and bill is a serialized product stamped with the full faith and credit of the United States.
Together, they form the supply chain of the world's financial system.
When a 10-year note matures, a new one is issued; when an old bond is redeemed, its replacement ensures continuity.
This **constant manufacturing cycle** keeps global capital flowing as reliably as electricity.

Through this mechanism, the Treasury does something no private company can:
it converts deficits into order, chaos into confidence.
The more it borrows, the more liquidity the world gains.
Debt becomes not a symptom of weakness but the structure of stability itself.

The Auction as Theater

Consider a typical refunding day.
At the Treasury's auction operations center, analysts watch as bids cascade across their screens.
A few whisper updates—"Strong demand from foreign accounts," "Dealers taking down more than expected."
Eight minutes later, the results hit the wire: *Bid-to-cover ratio 2.45, stop-out yield 4.12 percent.*

The room exhales.
Another $42 billion has been raised.
Somewhere across the world, traders adjust portfolios, economists recalibrate models, and a senator issues a press release claiming fiscal responsibility.
But the true statement has already been made, silently, in numbers.

That eight-minute auction represents the highest synthesis of democracy and capitalism ever engineered: elected officials decide how much to spend; unelected investors decide how much that

spending costs.
The dialogue is constant, public, and unforgiving.

The Human Ripple

A 0.10 percent rise in the 10-year yield might seem trivial.
Yet it adds roughly **$25 per month** to a $400,000 mortgage, increases corporate borrowing costs by billions, and shifts pension-fund valuations across continents.
The consequences of a single Treasury auction ripple through every household and every economy that pegs its rates to the dollar.

When the Treasury borrows, the world adjusts.
And when the world doubts, the Treasury pays more.
This feedback loop is not abstract policy—it is the everyday metabolism of global capitalism.

The Unspoken Code

The entire system operates on an unspoken covenant: that the U.S. will always meet its obligations in full and on time.
This assumption underpins everything from trade finance to credit-default models.
It is the reason an oil tanker sailing under a Liberian flag can be insured in London using Treasury yields as a benchmark.

That covenant was tested in 1979 when a clerical error delayed $120 million in Treasury-bill payments.
Yields spiked instantly, and panic spread until the glitch was resolved.
The lesson was unforgettable: even the suggestion of default was intolerable.
The Iron Law of Separation had to be matched by an Iron Law of Punctuality.

Debt as America's Language of Power

The rest of the world projects strength through armies or empires; the United States projects it through auctions.

Each sale of a Treasury bond is a quiet declaration of supremacy:
We owe, therefore we lead.

Every nation on earth holds U.S. debt because doing so grants access to the system itself—to liquidity, pricing, and safety.
By manufacturing debt at scale, the United States manufactures global dependence.
Its liabilities are everyone else's assets.
That inversion—power through debt—is the heart of the dollar paradox.

The Moral Accounting

The Treasury's factory of debt is, at its core, an ethical machine.
It turns political promises into math and forces ambition to answer to arithmetic.
The auction is not a loophole; it is the conscience of democracy.

Each time the Treasury pays interest, it is repaying more than money—it is repaying trust.
And each time investors accept a lower yield, they are casting a vote of faith that the United States still values restraint over convenience.

In this way, debt becomes the mechanism through which virtue survives politics.
It is the contract that keeps the nation's ideals tethered to its numbers.

The Dollar as Weapon

The Treasury manufactures debt; the market prices it; the world buys it.
But the story does not end there.
Because every other country holds U.S. debt to secure its own stability, the United States wields an extraordinary, often invisible power: the ability to weaponize the dollar system itself.

Chapter 5

The Federal Reserve: The Independent Printer

The Paradox at the Core

If the **Treasury** is the manufacturer of America's debt, the **Federal Reserve** is its banker and broker—the custodian that ensures every bond the government creates keeps circulating through the bloodstream of global finance.

Yet the Fed's role is defined by contradiction. It must stabilize the system built on Treasury debt while being legally forbidden from creating that debt itself. It may **buy** and **sell** the securities that fund the government, but it may never fund the government directly. Its actions must occur only after the market has spoken.

The entire drama unfolds in the **secondary market**—that vast and invisible arena where trillions of dollars of Treasury securities change hands daily, long after the initial auctions end. Here, the Fed's traders sit at the heart of a machine that never sleeps, guiding interest rates with gestures measured in billion-dollar increments.

Inside the Fed's Trading Room

At 8:30 a.m. each weekday, the trading desk at the **Federal Reserve Bank of New York** hums to life. Giant displays track every Treasury maturity in existence: two-year notes, five-year notes, 10-year bonds. Traders watch the color-coded lines of yield curves shift by fractions of a basis point. The data looks clinical, but behind each movement lies the pulse of the global economy.

Here, the Fed implements monetary policy through a modern framework that combines administered interest rates, standing facilities, and balance-sheet operations. The trading desk remains central to execution, but the day-to-day mechanism is no longer the pre-2008 routine of constantly fine-tuning scarce reserves through Treasury purchases and sales.

The Fed's Dual Imperative

By law, the Federal Reserve pursues two mandates: **price stability** and **maximum employment.** These goals are deliberately broad—flexible enough to adapt, strict enough to prevent political capture.

To fulfill its mandate, the Fed sets a target range for the federal funds rate. Since 2019, it has implemented that target in an ample-reserves regime: rather than fine-tuning the quantity of reserves each day, it relies primarily on administered rates—especially the interest rate on reserve balances (IORB)—to keep overnight rates within the target range.

Open-market operations still matter, but their role depends on the objective. Treasury purchases or sales can change the Fed's balance sheet, supply reserves, support market functioning, or provide monetary accommodation; they are no longer the routine day-to-day lever used to steer the federal funds rate as they were in the pre-2008 scarce-reserves system.

Open Market Operations: From Scarce to Ample Reserves

1. Before 2008, reserves were scarce and the Fed routinely used open-market purchases and sales to adjust reserve supply and keep the federal funds rate near its target. Buying securities added reserves; selling securities drained them.

2. In today's ample-reserves framework, IORB is the main tool for controlling short-term rates, while facilities such as the overnight reverse repo facility and the standing repo facility help keep money-market rates within the desired range and supply liquidity when needed.

Open-market purchases and sales still change reserve supply and the Fed's balance sheet, but they should not be confused with the old daily reserve-fine-tuning mechanism. The operating framework changed; the Fed's responsibility for monetary control did not.

The Legal Firewall

The distinction between these operations and direct financing is subtle but sacred.

- In **direct financing**, the Fed would hand money to the Treasury's checking account—the TGA—eliminating all market discipline.
- In **Open Market Operations**, the Fed interacts only with existing securities, already priced by investors.

Intent and sequence preserve legality. The Treasury must first face the public; only later can the Fed manage the aftermath. That order of operations—auction first, stabilization second—is the invisible backbone of the **Golden Guardrail**.

The Balance Sheet: The World's Anchor

Every purchase the Fed makes adds to its **balance sheet**—the largest single ledger in existence. Each entry records a trade that ripples across continents.

- **Assets:** Mostly U.S. Treasury securities and, since 2008, government-guaranteed mortgage-backed securities. These holdings give the Fed its leverage to move markets.
- **Liabilities:** Two colossal categories—**Federal Reserve Notes** (the cash in your wallet) and **Bank Reserves** (the digital deposits banks hold at the Fed).

When the Fed buys Treasuries, both sides expand: assets rise by the bonds purchased; liabilities rise by the reserves created to pay for them. Money enters the system not through a printing press but through accounting entries.

This balance sheet—now several **trillion dollars**—is the modern map of trust. It shows that every dollar in circulation is ultimately backed not by gold or oil, but by the promise that U.S. Treasuries remain valuable, liquid, and universally accepted.

Quantitative Easing: Power and Peril

Since the 2008 crisis, the Fed has used large-scale asset purchases, known as **Quantitative Easing (QE)**, to lower long-term interest rates when short-term rates hit zero. The mechanics are simple: buy vast quantities of Treasuries, flood the banking system with reserves, and signal to markets that credit will stay cheap until stability returns.

QE is not cost-free. Done too aggressively, it risks inflating asset bubbles and eroding faith in the currency. Yet without it, financial plumbing can seize. Each round of QE is therefore a tightrope walk between rescue and excess. The balance sheet becomes both lifeboat and warning sign.

Why the Fed Buys What It Cannot Fund

To outsiders, the Fed's constant presence in the Treasury market looks like hypocrisy: *How can the central bank claim independence while holding trillions in government debt?*

The answer lies in motive. The Fed buys not to finance deficits but to maintain the **liquidity of collateral** on which the entire financial world depends. Without an ample, functioning Treasury market, credit everywhere would freeze. The Fed's loyalty is not to the Treasury; it is to the system.

Its purchases, therefore, are not charity but maintenance. The Fed is the custodian that ensures the global engine of credit never runs dry, even as it refuses to fill the Treasury's gas tank directly.

The Collateral That Runs the World

To most people, Treasury securities are investments.

To the financial system, they are oxygen—**the universal collateral** that keeps the global machinery of credit alive.

Every night, across trading floors from London to Hong Kong, billions of dollars in short-term loans are negotiated in seconds. None of these loans would exist without Treasuries. They are not just the safest asset; they are the system's *permission slip to lend.*

Without them, the dollar-based economy would suffocate.

The Repo Market: The Hidden Engine

This invisible world is called the **Repurchase Agreement (Repo) Market**—a network where institutions lend and borrow cash, usually overnight, using Treasuries as collateral.

The concept is deceptively simple: one party sells a Treasury security and agrees to repurchase it the next day at a slightly higher price. The difference is the interest rate on that overnight loan.

Every major bank, hedge fund, and central bank participates. The scale is breathtaking—**trillions of dollars each day**, cycling through balance sheets at the speed of code.

The math may be mechanical, but the meaning is psychological: each transaction represents a vote of confidence that the Treasury collateral is still unquestionable. The entire world's credit supply depends on that belief.

Why Treasuries Dominate Collateral

Three qualities make Treasury debt supreme in this ecosystem:

1. **Safety.** They carry no credit risk; default is unthinkable.
2. **Liquidity.** They can be sold instantly, at scale, in any market condition.
3. **Transparency.** Every price, every auction, every yield is public.

An investor lending $100 million overnight to a bank will accept no substitute. A Treasury bill ensures repayment; a corporate bond introduces doubt. The global financial system therefore requires a **continuous supply** of new Treasury securities just to function.

If the Treasury ever ran a surplus large enough to eliminate debt issuance, the Repo Market would collapse from lack of collateral. Ironically, America's deficits are the lubricant of global finance.

The Repo Chain Reaction

When Treasury collateral tightens—whether from heavy investor hoarding, high foreign demand, or a government shutdown—Repo rates spike.
A single percentage-point move in Repo can ripple through every other credit market, instantly raising borrowing costs for households and corporations alike.

In that moment, the **Federal Reserve** becomes not just the banker of last resort, but the **broker of last resort**—the institution responsible for restoring the flow of collateral through the pipes of the world economy.

CASE STUDY:
The 2008 Crisis — When Trust Evaporated

The 2008 financial crisis began as a housing problem and metastasized into a collateral problem. Banks and hedge funds held vast quantities of mortgage-backed securities once considered safe enough for Repo transactions. When those assets lost credibility, lenders refused to accept them.

Overnight funding froze. Firms that relied on continuous Repo financing—Bear Stearns, Lehman Brothers—collapsed. The global system, suddenly deprived of usable collateral, began to seize.

The Fed intervened with historic speed and scope through emergency lending facilities and, later, large-scale asset purchases. Outright purchases of Treasuries and agency securities paid the private sector with reserves; they did not inject the purchased Treasuries back into the market. Liquidity support instead came from reserves, emergency lending, repo-type facilities, and securities-lending arrangements that restored funding and market functioning.

Without those actions, even the Treasury market itself might have fractured, destroying the foundation of the global dollar system.

The Fed became the **buyer of last resort**, not to save the government, but to save the instrument that makes government borrowing possible.

CASE STUDY:
The 2019 Repo Shock — A Modern Warning

On an otherwise quiet Monday in September 2019, something strange happened. The overnight Repo rate—normally aligned with the Fed's target near 2 percent—suddenly spiked to **10 percent**. Banks stopped lending to one another. A brief panic swept through trading desks.

The cause was banal yet catastrophic in potential: a temporary cash shortage caused by corporate tax payments and a glut of Treasury issuance. There were plenty of Treasuries, but not enough dollars. The world's deepest market was suffocating on its own abundance of collateral.

Within hours, the Fed stepped in, announcing emergency Repo operations. It offered to lend cash to banks against Treasury collateral—essentially becoming a massive overnight counterparty to the entire system. The crisis evaporated as quickly as it began.

The lesson was profound: the Treasury can manufacture the debt, but only the Fed can guarantee its **continuous usability**. The central bank must stand ready not merely to buy or sell, but to ensure that Treasuries never lose their function as the world's collateral of trust.

Why the Repo Market Proves the Golden Guardrail

Every overnight Repo transaction—every $100 million swapped for a T-Bill—is a vote of faith in the Iron Law of Separation.
It says: *We trust that the U.S. will not inflate away its debt. We trust that the Fed will never fund the Treasury directly. We trust that the system is self-disciplined.*

If that trust ever cracked—if investors believed the U.S. might monetize its deficits or politicize its central bank—the Repo Market would seize within hours. Interest rates would explode, global credit would dry up, and trillions in shadow-banking transactions would collapse.

In that sense, the Repo Market is the world's daily stress test of American integrity.
Every evening, banks and funds effectively ask: *Do we still believe in the system?*
And every morning, when the trades unwind smoothly, the answer is yes.

The Fed's Role as Market Custodian

The Federal Reserve's power is therefore both limited and absolute. It cannot create political will, raise taxes, or approve spending. But it can—and must—preserve the liquidity of the instrument upon which all of that depends.
When crises erupt, it moves with quiet violence: buying Treasuries, injecting cash, extending repos, and absorbing risk until stability returns.

It acts not as master but as **custodian of credibility**—the silent broker who ensures that every act of faith in the dollar is rewarded with function, not failure.

The Global Shadow of the Fed

No central bank on earth moves alone.
When the Federal Reserve breathes, the world's markets inhale.

Every change in the Fed's balance sheet, every whisper of a rate decision, ripples outward across oceans, shaping exchange rates, credit flows, and national destinies.

A Fed rate hike in Washington tightens mortgages in Nairobi. A bond purchase in New York sends capital surging into São Paulo. Its balance sheet is the hidden weather system of global finance.

Foreign central banks watch the Fed's operations like astronomers tracking a star that anchors their orbit. They mimic its policies, adjust their currencies, and sometimes even defy domestic priorities just to maintain exchange-rate stability. The Fed's domestic mandate—price stability and employment—thus becomes the **world's de facto monetary policy.**

The Paradox of the Global Lender

The United States never set out to run the world's credit system. It happened because the Treasury manufactured the safest debt and the Fed became its perpetual broker.

Over time, the Fed's domestic duty morphed into a global one: to prevent dollar shortages abroad that could crash foreign economies and, by extension, boomerang back to America.

This unspoken responsibility manifests through **dollar swap lines**—emergency lifelines the Fed extends to foreign central banks in times of crisis.

During 2008 and again in 2020, the Fed opened these channels to Europe, Japan, and emerging markets, allowing them to borrow dollars against their own currencies.

It was monetary diplomacy by spreadsheet: quiet, technical, and world-saving.

Each swap line reaffirmed the hierarchy of global finance: the dollar on top, Treasuries beneath it, and every other currency somewhere below, orbiting both.

The Cost of Dominance

This dominance is not free.
Maintaining the dollar's supremacy requires the United States to remain the supplier of last resort for the world's safe assets—meaning it must always have debt to sell.
That debt, paradoxically, is both a liability and an export.

Foreign governments, corporations, and investors hold more than **$25 trillion** in U.S. securities, not out of charity but necessity. Their banking systems use Treasuries as collateral; their pension funds use them as benchmarks; their trade payments settle in dollars backed by them.
Every new Treasury bond sold is another link in the chain of dependency.

The cost for America is subtle but immense:
it must accept permanent deficits and a permanently strong currency, making its exports pricier and its domestic manufacturing less competitive.
In exchange, it earns something greater than trade surpluses—**global obedience to its monetary rulebook.**

When the Broker Becomes the Empire

The Fed never raised a flag over a foreign capital.
Yet its influence reaches deeper than any occupying army could.
When the Fed tightens rates, capital flees emerging markets, currencies collapse, and governments fall.
When it eases, bubbles inflate from New York to New Delhi.

Its governors rarely speak of power, but every policy meeting in the Eccles Building is a geopolitical event.
A single phrase—"higher for longer," "data dependent," "quantitative tightening"—can shift billions in minutes and decide which nations prosper or panic.
In this sense, the Federal Reserve is both **the world's central bank**

and its **chief enforcer.**
Its power lies not in coercion, but in the quiet inevitability of math.

The Invisible Alliance

The relationship between the Treasury and the Fed is a masterpiece of American design: tension that sustains stability.
They do not love each other; they respect each other's boundaries.
The Treasury creates the debt that disciplines politicians; the Fed manages that debt to discipline markets.
Together they form the machinery of credibility—the "banker and broker" of a system whose product is trust itself.

Each relies on the other but cannot dominate.
The Treasury's auctions give the Fed the instruments it needs to manage liquidity; the Fed's market operations keep those instruments functional and safe.
Their cooperation, enforced by law and necessity, is what keeps the Iron Law of Separation alive in practice.

The Self-Imposed Tax of Power

The United States pays for this system every day.
The interest on its debt—nearly **$1 trillion annually**—is not merely a budget line.
It is the **rent America pays for global leadership.**
Each coupon payment is a dividend distributed to the world for trusting the dollar.

That cost can never disappear.
If the debt were paid off entirely, the collateral of global finance would vanish, the Repo Market would seize, and the world's liquidity engine would stall.
America's deficits are not a sign of failure—they are the structural price of empire without conquest.

The Moral Paradox of the Printer

The Fed's greatest virtue is restraint.
It can conjure infinite dollars, yet it chooses not to.
Every crisis tests that discipline.
Every recovery reaffirms it.

Its balance sheet may swell to rescue markets, but its authority depends on the promise that expansion is temporary, never political. That self-denial is the final form of the Golden Guardrail: **the willingness of infinite power to limit itself.**

The Quiet Empire

When future historians trace the 21st century, they may not dwell on wars or elections but on the architecture of trust that underpinned global commerce.
They will see that the most powerful weapon ever created was not a missile or algorithm but the humble Treasury bond—backed by the credibility of a central bank that refused to print for politics.

The Federal Reserve is not the world's conqueror; it is its custodian.
It enforces stability without declaring it, governs without governing, and maintains order through math.
Its empire is invisible, its rule accepted, its victory continuous.

The Dollar as Weapon

The Golden Guardrail keeps the Spender honest and the Printer restrained.
But the story of the dollar does not end with self-discipline.
It extends outward—into the realm of power projection.
For when every other nation depends on your currency for safety, that currency becomes a weapon.

Chapter 6

The Unholy Alliance: The Debt Market's Three-Party System

The Triangle That Rules the Dollar

Every empire in history has relied on a delicate balance of fear. Rome had its Senate and legions; Britain its merchants and admirals. America has something stranger: a **three-party financial system** that keeps itself in check by permanent mistrust.

The **Treasury**, the **Federal Reserve**, and the **Market**—a constellation of Primary Dealers and investors—form a triangle of incentives that never aligns yet never breaks.
Each possesses a form of power the others need but cannot fully control.
Their mutual friction is the hidden architecture that sustains the dollar's supremacy.

At its heart lies the paradox first explored in earlier chapters: the U.S. must borrow endlessly not because it is weak, but because that debt is the machinery of global order. The Unholy Alliance is the mechanism that ensures that borrowing remains painful enough to stay credible.

The Three Characters of the Drama

1. **The Spender – The U.S. Treasury**

It wields the political will of a democracy that always promises more than it taxes. It creates obligations—wars, welfare, infrastructure—and must find cash to fulfill them.

2. **The Market – The Primary Dealers and Global Investors**
   It demands profit and security. It funds governments only when the price of risk feels fair. Its loyalty lasts exactly one auction at a time.

3. **The Printer – The Federal Reserve**
   It controls the money supply, guards against inflation, and smooths liquidity shocks—but must never directly pay the Treasury's bills.

These three are bound by necessity but divided by design. Their alliances shift like tectonic plates—cooperating in crisis, colliding in calm, forever preventing any single hand from resting on the printing press.

Where Politics Meets the Market: The Iron Gate

The relationship between the **Treasury** and the **Primary Dealers** is the first fault line in the system. It is the **Iron Gate of the Auction**, the narrow passage through which every dollar of public spending must pass before entering circulation.

Every month, the Treasury announces its borrowing schedule. Every Primary Dealer studies it like scripture. Inflation forecasts, Fed guidance, oil prices, even election polls feed into their bidding models. When the auction clock starts, the Dealers decide—silently, mathematically—how much trust the United States deserves today.

The Dealers' Veto

Their power is subtle but absolute.
If they judge Washington reckless, they demand higher yields. Those yields instantly raise the cost of every future deficit and become a political embarrassment in budget hearings.
If they are confident, yields fall, and politicians claim fiscal virtue.

No vote in Congress wields such immediate consequence. The **auction result** is the Market's veto power—an unspoken referendum on government behavior.

Each higher yield is a penalty; each lower one, a reward. The system thus turns profit motive into discipline. The Dealers act out of self-interest, but the outcome enforces public restraint.

The Treasury's Need for Predictability

Because of this dependence, the Treasury behaves like an addict under contract: it must feed its financiers consistency. Surprises are punished brutally.
Unexpected borrowing, erratic auction sizes, or opaque fiscal forecasts all raise yields within hours. Predictability is currency.

To protect that credibility, the Treasury schedules issuance months in advance, releases refunding statements on precise dates, and leaks nothing. The Dealers, in turn, price certainty into every bid. The relationship resembles diplomacy more than commerce—ritualized, tense, and bound by mutual necessity.

How the Market Teaches Humility

When Congress spends beyond reason, the punishment is swift but impersonal: yields climb, debt-service costs swell, and the illusion of free money evaporates.

By the time those numbers reach taxpayers as rising mortgage rates or a weaker stock market, the message has already been delivered: the Market has spoken.

This is why every Treasury secretary, regardless of ideology, bows to "market confidence." It is not a metaphor; it is survival. Lose the Dealers' trust, and the United States loses its cheapest funding source. The Iron Gate closes.

The Price of Obedience

The Treasury's obedience to transparency is expensive. It cannot disguise its borrowing, and it must expose every move to global judgment. Yet that exposure is what makes U.S. debt the safest asset alive. Investors trust what they can see, even when they dislike it.

In that way, democracy's chaos becomes a feature, not a flaw. The world accepts the dollar precisely because its disorder is public, its auctions real, its interest rate a mirror of collective belief.

The Engine of Liquidity: The Fed and the Dealers

If the Treasury's auction is where discipline begins, the **relationship between the Federal Reserve and the Primary Dealers** is where survival happens.

The Fed ensures that the Dealers who finance the government never run out of oxygen—**cash.**

The Dealers' balance sheets are the capillaries of the entire dollar system.

They absorb trillions in new Treasury debt each month, using it as inventory, collateral, and product. Without constant liquidity, that pipeline would seize, sending shockwaves through every corner of global finance.

Every day, the Federal Reserve Bank of New York's trading desk implements FOMC decisions and operates the facilities that connect monetary policy to money markets. Dealers watch those operations closely, but they do not receive an automatic promise of rescue.

In the ample-reserves regime, the Fed does not ordinarily steer overnight rates by buying Treasuries whenever cash is scarce and selling them whenever cash is abundant. IORB is the main rate-control tool; standing repo operations can supply cash against eligible collateral when funding markets tighten, while the overnight reverse repo facility can absorb cash from approved counterparties.
Outright Treasury purchases and sales remain available for balance-sheet management, monetary accommodation, and market-functioning objectives, but they are not the routine life-support mechanism for Primary Dealers.

Through this framework, the Fed can influence short-term rates and relieve systemwide funding stress without turning the Treasury market into a direct financing channel for the government.

These are the **Open Market Operations** described in earlier chapters, but here they function as life support.
Through these transactions, the Fed doesn't just steer interest rates; it guarantees that the financial arteries never clog.

The Dealer's Privilege
Being a **Primary Dealer** is an extraordinary privilege.
Only about two dozen institutions on Earth hold this status. They sit at the intersection of politics and monetary power, able to transact directly with both the U.S. Treasury and the Federal Reserve.

Their reward is access—direct trading rights with the central bank and a central role in Treasury markets.
Their obligation is service—constant participation, constant quoting of prices, constant readiness to supply liquidity.

Primary Dealers are important counterparties in Fed repo and reverse-repo operations, but they are not the only eligible counterparties. Depending on the facility, approved depository institutions and other counterparties may also participate. A Dealer holding Treasuries can obtain cash against eligible collateral when it meets the terms of the relevant facility.

The Feedback Loop That Keeps the Dollar Alive

1. **The Treasury needs cash** → It issues bonds.
2. **The Dealers buy the bonds** → They distribute or repo them for financing.
3. **The Fed provides the backstop** → It buys or lends against those same bonds to manage liquidity.

The loop is self-sustaining, yet every step preserves independence.
The Treasury cannot borrow directly from the Fed.
The Dealers must price the risk through auctions.
The Fed must transact only after the market has spoken.

The brilliance of the system lies in its circular dependency: each participant relies on the others but cannot dominate.
Remove one corner of the triangle and the architecture collapses.

How Liquidity Becomes Trust

To global investors, this arrangement is the ultimate guarantee.
When they hold a U.S. Treasury, they know that:

- The **Treasury** will honor it.
- The **Dealers** will trade it.
- The **Fed** will make it liquid.

No other asset on Earth enjoys that three-layered security.
It is why Treasuries form the core collateral for trillions in repo transactions and why every central bank on the planet keeps them in reserve.

Liquidity, in this system, is not just a financial condition—it is a **moral promise**.
The Fed enforces that promise daily, one repo at a time.

When the Loop Falters
Occasionally, the loop shows its fragility.
In 2019, when Repo rates spiked above 10 percent overnight, the market momentarily doubted that liquidity was infinite.
The Fed intervened with surgical precision—launching massive repo operations that calmed the panic within hours.

The same happened during the pandemic panic of 2020, when the Treasury issued record debt and investors sold even "safe" assets to raise cash.
The Fed's traders responded by buying $1 trillion in Treasuries in a matter of weeks.
Their speed prevented the ultimate paradox: a loss of confidence in the very asset designed to represent safety.

Each time, the system bent but did not break.
Each time, the Fed proved that liquidity is not a luxury—it is a law.

The Moral Cost of Liquidity
This guarantee, however, carries a hidden cost.
By ensuring that the Market will never truly fail, the Fed risks teaching it that failure no longer exists.
Moral hazard—the quiet expectation of rescue—lurks beneath every bailout, every facility, every crisis response.

Yet the Fed cannot withdraw. To refuse intervention would be to let trust itself collapse.
So it continues the ritual: enforcing discipline in peacetime, providing

salvation in panic, and hoping that balance will survive the next storm.

The Dealers may privately curse its caution, but they depend on it as devoutly as the Treasury depends on their bids.
Together, they sustain a liquidity machine that has replaced conquest as the foundation of global power.

The Firewall: The Treasury and the Fed

Among the three players in the Unholy Alliance, none stand closer yet remain more separated than the **Treasury** and the **Federal Reserve**.
Their offices sit mere blocks apart in Washington—neighbors by geography, strangers by law.
The Treasury holds its checking account, the **Treasury General Account (TGA),** at the Fed itself, yet cannot ask the Fed to fill it.

Every transfer, every payment, every war bond redemption must be funded with real dollars—either raised from taxpayers or borrowed through auctions.
When the TGA balance runs low, Treasury officials cannot pick up the phone and request a deposit.
They must face the Market.
That mechanical humiliation is the design, not a defect.

The proximity is symbolic: the Spender can see the Printer through the glass but cannot touch it.
That barrier is the Iron Law of Separation incarnate—the legal wall that ensures money creation serves **monetary policy**, not **political convenience.**

The Line in the Sand: No Direct Funding

The Federal Reserve Act is explicit: the Fed may buy Treasury securities only "in the open market," never directly from the Treasury.
That single clause—just a few dozen words—forms the constitutional firewall of American finance.

If that rule were erased, Congress could spend without restraint, the Treasury could sell bonds straight to the Fed at zero yield, and inflation would follow faster than law could react.
History's graveyard—Weimar, Zimbabwe, Venezuela—begins with that shortcut.

Instead, the U.S. accepts the pain of separation.
Every deficit must face the discipline of an auction.
Every borrowing decision must pass through the Market's fire.
It is slow, costly, and inefficient—and that is exactly why it works.

The Debt Ceiling Spectacle

The **Debt Ceiling** is the most visible expression of this architecture—a recurring political theatre that terrifies markets and reassures them simultaneously.

Each time the ceiling nears, cable networks scream of "default" and "crisis."
Yet beneath the drama lies purpose.
The ceiling forces Congress to confront the cumulative cost of its choices in public view.
It is the ritual confession of fiscal sin.

When the Treasury hits the limit, it cannot call the Fed for rescue.
It must juggle internal accounts, delay payments, or plead for legislative relief.
The Fed watches helplessly, forbidden to intervene.
This public tension—the visible discomfort of two institutions unable to save each other—is the system proving its independence.

Pain as Credibility

To the outside world, these spectacles look like dysfunction.
To insiders, they are discipline.
Every crisis that ends with the United States still paying its bills reinforces faith that the wall still stands.
The pain itself becomes proof of honesty.

Markets may panic during the standoff, but the eventual resolution—always at the eleventh hour—reminds the world that America will debate everything *except* its willingness to honor its debt. That distinction separates democracy's noise from collapse's silence.

The Ultimate Check and Balance

The genius of the Unholy Alliance is that it transforms distrust into stability:

- **The Spender (Treasury)** is checked by the Market's demand for higher yields.
- **The Market (Dealers)** is stabilized by the Printer's guarantee of liquidity.
- **The Printer (Fed)** is legally forbidden to finance the Spender.

Each fears the other.
Each depends on the other.
Together they form a self-correcting triangle in which power cannot accumulate without consequence.

The result is not harmony but **managed friction**—a constant hum of tension that prevents the U.S. from succumbing to the political temptation of free money.

The Unholy Alliance in Motion

Watch the cycle unfold:
Congress votes to spend.
The Treasury issues bonds.
Dealers bid and distribute.
The Fed calibrates liquidity.
Interest rates adjust.
The public feels the cost.

No committee coordinates it; no agency commands it.
The system functions because every participant acts selfishly within

limits that force collective discipline.
It is capitalism's most elegant contradiction—order emerging from competition, trust born of suspicion.

The Price of Supremacy

This machinery is expensive.
The annual interest on the national debt, now approaching **one trillion dollars**, is not merely an accounting line—it is the toll America pays to keep its empire of trust intact.
Each coupon payment is a renewal fee for global confidence.

The world lends to the United States because it believes that the triangle will never collapse—that the Printer will never fund the Spender directly, that the Market will always demand its due, and that the Treasury will always pay.

The cost is staggering, but the alternative—unquestioned political control over money—is history's oldest disaster.
Pain is the price of permanence.

Why the System Endures

Other nations envy America's privilege but rarely its discipline.
They see the benefits of dollar dominance without grasping the architecture of restraint that sustains it.
The Unholy Alliance endures because it converts mistrust into mechanism.
It forces humility on the world's most powerful government.

As long as the Treasury must borrow, the Dealers must price, and the Fed must refuse temptation, the dollar will remain untouchable.
The day that pain disappears—the day borrowing feels easy, auctions lose fear, or printing becomes political—that supremacy will begin to rot.

The Dollar as Weapon

This chapter has mapped the architecture of restraint—the inner engineering that keeps America's currency from devouring itself. But restraint is only half the story.

When the same system that enforces discipline at home extends abroad, it becomes something else entirely: power projection.

The dollar, born as a tool of order, evolved into the world's most formidable instrument of coercion.

This is the moment the Guardrail becomes a weapon.

Chapter 7

The 1951 Accord: The Day the Printer Fought Back

The Crisis Before Independence

The Federal Reserve's independence—the sacred wall that now defines modern finance—was not born from theory or calm deliberation.
It was wrestled into being by conflict.
The year was 1951, and America's post-war prosperity was already showing cracks.
Behind the celebratory headlines of victory lay an economy flooded with cheap money, a government addicted to borrowing, and a central bank that had become little more than a printing press wearing a necktie.

The Golden Guardrail, conceived to keep politics out of money, had collapsed in silence.
The Spender had captured the Printer.

The Age of Pegging

During World War II, patriotism demanded obedience.
To finance the war, the Treasury needed endless cash—and it demanded that the Fed guarantee low borrowing costs.
The policy that followed was called **interest-rate pegging**: the Fed promised to buy any Treasury securities necessary to cap yields at politically acceptable levels.

- **Short-term bills:** fixed around ⅜ percent.
- **Longer-term bonds:** capped near 2½ percent.

The intent was patriotic; the result, corrosive.
By turning the Fed into a guaranteed buyer, the Treasury stripped the Market of discipline.
Every bond carried an implicit promise: if no investor wanted it, the Fed would.

That policy kept wartime borrowing cheap, but when peace returned, the machinery of inflation roared to life.

The Price of Victory

By 1947, consumer demand exploded.
Factories shifted from tanks to toasters, soldiers became homeowners, and dollars flooded the economy.
Prices rose at double-digit rates.
Yet the Fed's hands were tied—it could not raise interest rates without defying its orders to keep yields low.

Every bond it bought to hold rates down poured more liquidity into an already overheated system.
Inflation became the new enemy, but the central bank was fighting with its weapon locked away.

Inside the Federal Reserve Bank of New York, frustration turned to alarm.
Economists warned that the policy designed to defend national security was now endangering economic stability.
They could see what the public could not: a monetary time bomb ticking beneath the post-war boom.

The Shadow of War Returns

Then, in June 1950, North Korea invaded the South.
Once again, Washington needed instant money for war.
Treasury Secretary **John W. Snyder**, a close ally of President Truman, ordered the Fed to maintain its wartime peg.
He argued that raising rates during conflict would be "unpatriotic"—that cheap credit was as vital as ammunition.

To the Fed, this was sacrilege.
Its leaders had endured five years of inflation, five years of lost autonomy.
They knew that surrendering again would destroy whatever credibility remained.

The confrontation was no longer theoretical.
It was personal, political, and imminent.

A Quiet Mutiny

Fed Chairman Thomas B. McCabe, New York Fed President Allan Sproul, Marriner Eccles, and other Federal Reserve officials increasingly resisted continuation of the wartime rate peg, arguing that it was fueling inflation and constraining independent monetary policy.

The dispute became increasingly public. Treasury officials emphasized the need to finance the government at manageable rates, while Fed officials argued that continued support of the peg was impairing the central bank's ability to restrain inflation.

The lines were drawn: **the Spender versus the Printer**.

The Public Break

At the January 1951 White House meeting, President Truman pressed the Federal Reserve to support the government's financing needs during the Korean War. Fed officials resisted continued unconditional support of the bond-price peg and argued that inflation control required greater freedom over monetary policy.

The meeting did not resolve the dispute. Instead, conflicting public accounts of what had been agreed pushed the institutional conflict between the Treasury and the Federal Reserve into the open.

What had once been an internal argument over debt management was now a visible confrontation over who would determine monetary conditions after the war.

The Breaking Point

Within weeks, pressure became unbearable.
Inflation topped 10 percent.
Long-term bond prices wobbled as investors doubted the government's will to defend the dollar.
Foreign holders of U.S. debt—then a new phenomenon—began demanding higher yields.

Something had to give.
Either the Fed would reclaim its independence, or the credibility of American finance would disintegrate.

The answer arrived in March 1951.

The Day the Printer Fought Back

On March 3, 1951, the dispute moved toward resolution. Treasury Secretary John W. Snyder had agreed to negotiate an understanding with the Federal Reserve but was hospitalized for cataract surgery.

In his absence, Assistant Secretary of the Treasury William McChesney Martin Jr. led the Treasury's negotiations with Federal Reserve representatives Robert Rouse, Woodlief Thomas, and Winfield Riefler.

Federal Reserve Chairman Thomas B. McCabe still headed the Board of Governors; Martin was negotiating from the Treasury side, not as Fed chairman. The compromise ended the Fed's obligation to support government bond prices indefinitely and restored room for monetary policy to operate separately from Treasury debt-management goals.

Martin was a Treasury official charged with helping find a workable compromise. One month later, President Truman appointed him chairman of the Federal Reserve Board.

The Treasury–Federal Reserve Accord of 1951.

The Accord: Liberation in Legal Form

The document itself ran only a few paragraphs.
It did not proclaim independence or name villains.
It simply **released the Federal Reserve from its obligation to peg interest rates** on government bonds.

Those few sentences restored the natural hierarchy between the Spender and the Printer:

- The Treasury would issue debt and submit to market pricing.

- The Federal Reserve would manage monetary conditions without political interference.
- The Market would again become the referee, setting rates based on trust rather than decree.

The symbolism was profound. America had fought two world wars to defeat tyranny abroad; now it had quietly defeated a fiscal tyranny at home.

The Men Behind the Accord

One month after the Accord, **William McChesney Martin Jr.** became chairman of the Federal Reserve Board. He was only 44 years old—slender, courteous, and deceptively mild. Yet beneath the surface was iron discipline.

"The job of the Federal Reserve is to take away the punch bowl just as the party gets going."

That single line captured the spirit of the Accord: the commitment to inflict discomfort when prosperity became intoxication.

Snyder represented the Treasury's determination to keep government borrowing costs low; McCabe and the Federal Open Market Committee represented the central bank's demand for greater monetary independence. Martin's role was to help bridge those positions from the Treasury side.

President Harry S. Truman ultimately accepted the settlement. He still needed to finance the Korean War, but the government also needed a monetary framework capable of restraining inflation.

Monetary Supremacy Restored

The Accord did not merely end a policy—it redefined power.
For the first time in American history, **monetary policy** became a distinct branch of governance, equal to but separate from **fiscal policy**.

The Fed could now raise or lower interest rates, buy or sell Treasuries, and adjust the money supply without permission from the White House or the Treasury.
Its purpose shifted from financing the government to protecting the currency itself.

This was the formal birth of the **Iron Law of Separation**: the legal and operational divide that ensures no political hand can reach the printing press.

The Immediate Consequences

Freedom came with pain.
Almost overnight, interest rates began to rise.
Bond prices fell.
The Treasury, once accustomed to cheap borrowing, faced a new reality: market discipline.

Within months, the cost of servicing the national debt increased. Deficits widened. Politicians fumed.
But beneath the short-term discomfort lay the long-term dividend—**credibility**.
Investors, at home and abroad, began to believe again that the United States would defend its currency even when it hurt.

The dollar, which had been wobbling against gold and foreign currencies, stabilized. Inflation began to ease. And the Fed, newly empowered, gained a reputation that would shape markets for generations.

The Irony of Power

The Treasury had sought to maintain control to protect the nation; in doing so, it had endangered it.
The Fed had defied the government to save the government's money from the government itself.
That irony—self-restraint as salvation—became the cornerstone of American economic identity.

In the years that followed, the relationship between the Treasury and the Fed was permanently recast.
The two institutions continued to share buildings, staff, and even data—but never again power.

When future Treasury secretaries tried to pressure the Fed, they encountered polite deflection and institutional steel.
The Accord had drawn a line that no one could cross without shattering confidence.

The Global Echo

The world watched and took note.
In London, the Bank of England studied the Accord as a model for rebuilding credibility after postwar devaluation.
In Tokyo and Bonn, finance ministries debated whether they too should separate their central banks from their treasuries.
The American experiment was proving contagious.

By formalizing independence, the United States had invented a new kind of power: monetary democracy.
The Fed was no longer the government's instrument—it was the government's conscience.

The Aftermath: The Pain of Freedom

When the ink on the Accord dried, the real work began.
The Treasury had been unshackled from cheap credit; the Fed had reclaimed its independence.
But liberation always comes with pain.

By late 1951, bond prices fell sharply as yields rose to meet market reality. Investors who had grown fat on fixed, government-protected returns watched their holdings shrink.
Congress demanded hearings. Headlines screamed that the Fed had "crashed the bond market."

Yet beneath the noise, a miracle was unfolding: inflation began to recede. The dollar, no longer a captive currency, started to regain

its global prestige.
For the first time in modern history, the United States was proving that a democracy could choose long-term stability over short-term convenience.

The market had rediscovered fear—and with it, trust.

The Accord's Quiet Revolution

The Accord did not simply change a policy—it rewrote the Constitution of money.
It transformed the Fed from a subordinate agency into an independent guardian of value, permanently altering the balance of power among the nation's financial institutions.

From that moment forward:

- **The Treasury** became the Spender—obligated to face the pain of every deficit in public auctions.
- **The Market** became the Judge—pricing that pain and punishing excess through yields.
- **The Fed** became the Arbiter—regulating liquidity but barred from financing indulgence.

The resulting geometry—three powers in perpetual tension—became the **Three-Party System** described throughout this book. Its creation was not academic; it was the scar tissue left by the inflationary wounds of the 1940s.

Institutionalizing the Iron Law

The 1951 Accord became the legal precedent for the **Iron Law of Separation.**
Every subsequent reform—from the 1978 Federal Reserve Reform Act to the 2010 Dodd-Frank Act—traced its lineage back to this moment.

The principle is simple, the enforcement relentless:
The hand that spends must never control the hand that prints.

That rule was tested repeatedly in the decades that followed—during the stagflation of the 1970s, the debt explosion of the 1980s, and the financial crises of the 21st century.
Yet each time, the system held. Independence bent but never broke.

The 1951 Accord was the blueprint that taught every future Fed chair—from Volcker to Powell—that credibility is built not by pleasing presidents, but by defying them when necessary.

The Price of Principle

The Accord also created a permanent tension at the heart of American politics: every president since Truman has wished, at some point, that it had never been signed.

- In the 1960s, Lyndon Johnson begged the Fed to hold rates down to finance the Great Society and the Vietnam War.
- In the 1970s, Richard Nixon bullied the Fed into delaying rate hikes before his re-election—a move that unleashed double-digit inflation.
- In the 1980s, Ronald Reagan praised Paul Volcker for slaying inflation but quietly fumed at the recessions his policies caused.
- In the 2000s, presidents of both parties learned that the Fed's chairmanship could make or break their legacies.

Every generation of politicians rediscovers the same frustration: the central bank's loyalty is to the currency, not to the campaign.

That frustration is the system working exactly as designed.

From Inflation Fighter to Global Anchor

As the decades passed, the 1951 Accord's influence spread beyond U.S. borders.
By the 1960s, the dollar had become the foundation of the global monetary system under Bretton Woods.
When that system collapsed in 1971 and currencies began to float, it

was the **Federal Reserve's credibility**, not the gold standard, that kept the dollar dominant.

Foreign central banks began to mirror the Accord's principles: independence, transparency, and inflation targeting.
In Tokyo, Frankfurt, and London, monetary authorities studied the American model not as a policy but as a survival manual.
By freeing its central bank, the United States had unwittingly exported the blueprint for modern capitalism.

The Accord's Moral Legacy

There is a moral dimension to this story often missed by economists.
The 1951 Accord was the moment when America declared that *integrity has a cost—and we will pay it.*

It enshrined the idea that restraint is not weakness but strength, that the power to print money must be tempered by the willingness to suffer its consequences.
It proved that discipline could coexist with democracy—that a nation could govern its appetites without surrendering to them.

In a century defined by excess, that commitment became the true reserve asset of the world: credibility.

The Accord as Origin Story

Every modern feature of the dollar system—the open auction, the Fed's balance-sheet operations, the Repo Market's trust in collateral—traces its lineage back to this single event.
The Accord was not the end of conflict; it was the codification of permanent tension.
It forced the Spender, the Market, and the Printer into a perpetual triangle where each fears the other just enough to keep faith alive.

The pain of the national debt, the spectacle of the debt ceiling, the independence of the Federal Reserve—all of it is the living echo of that March afternoon in 1951 when the Printer finally said "no."

The Dollar as Weapon

By freeing itself from political control, the Federal Reserve secured the dollar's integrity.
But independence created a new form of power—one that extended far beyond national borders.
The same system that protected the currency at home became a tool of influence abroad.

The institutions born from discipline evolved into instruments of deterrence, sanctions, and global leverage.
This is where monetary independence becomes geopolitical dominance—the moment America's moral restraint turned into strategic force.

PART II

The Mechanics of the Ritual and Its Hidden Costs

Chapter 8

The Collateral Crisis and the Repo Market Engine

From Doctrine to Machinery

The previous chapters built the architecture of restraint — the Iron Law separating the Printer from the Spender, the Golden Guardrail enforcing market pain.
Now the focus shifts from politics to plumbing: how those moral constraints became the world's most powerful financial engine.

In this second act, philosophy gives way to physics.
Here, the U.S. national debt is not theory or metaphor — it is the working material of the global system.
Every bond, every bill, every note is a moving part in a machine that converts American obligations into worldwide liquidity.

The paradox sharpens: the greater America's debt, the safer the world feels.

The Mountain of Safety

To most citizens, the roughly $38 trillion national debt is a monument to excess.
To global finance, it is infrastructure — a colossal reservoir of risk-free collateral that keeps credit flowing across continents.
These securities circulate like electrical current: pledged, borrowed, rehypothecated, and returned billions of times each day.

Without them, the modern economy would darken overnight.
Every loan, every derivative, every corporate payroll depends on the silent pulse of U.S. Treasuries moving through the financial bloodstream.

The Repo Market: The Invisible Exchange

This pulse has a name: the **Repurchase Agreement (Repo) Market** — the quiet giant beneath every other market.
It dwarfs global stock exchanges in volume yet remains largely unseen, because it operates not in months or years but in hours.

A **Repo** is, in essence, an overnight secured loan:

1. The borrower sells a Treasury to a lender.

2. The borrower promises to repurchase it the next day at a slightly higher price.
3. The tiny price difference is the interest — the **Repo rate**.

To lawyers it is a sale; to financiers it is a loan; to the world it is oxygen.
Trillions of dollars move through this mechanism every 24 hours, balancing the liquidity of banks, hedge funds, and central banks alike.

The Anatomy of a Single Night

At 9 p.m. New York time, a large money-market fund lends $10 billion in cash to a major bank.
The bank hands over $10 billion in Treasury bills as collateral.
At 8 a.m. the next morning, the trade reverses — the bank repays the cash plus a few thousand dollars in interest, and the collateral returns.
The transaction lasts barely eleven hours, but multiplied across thousands of institutions, it becomes the circulatory system of capitalism.

Every night, this ritual repeats.
Every morning, the world wakes to find its credit supply refreshed.

Why Only Treasuries Will Do

Three qualities make U.S. Treasuries the supreme collateral of the Repo universe:

1. **Risk-Free Status.** Because the U.S. issues its own currency, default in dollar terms is impossible. That legal reality, enforced by the Iron Law of Separation, gives Treasuries an unmatched credit rating.
2. **Liquidity.** The Treasury market trades in trillion-dollar depth. A bond can be sold in seconds without moving its price. That immediacy is priceless when billions hinge on timing.

3. **Fungibility.** A 10-year note issued last week is identical to one issued last year. Standardization makes automation possible; automation makes scale unstoppable.

Together these traits create what traders call **the risk-free asset** — not a metaphor, but a working component. Without it, overnight lending would seize, and the global credit machine would choke.

The Tyranny of Perfection

Because Treasuries are flawless, everything else is judged against them.
They define the **risk-free rate**, the baseline for pricing every mortgage, bond, and derivative on earth.
A single basis-point move in this rate shifts the valuation of trillions.

This perfection breeds dependence.
Every institution, from a Tokyo bank to a Chicago hedge fund, structures its balance sheet around the assumption that Treasuries will always be available, always liquid, always beyond question.
When that assumption trembles, so does the world.

The Debt as Utility

Seen from the inside, America's debt is less a burden than a public utility.
It supplies the raw material — collateral — that lubricates global finance.
If issuance slows or the Fed removes too many bonds through Quantitative Easing, the system experiences **collateral scarcity**: too much cash chasing too few Treasuries.

Interest rates in the Repo Market spike, loans stall, and liquidity evaporates.
Paradoxically, the remedy is **more debt**, not less.
The world needs a constant flow of new Treasury securities to keep credit alive.

The mountain that looks terrifying from afar is, up close, the scaffolding that holds civilization's economy together.

The Collateral Paradox

The stability of the global dollar system depends on an irony so profound that it defies common sense:
Too much cash can be as dangerous as too little.

When the Federal Reserve floods the banking system with liquidity, it does not create more Treasury securities—it removes them.
Each bond the Fed buys through **Quantitative Easing (QE)** disappears from circulation, tucked safely onto the Fed's balance sheet.
The money supply expands, but the supply of usable collateral shrinks.

The result is a bizarre kind of famine in the midst of plenty: markets swimming in dollars but starving for something risk-free to anchor them.

The World Runs on Collateral

Collateral is to finance what oxygen is to biology: invisible until it's gone.
Every short-term loan, every hedge, every derivative contract relies on a high-quality asset—usually a Treasury security—to guarantee repayment.
Remove enough of that collateral and the system begins to suffocate.

In ordinary times, the Treasury continually issues new debt, providing fresh inventory for the Repo Market.
But during QE, the Fed buys those same securities in bulk, sterilizing their availability.
The world ends up with cash-rich balance sheets but not enough pristine collateral to keep short-term lending fluid.

This mismatch doesn't cause headlines—until it does.

The Mechanics of Scarcity

When a specific Treasury security is scarce, borrowers may pay a premium to obtain it, which typically appears as a repo rate below the general-collateral rate. Broad repo rates rise for a different reason: cash providers demand more compensation when readily available cash or reserves are insufficient relative to financing needs. In September 2019, the stress was principally of the second kind.

The stress ripples through every layer of finance:

- Money-market funds can't lend efficiently.
- Banks hoard Treasuries instead of circulating them.
- Hedge funds face margin calls as funding costs soar.

A Repo market designed to hum quietly at two percent can suddenly roar to ten.

And that is precisely what happened in **September 2019.**

CASE STUDY: The 2019 Repo Shock

It began without warning.
Monday, September 16th, 2019—an unremarkable trading day in late summer.
By midafternoon, traders noticed something strange: the overnight Repo rate, normally hovering around the Fed's 2% target, was climbing fast.
By nightfall it hit **10%**.

On Wall Street, that number was incomprehensible.
The world's safest lending market had just gone off-script.
Phones lit up across New York, London, and Hong Kong as desks scrambled to secure cash.

The causes were mundane yet lethal in combination:

- **Corporate tax payments** had drained reserves from the banking system as firms wired billions to the U.S. Treasury.
- **A large Treasury auction** had settled the same week, increasing Dealers' financing needs. The result was a sudden mismatch between financing demand and the supply of readily available cash. Treasury collateral was abundant; what became scarce at the margin was balance-sheet capacity and reserves that institutions were willing or able to deploy into repo.

Inside the Panic

At 6:00 p.m., funding desks at major banks began refusing new Repo trades.
By 9:00 p.m., hedge funds that relied on overnight financing were frozen out entirely.
The heart of the dollar system—a $4 trillion daily market—was seizing.

For the first time in over a decade, traders uttered a phrase that had not been heard since 2008:
"The pipes are clogged."

Every hour that passed risked contagion.
Without Repo financing, institutions would be forced to sell Treasuries en masse to raise cash, driving bond prices down and yields up.
In a market built on trust in liquidity, that spiral would be catastrophic.

The Fed Steps In

At dawn on September 17th, the Federal Reserve intervened.
In a single announcement, it offered to lend **$75 billion** in overnight cash through emergency Repo operations—exchanging dollars for Treasury collateral.
The effect was instantaneous: rates collapsed back toward normal.

Over the next several days, the Fed repeated and expanded the operation, supplying hundreds of billions of dollars of repo financing. It was not rescuing banks from insolvency and it was not curing a shortage of Treasury collateral; it was relieving a cash-and-reserve funding squeeze against abundant collateral. The intervention restored circulation to the market's funding channels.

The Lesson of 2019

The 2019 crisis changed how policymakers viewed debt forever.
It proved three truths that underpin the Dollar Paradox:

1. **Debt is Utility.**
   The national debt isn't a burden; it's working capital for the planet. When supply falters, markets suffocate.

2. **The Fed as Guarantor.**
   The central bank's role is not to finance deficits but to preserve the liquidity of the debt that finances everything else.

3. **Pain as Price.**
   The cost of paying interest on trillions of dollars of debt is the operational fee for keeping this collateral engine running.

In effect, the U.S. pays rent to itself for global stability.
The interest bill is not a fiscal flaw—it's the receipt for credibility.

The Quiet Aftershock

When the panic passed, Wall Street exhaled—but the memory lingered.
Behind closed doors, central bankers and market participants began to accept a new reality: the world's financial system was now permanently dependent on the Fed's ability to act as **backstop to collateral**.
Without that implicit guarantee, trust in the dollar's plumbing would vanish.

The 2019 episode became the prelude to a far greater test: the pandemic of 2020, when the entire global financial system would again turn to Treasuries—and nearly drown in its own demand for them.

When Liquidity Becomes Power

Every empire has its lever of control.
For Rome, it was roads and legions.
For Britain, it was ships and trade routes.
For the United States, it is **liquidity**—the ability to supply or withhold the world's most trusted collateral at will.

The global financial system runs on U.S. Treasuries as surely as an engine runs on oil.
And the valve that controls that flow—the Repo Market—sits under American jurisdiction.
Whoever governs that valve governs the price of trust itself.

Collateral as Currency

Over time, the Repo system evolved into something more profound than a credit tool.
Treasuries became a form of **shadow money**—a parallel currency that institutions trade, pledge, and hoard just as individuals hoard cash.

This shadow money circulates through global finance in enormous volume.
Each Treasury security pledged in a Repo becomes the base for multiple other transactions, each layering new credit upon the same foundation.
The system multiplies liquidity without multiplying risk—so long as everyone believes that collateral will always be honored.

That belief, however, has an address: Washington, D.C.

The Global Web of Dependence

From Frankfurt to Singapore, from Riyadh to Santiago, the same logic repeats:
Banks, pension funds, and sovereign wealth managers treat U.S. Treasuries as the universal reserve asset.
Their local currencies may fluctuate; their economies may stumble.

But as long as they hold Treasuries, they remain plugged into the world's financial bloodstream.

This dependence gives the United States a power that no empire has ever held in peacetime: the ability to project influence not through armies, but through **access to collateral**.
By controlling the supply, the pricing, and the convertibility of the safest asset, America dictates the terms of global liquidity.

The Fed's Hidden Diplomacy

Every major crisis abroad now triggers a familiar sequence: a rush into dollars, a shortage of Treasuries, and eventually, the Federal Reserve's quiet intervention.
Through **swap lines** and **repo facilities** extended to foreign central banks, the Fed supplies dollars and accepts Treasuries in return. These actions are not charity; they are strategy.

When the Fed lends dollars to Europe or Asia against Treasury collateral, it reinforces two truths:

1. The dollar is indispensable.
2. The collateral that underpins it remains within the Fed's orbit of control.

The Fed's balance sheet has thus become a tool of statecraft, its liquidity programs a form of diplomatic leverage.

The Pandemic Stress Test

In March 2020, as markets convulsed under pandemic panic, the global race for cash turned into a **dash for Treasuries**.
Investors sold even safe assets to raise dollars, driving Treasury prices down and yields up in a moment of paradoxical chaos.

For a brief, terrifying week, the world's safest asset became the hardest to sell.
The Repo Market—a system built on the premise that Treasuries are always liquid—teetered on the edge of collapse.

The Federal Reserve responded with a rescue so massive it defied imagination:
It purchased more than **$1 trillion** of Treasuries in weeks, reopened swap lines with foreign central banks, and launched a standing **Foreign and International Monetary Authorities Repo Facility** to lend dollars abroad against Treasury collateral.

In effect, the Fed globalized its backstop.
The central bank of the United States had become the central bank of the world.

The Geopolitical Dividend

Each intervention, though framed as stabilization, carries an unmistakable message: the world's access to liquidity depends on America's permission.
If the U.S. Treasury market is the engine, the Fed is the ignition key.

That key can be turned gently—to ease crises—or sharply—to apply pressure.
When nations defy U.S. sanctions or challenge dollar hegemony, they find that the channels of credit, settlement, and collateral narrow swiftly.
No decree is necessary. Markets enforce obedience automatically, because access to Treasury collateral is synonymous with survival.

In this way, the **Repo Market**—once a technical curiosity—became the quiet battlefield of modern geopolitics.

The Moral Irony of Power

This architecture of control did not emerge from conquest or conspiracy.
It arose from the same institutional discipline that once separated the Spender from the Printer.
The Iron Law that prevented political abuse at home evolved into a system that ensured strategic dominance abroad.

America's restraint became the world's reliance.
Every nation that uses the dollar, every investor that covets Treasuries, is participating in the same paradox: trusting the power that disciplines itself.

The U.S. does not need to threaten force; its credibility is the weapon.

The Cost of Empire Without Conquest

This dominance, however, demands continuous sacrifice.
The United States must remain willing to issue debt, tolerate deficits, and maintain a market large enough to absorb the world's savings.
The interest it pays on that debt—nearly a trillion dollars annually—is not the price of failure but the fee for global leadership.

Every Treasury auction, every Fed operation, is a renewal of that pact: America borrows, the world lends, and trust circulates like blood.
The arrangement persists not because of faith in virtue but because there is no alternative machine large enough to replace it.

The Dollar as Weapon

The collateral engine made the United States the financial core of the planet.
But with power came temptation.
If access to collateral could preserve stability, it could also enforce policy.
The same tools that kept markets alive could, in different hands, become instruments of economic coercion.

Liquidity became leverage, sanctions replaced soldiers, and the dollar—once a covenant of trust—became the sharpest weapon in the modern arsenal of power.

Chapter 9

The Stealth Tax: Interest Rate Parity and the Hidden Cost of Borrowing

The Hidden Toll of Stability

Every empire leaves its mark in taxes.
Rome demanded grain, Britain demanded gold, and the United States—without ever saying so—demands interest.

Unlike other empires, America's tax is invisible.
It is not levied by customs officials or armies but by spreadsheets and screens, collected through the mechanics of global finance.
This is the **Stealth Tax**—the quiet surcharge the rest of the world pays for the privilege of living inside a dollar-denominated system.

It cannot be voted away or negotiated at the United Nations.
It is enforced automatically every time a bond is issued, a loan is priced, or a currency is converted.
It is the price of stability in a world that cannot function without the U.S. Treasury market as its anchor.

The Dollar's Silent Authority

The world's governments and corporations may print their own currencies, but they borrow in dollars.
And because they borrow in dollars, they live under the discipline of U.S. interest rates.

Every time the U.S. Treasury conducts an auction, the resulting yield ricochets across the planet:

- Mortgage rates in Canada adjust within hours.
- Sovereign bond spreads in Brazil widen overnight.
- Infrastructure projects in India suddenly become more expensive.

No presidential decree is required; the signal is mechanical.
The cost of capital everywhere else is pegged, directly or indirectly, to the yield curve of the United States.

This is how power expresses itself in the twenty-first century: not through armies, but through basis points.

Revisiting the Exorbitant Privilege

In 1965, the French finance minister Valéry Giscard d'Estaing coined the phrase *l'exorbitant privilège* to describe America's ability to live beyond its means.
Six decades later, that privilege has evolved into something even larger: the ability to make the rest of the world finance its own dependence.

Traditionally, economists described this privilege in two parts:

1. **Purchasing Power.** Because the dollar is the global medium of exchange, the United States can buy foreign goods simply by creating its own currency. Every other nation must first earn dollars to trade.
2. **Cheap Financing.** Because investors everywhere crave U.S. Treasuries, the government can borrow at rates perpetually lower than its peers.

But these two advantages describe only the visible part of the equation.
Beneath them lies the **Stealth Tax**—the systemic markup everyone else must pay because U.S. debt defines the global benchmark.

The Low-Cost Hegemon

Imagine the world's financial system as a pyramid.
At its apex sits the U.S. Treasury yield, the purest expression of risk-free return.
Every other borrower—from the government of Germany to a start-up in Nairobi—must pay a **spread** above that yield to compensate lenders for risk.

That spread is unavoidable.
Even the most disciplined foreign government cannot borrow at the same rate as the United States because the very act of being "non-U.S." introduces a premium: less liquidity, less depth, less trust.

The result is structural asymmetry.
The U.S. funds its debt at 3 percent while much of the world pays 5 to 10 percent—or more—for the same dollars.
The difference flows silently toward Washington in the form of cheaper imports, stronger credit ratings, and lower fiscal pressure.

It is, in essence, a **permanent interest differential** built into the architecture of global finance—a toll on every bridge that crosses into the dollar zone.

The Mechanics of the Hidden Toll

When investors buy a foreign bond, they compare its yield not to zero but to the yield on a U.S. Treasury of equal maturity.
The Treasury yield is the **risk-free rate**, the base cost of money for the world.
Every other rate is simply:

Borrowing Rate = U.S. Treasury Yield + Credit Spread.

- The **Treasury Yield** is what the world trusts.
- The **Credit Spread** is what the world fears.

That spread—the few percentage points of additional cost—constitutes the Stealth Tax.
It is not collected in cash, but in opportunity.
Every school not built, every highway delayed, every business that cannot refinance its loans because the base rate has moved a quarter of a point higher—those are the real payments of this invisible tax.

The Global Lever

Whenever the Federal Reserve raises or lowers its policy rate, or whenever the Treasury increases debt issuance, the entire pyramid adjusts.
A single 100-basis-point move in the 10-year Treasury yield adds billions in financing costs across Europe, Asia, and Latin America.

When yields rise sharply:

- Global corporations postpone bond offerings.
- Developing nations scramble to defend their currencies.
- Commodity prices oscillate as traders reassess carrying costs.

The Fed's decisions, made in a conference room on Constitution Avenue, echo through capitals worldwide within hours.
The Stealth Tax is thus not a conspiracy but a **systemic reflex**—a global financial tide that rises and falls with U.S. policy.

The Safety Drag

Higher U.S. rates also trigger what economists call a **flight to safety**. Investors pull money from riskier assets—emerging-market bonds, corporate loans, equities—and pour it into Treasuries.
Capital that once financed growth in São Paulo or Johannesburg rushes back to New York, seeking the comfort of liquidity.

For emerging economies, the result is a one-two punch:

1. Their borrowing costs rise because U.S. yields rise.
2. Their currencies weaken because capital flees to dollars.

What began as a domestic policy adjustment in Washington becomes an international austerity wave.
The paradox deepens: America's pain relief is the world's recession.

Prelude to Parity

These dynamics are connected to an important no-arbitrage principle called Interest Rate Parity. In its covered form, the relationship links interest-rate differentials to spot and forward exchange rates: once currency risk is hedged, comparable returns across currencies should not offer a free riskless profit. It does not require national interest rates themselves to be equal.

The Law of Parity: Gravity of Money

In physics, gravity pulls everything toward a center of mass. In global finance, the dollar's depth gives U.S. rates enormous gravitational influence—but Interest Rate Parity is more precise than the metaphor. It describes how interest-rate differences and exchange-rate hedges fit together, not a rule that every country's rate must converge on the U.S. yield curve.

The principle is deceptively simple: when two comparable investments are expressed in different currencies, a fully hedged investor should not be able to lock in a risk-free gain merely by choosing the currency with the higher interest rate. If such a gap appears, arbitrage tends to close it through the spot and forward foreign-exchange markets.

Banks, asset managers, hedge funds, and other market participants enforce this relationship through borrowing, investing, and hedging. Real-world frictions can create deviations, but the covered relationship remains a core benchmark in global funding markets.

The Mechanism of Equalization

Consider a basic example. Suppose comparable U.S. dollar assets yield 4 percent while comparable yen assets yield 1 percent. A Japanese investor might convert yen to dollars and buy the higher-yielding asset, apparently earning a 3-percentage-point advantage.

Covered Interest Rate Parity closes the riskless version of that trade through the forward market. If the investor locks in the future dollar-to-yen conversion with a forward contract, the forward exchange rate normally reflects the interest-rate differential, offsetting the apparent extra return.

The key is the hedge: the forward rate, not an assumption that the future spot dollar will simply appreciate, removes the arbitrage opportunity. Market frictions, balance-sheet costs, and regulation can cause temporary deviations, but there is no automatic free spread.

This self-correcting mechanism contributes to the dollar's gravitational pull because the deepest dollar funding and hedging markets sit at the center of global finance. It reinforces the importance of U.S. rates without making them a compulsory rate for every country.

The Paradox of Safety and Surrender

The result is not global equality but powerful global transmission. National central banks retain their own policy rates, yet they operate in a world of mobile capital, exchange-rate pressure, dollar funding needs, and investor comparisons. Those forces can sharply constrain policy choices without erasing monetary sovereignty altogether.

Every finance minister learns the practical version of the lesson: the Federal Reserve moves, and the effects travel. Not because Interest Rate Parity mechanically forces obedience, but because dollar funding, hedging costs, capital flows, and risk appetite transmit U.S. monetary conditions across borders.

When Parity Becomes Punishment

For emerging markets, this synchronization is brutal.
Their credibility gap—the distance between the yield on U.S. Treasuries and their own sovereign bonds—is wide to begin with. When U.S. rates rise, that gap widens further, inflicting a two-fold injury.

1. **The Borrowing Squeeze**
   Their cost of issuing new debt jumps immediately. A 1-percent increase in the U.S. benchmark can add billions to annual interest bills for nations already running tight budgets. Infrastructure projects stall. Social spending shrinks. Capital investment freezes.

2. **The Currency Shock**
   As investors rush to the relative safety of the dollar, local currencies weaken.
   For governments and corporations that have borrowed in dollars—a common practice in the developing world—this is catastrophic.

Their debts, fixed in dollar terms, swell in local currency value.

This is the double pressure created by tighter U.S. monetary conditions: higher global funding costs and, for many economies, weaker local currencies—especially painful when governments or companies carry large dollar-denominated debts.

Case Illustration:
The Fragility of the Global South

When the Federal Reserve began raising interest rates in 2022 to fight post-pandemic inflation, the tremors were immediate and global.

- **Egypt** saw its foreign-exchange reserves fall by nearly one-third as investors pulled money back to the United States.
- **Pakistan** faced a 30-percent currency depreciation within months, pushing its external debt servicing costs into crisis territory.
- **Ghana**, once a poster child for African growth, defaulted on portions of its external debt by the end of 2022 after its borrowing costs doubled in less than a year.

None of these nations had printed recklessly or borrowed more than usual.
They were simply caught in the undertow of the Fed's rate hikes—a ripple from Washington that turned into a financial tsunami across continents.

The Stealth Tax is thus not an abstraction; it is measured in unemployment, austerity, and social unrest in countries that never cast a vote in the Federal Open Market Committee.

The Safety of the Few, the Cost of the Many

While developing nations scramble to defend their currencies, investors in New York, London, and Zurich enjoy a different reality. For them, higher U.S. yields mean better returns on safe assets. Money that once financed factories in Vietnam or wind farms in Brazil now flows into Treasury ETFs and money-market funds.

The same instrument—the Treasury bond—that stabilizes global finance also drains vitality from it.
Each rise in yield acts like a global gravity wave: stabilizing the center, destabilizing the periphery.

It is this structural inequality—built not on exploitation but on trust—that sustains America's financial dominance.
Every borrower abroad pays a few extra points of interest to underwrite the liquidity and credibility of the U.S. system.

The Dollar's Chain Reaction

In practice, the chain unfolds like this:

1. **The Fed raises rates** to fight inflation at home.
2. **U.S. Treasury yields rise.**
3. **Global capital shifts** out of riskier assets into Treasuries.
4. **Foreign currencies weaken.**
5. **Dollar-denominated debt burdens rise.**
6. **Emerging-market growth slows**, creating deflationary pressure abroad that later feeds back into cheaper U.S. imports.

The loop closes neatly: America cools its inflation while exporting its slowdown to the rest of the world.
The system stabilizes at a global cost invisible to domestic voters but painfully obvious in foreign ministries.

The Structural Asymmetry

This entire mechanism hinges on one immutable fact: the United States is the only issuer of the dollar, and the dollar is the only currency deep enough to absorb global capital without distortion. That monopoly gives the U.S. an automatic bid for its debt and an automatic subsidy for its deficits.

In a sense, every emerging nation's currency depreciation is a **tribute payment** to that monopoly—an involuntary adjustment that re-prices the world's risk in America's favor.
No law mandates it. No treaty codifies it. It simply happens because mathematics leaves no alternative.

The Hidden Tribute

When historians of finance look back on the early twenty-first century, they will note that the world's most profitable export from the United States was not technology, nor oil, nor arms—it was **interest rates**.
Every Fed decision, every Treasury auction, is a small act of global taxation disguised as monetary policy.
The burden is distributed across millions of spreadsheets, billions of transactions, and entire national budgets.

The stealth tax is not moral; it is mechanical.
It functions because the U.S. built a system so credible that everyone else must use it, even when it hurts them.
And like all taxes, its collection is automatic.

The Final Constraint: The World on America's Clock

Every global financial system runs on someone's clock.
For the past eighty years, that clock has ticked to the rhythm of the U.S. yield curve.

Tokyo and Frankfurt open their trading days not with local data, but by checking what happened overnight in U.S. Treasury futures. Emerging-market bond auctions are priced not in isolation, but in

reference to yesterday's close of the 10-year note.
When Washington sneezes, the world holds its breath.

Dollar funding markets, hedging costs, and global portfolio flows transmit U.S. rate changes widely. Interest Rate Parity is one link in that transmission, not a rule tying every loan, credit-default swap, or sovereign bond to a single Washington-set rate. Even so, the U.S. yield curve remains the world's most influential financial reference point.

The Illusion of Sovereignty

For most countries, monetary sovereignty is a legal fiction.
Central banks may issue their own currencies, but they cannot detach from the gravitational pull of the dollar.

When the Federal Reserve tightens policy, the ripple effects arrive like an invisible embargo:
local borrowing costs rise, foreign exchange reserves dwindle, and domestic banks scramble to maintain liquidity.
Conversely, when the Fed eases, global liquidity surges, inflating asset bubbles from Buenos Aires to Bangalore.

Every financial boom and bust in the developing world is, in some measure, a shadow of American monetary weather.
It is why economists often call the Fed the **"central bank to the world."**

Yet this dependency is not colonialism by design—it is the collateral consequence of trust.
The world depends on the U.S. not because it is forced to, but because it must.

The Price of Credibility

The Stealth Tax functions because the U.S. has done what no empire before it ever managed: monetize credibility.
It turned trust itself into a financial product—issued, auctioned, and traded globally under the brand name *U.S. Treasury*.

Every investor who buys a Treasury bond is not lending money to a government; they are buying a piece of certainty.
That certainty commands a premium.
It allows the United States to fund trillion-dollar deficits at rates that would bankrupt lesser nations.

The same mechanism that keeps borrowing cheap at home keeps it expensive abroad.
Every time the Treasury auctions new bonds, the base rate of global finance resets around it.
That is the quiet miracle of the system: the more the U.S. borrows, the more the world aligns around its discipline.

The World's Hidden Subsidy

It is fashionable in political circles to decry the "cost of the debt." But the true cost of the debt is not borne by the United States; it is borne by everyone else.

Foreign central banks, pension funds, and corporations hold roughly half of all publicly traded U.S. Treasuries.
They do so not out of charity, but necessity.
Their participation keeps U.S. interest rates low, ensuring that America's fiscal burden is dispersed across the global balance sheet.

The Stealth Tax, therefore, is not a metaphor—it is a literal redistribution of financing cost.
By anchoring global credit to its own liabilities, the United States externalizes part of its debt service to the rest of the world.
The world pays more to borrow so that America can pay less.

The Golden Guardrail Revisited

This global structure rests on the same principle that keeps Washington's institutions honest: **discipline through pain**.

At home, the Treasury must borrow in the open market, facing investors who price every fiscal decision in real time.
Abroad, every other borrower must do the same—but their

benchmark is the U.S. Treasury itself.
The Golden Guardrail, which separates the Spender from the Printer domestically, extends outward into the world as a financial hierarchy:

- The **U.S. Treasury** faces the market but sets the base rate.
- **Developed nations** borrow just above it, paying for their proximity to credibility.
- **Emerging nations** borrow far above it, paying for their distance from trust.

The pain of interest—what the U.S. once accepted as a domestic cost of restraint—has become the global price of stability.

The Hidden Logic of the Paradox

In the early chapters, the paradox of borrowing was moral and political:
Why would a nation so powerful choose to borrow rather than print?
Now, its answer is mechanical and global:
Borrowing is what keeps the world orbiting the dollar.

If the U.S. printed freely, it would destroy the credibility that makes its debt indispensable.
If it refused to borrow, it would starve the system of the collateral that keeps global finance liquid.
By borrowing—and paying the price of interest—it maintains both its internal integrity and external dominance.

The Stealth Tax, then, is not an act of exploitation but of equilibrium.
It is how the world finances the credibility it cannot manufacture for itself.

The Empire of Interest

This arrangement defines the true character of the modern American empire.
It is not an empire of conquest, but of contracts.

Its territories are not lands but balance sheets.
Its tribute is not gold or oil but interest differentials—a quiet stream of payments flowing daily through the veins of the global financial system.

Empires of the past extracted wealth through force; the United States extracts it through trust.
That is the ultimate paradox: the only thing more profitable than domination is belief.

The Hidden Cost of Order

The world's dependence on U.S. debt has created the most stable, yet most unequal, financial order in history.
The United States bears the responsibility of maintaining credibility; the world bears the cost of financing it.
This is the final layer of the Golden Guardrail: the transformation of moral restraint into global leverage.

The interest paid on America's debt is the most efficient tax ever invented—voluntary, invisible, and universal.
It funds not war, but order; not colonies, but confidence.

And as long as the rest of the world prefers pain with stability to freedom with chaos, the Stealth Tax will continue to be paid, silently, in every loan, every bond, and every promise written in dollars.

PART III

The Breach of Trust: The Weaponization of the Dollar

YOUR JUDGMENT MATTERS

Before trust becomes a weapon, a brief pause.

You have now reached the point where the paradox comes into focus: America's debt is not simply a burden—it is part of the machinery that makes the dollar powerful. **Your judgment matters because readers—not institutions—decide which serious ideas travel.**

A brief, honest Amazon rating or review helps another curious reader decide whether this explanation is worth their time. It also shows which arguments changed the way people think about debt, trust, and American power.

One or two honest sentences are enough.

SCAN TO RATE OR REVIEW THE BOOK

amazon.com/review/create-review?asin=B0G2PNMVYC

Thank you for lending your judgment to the conversation.

Part III now asks what happens when the trust that made the dollar powerful becomes a weapon.

Chapter 10

The Weaponization of Trust: Sanctions and the End of the Golden Guardrail

The Quiet Contract Everyone Signed

Every system that holds the world together is built on a promise. For aviation, it is the promise of maintenance; for electricity, the promise of frequency.
For global finance, it is the promise that a U.S. Treasury is safe from everything except time.

Nobody ever signed this promise on paper. No treaty names it. No courtroom enforces it.
Yet for eight decades, the world behaved as if a contract existed between the United States and every holder of its debt:

- Your dollars will clear.
- Your bonds will trade.
- Your savings are not a bargaining chip.

This unwritten contract is what this book calls the **Golden Guardrail**—the institutional self-denial that made the dollar not only powerful, but trustworthy. America could print money, but chose to borrow; it could bully, but chose rules; it could punish, but chose predictability. And because it chose restraint, the world chose its bonds.

The cost of that restraint was the interest bill.
The dividend was dominion.

A Subscription to Credibility

In Part I, we showed that the United States pays interest not because it must, but because it prefers to—because the pain of paying markets is cheaper than the chaos of printing at will. That pain buys membership in a club with one member: the issuer of the world's ultimate safe asset.

Think about the extraordinary perks of that membership:

1. **Permanent Bid:** Every auction, everywhere, references Treasury yields. Demand is structural—insurance companies,

pensions, central banks, and money funds are obligated by their mandates to own U.S. paper.

2. **Policy Space:** Fiscal mistakes that would bury smaller nations become survivable for the U.S. because the market reflexively buys its debt in a crisis.
3. **Dollar Gravity:** When fear rises, capital runs *toward* Washington, not away from it, lowering America's funding cost precisely when others' costs explode.

But the dues for this club are steep: the U.S. must behave as if its bonds are **apolitical** even when its politics burn hot. The Golden Guardrail is not a statute—it's a stance. It says: *We separate money from mood.*

Three Promises That Made an Empire

To a central banker in Riyadh, a sovereign fund in Oslo, or a reserve manager in Bangkok, the value of a Treasury has always rested on three bedrock assurances:

1. **Guaranteed Liquidity.** Need cash at 3 a.m.? Sell the bond at a known price into the deepest market on earth. Proceeds arrive instantly through the Fedwire and custody pipes.
2. **No Counterparty Risk.** Coupons land on time. Redemptions settle on time. The issuer owns the printing press; nominal payment failure is not a risk variable.
3. **Apolitical Presumption.** Reserve assets were generally treated as financial infrastructure rather than ordinary political bargaining chips, although that presumption had exceptions. U.S. sanctions had previously blocked central-bank property, including Iranian assets in 1979 and Libyan assets in 2011.

The first two promises are technical. The third is moral. It is why adversaries who would not share a border could share a balance sheet. It let Beijing hedge a generation's worth of surpluses in U.S. paper. It let Saudi Arabia recycle oil revenues without fear of seizure. It let Brazil and India park rainy-day cash in an instrument that wasn't a vote.

Neutrality turned bonds into bridges.

Why Neutrality Was Non-Negotiable

There is a simple, brutal reason the United States guarded this principle so carefully: **the dollar's supremacy depends on users who don't like us.** If only friends bought Treasuries, the market would be smaller, shallower, and more volatile. The hallmark of a true reserve asset is that even your rivals prefer it.

Neutrality therefore was not charity; it was strategy. It converted adversaries into stakeholders, knitting hostile capitals into the same clearing network, the same settlement rails, the same accounting entries at the Fed and Euroclear. The more the world relied on those rails, the less likely it was to burn them.

The Golden Guardrail was America's soft armor.

How the Guardrail Was Built—And Policed

The guardrail took form through countless operational choices:

- **Custody Architecture:** The Federal Reserve Bank of New York's foreign official accounts, Euroclear in Brussels, Clearstream in Luxembourg, and global custodians in New York and London built industrial-grade pipes where reserves could be held, lent, pledged, and sold at machine speed.

- **Rule Consistency.** Across administrations, most sanctions targeted people, companies, banks, sectors, or governments without immobilizing the reserve assets of a major globally integrated central bank. Earlier cases involving Iran and Libya showed, however, that sovereign central-bank property was not legally untouchable.

- **Crisis Behavior:** In crashes—from 1987 to 2008 to 2020—the United States opened the spigots, extended swap lines, and stabilized settlement. It didn't ask who voted how. It asked what the plumbing needed.

Every one of those choices advertised the same creed: *Treasuries are the world's Switzerland.*

The Theology of the Safe Asset

"Safe" in markets is not an adjective; it is a religion.
Investors tithe to it daily—accepting lower yields, tighter spreads, harsher haircuts—because salvation in a panic is worth the cost. And like any religion, safety depends on faith in a higher principle.

For Treasuries that higher principle was **neutrality**.
Take away neutrality and a Treasury becomes just another rich country's bond—still liquid, still deep, but now politically *conditional.* The safe asset becomes a *permissioned* asset. Safety turns into privilege.

At that moment, every portfolio manager, reserve chief, and pension trustee must add a new line to the risk register:
"Access risk: Could our asset be frozen?"

Once that question exists, the religion begins to fracture.

The Cost of Breaking Your Own Rule

Why stress this so hard before we even reach 2022? Because the action that year did not just punish an aggressor; it **reversed America's own doctrine**. The United States had spent generations proving it would rather pay the political price of neutrality than risk the financial price of conditionality. We endured criticism for "letting bad actors hold our bonds" because the alternative—politicizing reserves—threatened the very basis of dollar power.

That is the central paradox of this chapter:

- The same restraint that made the dollar supreme also limited America's ability to wield it as a weapon.
- The moment the dollar became a weapon, it ceased to be purely a sanctuary.

In the pages that follow, we will trace the moment the guardrail bent, then broke—the day the safe asset revealed a trigger beneath its chrome.

Setting the Stage for a Line No One Crossed

By the late 2010s, the sanctions toolkit had grown sophisticated: SDN lists for individuals, sectoral sanctions for energy and finance, export controls for technology, and SWIFT restrictions for targeted banks. Central-bank assets had been blocked before, but never on the scale that would follow in 2022 against a major G20 economy.

The taboo was logical. Central-bank assets are the fire extinguishers of crises. In a run on a currency, reserves stabilize exchange rates; in a sudden stop, they pay for food and fuel. Freeze those, and you don't just hurt elites—you risk the safety of civilians, the stability of supply chains, and the integrity of settlement systems that bind other countries too.

The line was therefore not absolute. Iran in 1979 and Libya in 2011 were important precedents. What remained untested was whether the United States and its allies would immobilize reserves on this scale against a major nuclear power deeply integrated into global markets. That test arrived in February 2022.

The Day the Clock Stopped

At 10:58 a.m. Moscow time on February 24, 2022, Russian armor rolled across the Ukrainian border.
By the next sunrise, a different kind of war was under way — a financial one waged at light speed.

Within hours of the invasion, the White House and its G7 allies announced coordinated sanctions.
At first, they looked familiar: restrictions on oligarchs, banks, and exports. Markets barely flinched. This was sanction as usual — loud but containable.

Then came the sentence no one expected to hear:

"The United States and partners will impose measures to prevent the Central Bank of Russia from deploying its international reserves."

The translation was instant: *freeze the reserves.*

How Much Was at Stake

Roughly $630 billion stood behind the Central Bank of Russia as its prewar reserve stock. After the invasion, roughly $300 billion of Russian sovereign reserve assets were immobilized abroad, primarily foreign-currency securities and deposits held in G7 jurisdictions, with the largest share in Europe. Russia's domestically held gold was not simply seized or frozen by the G7 action.

For years, reserve managers had treated assets held in major financial centers as extraordinarily secure and liquid. The sanctions demonstrated that legal ownership and practical access are different questions when assets sit inside another jurisdiction.

The G7 action did not create the concept of blocking central-bank property, but it crossed a far larger threshold: coordinated immobilization of a substantial share of the reserves of a G20 nuclear power.

The Legal Mechanism of a Freeze

To the public, "freezing assets" sounds like a bank clerk pushing a button.
In reality, it is a bureaucratic cascade across multiple jurisdictions and institutions.

The Treasury's Office of Foreign Assets Control (OFAC) issued directives barring U.S. entities from transacting with the CBR or processing payments on its behalf.
Simultaneously, the European Union froze CBR assets held in Euroclear and other clearing houses, while the Bank of England did the same in London.
Within hours, major custodians — Citibank, JPMorgan Chase, and

BNY Mellon — received legal orders to suspend all CBR-related instructions.

No doors were broken down. No gold was hauled away. The assets remained where they were — immaculate, intact, and utterly inaccessible.

Russia's foreign savings had been turned into museum pieces: visible but untouchable.

From Sanction to Precedent

Within 24 hours, the ripple effects spread through every central bank in the world.
Reserve managers did not sleep. They called their custodians and asked quietly:

"If this were us — could you do the same?"

The answer, honestly given, was yes.
Custodians operate under the laws of their host countries. If Washington or Brussels orders them to freeze a foreign account, they must comply. The CBR discovered this first; everyone else understood it instantly.

The real shock was not that the West had acted against Russia — that was predictable in wartime — but that it had sacrificed the illusion of reserve neutrality to do so.
A door once opened can never again be said to be locked.

The Unthinkable Becomes Thinkable

The reserve architecture rested on the assumption that assets held through established custody channels would remain accessible in ordinary circumstances. The 2022 freeze exposed the jurisdictional limit to that assumption: legal access to foreign-held assets can be restricted by the authorities governing the custodians and settlement systems.

In a stroke, U.S. and European authorities had demonstrated that reserves were not owned so much as *hosted.*
Access depended not on balance sheet entries, but on political permission.
The safe asset had become a conditional asset.

Every nation with dollars in New York or euros in Frankfurt had to recalculate its risk.
The new question wasn't "How stable is the bond?" but "Who controls the switch?"

The Reversal of Neutrality

The Russia action was unprecedented in a narrower and more defensible sense: never before had a major G20 economy and nuclear power faced a coordinated reserve immobilization of this scale by the United States, the European Union, and other advanced-economy partners. It demonstrated that the dollar-centered financial system could be used strategically against a sovereign central bank of systemic importance.

For decades, Washington had promoted the dollar as the currency of trust.
Now it was using that trust as a lever of coercion.
The message was clear and global:
The U.S. will always honor its debts — but it reserves the right to decide who may collect.

The action did not erase an unbroken seventy-five-year tradition—earlier U.S. sanctions had blocked central-bank assets, including Iran's in 1979 and Libya's in 2011. What changed in 2022 was the scale, coalition breadth, and systemic significance of the target. The Treasury bond did not default; reserve managers were reminded that access can depend on the jurisdiction in which assets are custodied.

Shock Across the System

Inside finance ministries from Delhi to Riyadh, meetings began with one slide: "Exposure to U.S. Custody."
Reserve allocations were quietly reviewed. Portfolios that had been optimized for liquidity were now being reassessed for *survivability*.

Even U.S. allies felt unease. They might agree with the target today, but what if they disagreed tomorrow?
If the reserve asset could be frozen for Russia, what of Turkey in its next diplomatic spat, or Saudi Arabia in a regional crisis?

Markets did not crash — the dollar was too entrenched — but the psychology shifted.
The safe asset had gained a shadow.

The Symbolism of the Freeze

In strict accounting terms, the United States had not defaulted. The bonds continued to pay interest into blocked accounts. Not one coupon was missed.
But in moral terms, something greater than money was seized: credibility.

At unprecedented scale, the world saw that even a major central bank's reserve access could become an instrument of statecraft. The significance lay not only in the size of the sanction but in the systemic importance of its target. If a G20 central bank could be immobilized, every reserve manager had reason to think more carefully about access risk.

That is how a technical action became a historical one.
It was not the freeze of Russia's reserves; it was the freeze of an idea.

The Immediate Fallout

In the weeks that followed, Russia's ruble collapsed by over 40 percent before emergency capital controls and energy revenues stabilized it.
Moscow was forced to demand that foreign buyers of gas pay in

rubles rather than euros or dollars — a symbolic gesture that nevertheless exposed how deeply the dollar system had entangled the world.

Meanwhile, outside Russia, reserve managers were conducting their own rehearsals for self-defense.
Gold purchases surged. Asian finance ministers revived talk of regional swap lines and local-currency settlement.
None of this happened in press conferences. It happened in spreadsheets and quiet phone calls — the whispered language of fear among technocrats.

The Golden Guardrail had not been abolished by law; it had been abandoned by faith.

A Global Question No One Can Un-Ask

Every reserve manager from Beijing to Brasília now lives with the same unanswered question:

"If the United States could freeze Russia, what would stop it from freezing us?"

The power of that question is not that it will ever be answered, but that it will never again be unasked.
That is how trust dies in international finance — not with a collapse, but with a conditional clause.

The Illusion of Sovereign Savings

To understand the magnitude of what the 2022 reserve freeze revealed, we must start with the quiet fiction that underpins modern sovereignty.
Every nation imagines that it *owns* its reserves — that the dollars and euros listed on its balance sheet are real assets sitting securely in vaults under its control.
In truth, the vast majority of global reserves exist as electronic entries held in **foreign custody**.

When a country says it has "$300 billion in foreign exchange reserves," what it really has is a digital ledger showing claims on assets — assets that are *legally housed* inside Western institutions. The owner can give instructions, but cannot execute them directly. Like a pilot in a cockpit, the central bank has the controls — but someone else owns the runway.

The Architecture of Custody

The global reserve system evolved after World War II around a network of trust-based custodians.
These institutions—part bank, part vault, part clearinghouse—form the circulatory system of world finance.

The hierarchy looks roughly like this:

1. **The Asset.**
   The reserve itself is usually a U.S. Treasury bond or other highly rated sovereign security. It is not physical paper but an entry in the Federal Reserve's book-entry system or a European clearinghouse such as Euroclear or Clearstream.

2. **The Holder.**
   The owner is a foreign central bank — for example, the Central Bank of Russia, the People's Bank of China, or the Saudi Arabian Monetary Authority. The holder appears as the beneficial owner of record.

3. **The Custodian.**
   The custodian is the institution that actually *holds* the securities and processes transactions — JPMorgan Chase, Citibank, the Federal Reserve Bank of New York, or Euroclear in Brussels.

This setup has always been seen as neutral infrastructure, akin to air-traffic control.
But as the 2022 sanctions proved, neutrality is a choice — not an engineering property.

The Fragility Hidden in Efficiency

The system's elegance is also its vulnerability.
To make the global financial machine efficient, reserves are **centralized** within a few highly regulated Western hubs.
This concentration allows for speed, liquidity, and transparency.
It also gives the host jurisdictions enormous power.

When the U.S. Treasury or the European Union issues a legal directive, the custodians must comply immediately.
There is no appeals process, no international court of override.
A sovereign's national savings are thus *legally subject* to the laws of the custodian's domicile.

The same architecture that made Treasuries universal made them **controllable.**

The Ledger of Truth

To see this more clearly, imagine how a reserve transaction actually unfolds:

- The Central Bank of Russia places an order to purchase $10 billion in 10-year U.S. Treasury notes.
- A primary dealer executes the trade.
- The securities are delivered not to Moscow but to an account at **Euroclear** or the **Federal Reserve Bank of New York,** listing the CBR as the beneficial owner.
- The Fed's systems confirm ownership electronically. No physical certificates exist.

Everything is digital, instantaneous, and traceable.
That digital purity, once seen as a triumph of modern finance, became the mechanism of immobilization in 2022.
When OFAC issued its directive, custodians did not have to move trucks or guards — they simply **ignored commands from a blacklisted account.**

In one administrative instant, national wealth became frozen code.

When Ownership Means Permission

This revelation horrified reserve managers around the world. They realized that the difference between **ownership** and **permission** was smaller than a line of software code.
A reserve asset under Western custody was not an instrument of sovereignty; it was a contract of trust.

As one former central banker put it privately,

"We thought we were holding dollars. In reality, we were holding an opinion — and that opinion could change."

This was not paranoia; it was simple operational fact.
The West had proven that custodianship was conditional, and that the world's assets could be immobilized without a default, without a court order, and without warning.

The Sovereign Paradox

Foreign reserves are supposed to be the ultimate defense mechanism — the firewall that protects a nation during crisis.
But the 2022 seizure revealed a paradox: the firewall itself was wired into another nation's control room.

- A developing economy borrows abroad in dollars.
- To defend its currency, it accumulates dollar reserves.
- To hold those reserves, it must use Western custodians.
- Those custodians are governed by Western laws.

The very act of seeking safety from market volatility makes the sovereign dependent on the political discretion of another power. That dependency is invisible until the day it isn't.

Why Gold Became Romantic Again

In the wake of the freeze, a curious nostalgia gripped global finance. Gold—long dismissed as a barbarous relic—suddenly looked like freedom.

Gold cannot be blocked by OFAC or Euroclear.
It cannot be de-platformed.
It does not rely on any digital ledger controlled by another jurisdiction.

The irony is profound: seventy years of technological advancement had produced a monetary system so efficient, so digitized, and so transparent that it could be turned off by decree. In that sense, gold's greatest weakness — its physicality — became its one unhackable strength.

The Quiet Panic in the Halls of Trust

After the Russian reserves were immobilized, custodians fielded a flurry of discreet inquiries.
Central banks that would never admit to anxiety in public wanted to know if their assets were legally protected.
The honest answer was unsatisfying: *It depends.*

It depends on political relations.
It depends on jurisdiction.
It depends, most dangerously, on precedent.

In that moment, the notion of the Golden Guardrail transformed from an assumption into a question mark.

The Geopolitical Default

When Power Replaces Insolvency

In finance, default used to mean failure.
It was the end of credibility — a declaration that the borrower could not pay.
But in 2022, the world witnessed a new kind of rupture: one born not of weakness, but of overwhelming power.

The United States did not default on its obligations.
It paid interest precisely on time, in full, into accounts that Russia could no longer touch.
The payments landed, settled, and vanished into legal limbo — immaculate but unusable.

This was a new category of event, one that the bond markets had no word for.
It was not insolvency. It was **excommunication.**
A sovereign state had been banished from the monetary network that made its assets liquid.

The Anatomy of a Financial Default

Before examining this new form of rupture, it helps to recall what a traditional default looks like.

In a **financial default**, the issuer fails in its basic duty: to pay interest or principal when due.
That failure signals mismanagement, insolvency, or inflationary collapse.
Markets respond with panic — yields spike, credit ratings collapse, and the borrower is forced into restructuring.

But crucially, this kind of default, painful as it is, has a known path to recovery.
Debt can be renegotiated, creditors can accept haircuts, and a new cycle of trust can eventually begin.
Even Argentina, the most prolific defaulter of modern times, still finds lenders.
Financial sin, it turns out, is forgivable.

The Nature of the Geopolitical Default

The **Geopolitical Default** of 2022 was different in every respect.
It was not about *ability* to pay, but *permission* to receive.
The United States and its allies did not question Russia's solvency — they disabled its access.

Under a traditional default, the borrower is the sinner.
Under a geopolitical default, the borrower becomes the judge.
The issuer (the United States) decides who is worthy to collect on the world's safest asset.

The result is a distortion far more destabilizing than a financial failure, because it attacks the core assumption that the safe asset is *neutral.*

Comparing Two Ruptures

Metric	Financial Default (Solvency)	Geopolitical Default (Trust)
Core Issue	Inability of the issuer to pay.	Unwillingness of the custodian to release payment.
Asset Condition	Risky – the bond loses value.	Conditional – the bond's value depends on political alignment.
Trigger	Fiscal weakness or crisis.	Political decision by dominant powers.
Systemic Damage	Hurts specific creditors; can be restructured.	Hurts all non-aligned holders; fractures global trust.
Restoration Path	Economic reform and negotiation.	None – trust, once politicized, cannot be depoliticized.

The freeze of Russia's reserves thus did not just inflict pain on one nation; it rewrote the legal DNA of the safe asset.
From that point forward, the U.S. Treasury bond — the keystone of the global system — acquired a new risk factor: **access risk.**

Access Risk: The New Variable

Access risk means that a holder of an asset may be prevented from using it, even if the issuer performs flawlessly.
This was the unpriced variable that every reserve manager now had to model.
It was not in the equations of the 1980s or 1990s.
It did not appear in the Basel regulations.
But after 2022, it had to be estimated, managed, and hedged — politically.

For most institutions, that meant reducing exposure.
Not selling everything — that would be impossible — but quietly adjusting the composition of reserves to include assets that could not be switched off by decree.

Gold, yuan bonds, commodity swaps, and local-currency reserves gained small but significant weight.
Each shift was a silent vote of no confidence in the permanence of neutrality.

The Frozen Is Worse Than the Fallen

A conventional default creates losses but also clarity.
Creditors know what has failed and can begin to rebuild around the wreckage.
A freeze creates paralysis — the money exists, but cannot move.
It is Schrodinger's balance sheet: alive and dead at the same time.

For global finance, this limbo is far more corrosive than a default.
A default punishes recklessness; a freeze punishes independence.
And that distinction reshapes behavior across continents.

If a country believes its reserves can be weaponized, it does not reform — it re-arms.
It diversifies. It hoards commodities. It builds alternative payment systems.

This is precisely what we saw after 2022: a geopolitical contagion of caution spreading through every central bank corridor.

The Loss of a Collective Illusion

Before the freeze, the world shared a collective illusion: that global finance was a *technocracy*, not an *ideology*.
Money was math; politics was policy.
The reserve system was the bridge between them.

After the freeze, that bridge became a border.
Each nation had to choose which side of the financial divide it stood on — not through ideology, but through custody.

Even countries that supported the sanctions privately feared the precedent.
They understood that credibility, once politicized, is a non-renewable resource.
The moment it is spent, it cannot be printed again.

The Market Learns Faster Than Diplomacy

Within months of the freeze, financial markets began to price in the change, even if economists hesitated to name it.
Spreads on non-G7 sovereign bonds widened slightly, not because of inflation or fiscal risk, but because of *custodial risk*.
Meanwhile, gold demand surged to multi-decade highs, not from retail buyers, but from central banks.

Quietly, global capital was voting on the meaning of "risk-free."
The old definition — "the United States will always pay" — was no longer enough.
The new definition was darker: "the United States will always pay, unless it decides not to let you collect."

That difference, though subtle, is the fault line of the new era.

The Logic of Distrust

In the old order, the dollar system was a kind of voluntary empire — nations joined because it was safer inside than outside.

The Russia episode introduced a new equation: **safety equals dependence.**
That is not an appealing formula for rising powers that prize autonomy.

From Beijing's Belt and Road ambitions to Riyadh's petro-yuan experiments, the same motive animates all these projects: the desire to escape the vulnerability of permissioned safety.
That desire is now structural, not rhetorical.

The freeze transformed diversification from a political statement into a risk-management necessity.

The Echo of the 1930s — In Reverse

Historians of money will recognize the parallel: in the 1930s, countries hoarded gold and built capital controls because they no longer trusted the British pound.
In the 2020s, they are doing the same — but this time, the target of diversification is the dollar itself.
The empire of sterling collapsed because London ran out of gold.
The empire of the dollar is challenged not because Washington ran out of money, but because it ran out of *neutrality.*

The Erosion of the Golden Guardrail

The Great Recalibration

In the months after the Russia reserve freeze, global finance underwent something like a controlled panic — silent, methodical, but profound.
There was no crisis headline, no public revolt. Instead, deep inside central banks and sovereign wealth funds, the gears began to shift.

Every nation that held significant dollar reserves performed the same mental audit:

"If trust can be revoked, what can't be?"

That question catalyzed the largest reallocation of official capital since the 1970s oil shocks.

Not a rush for the exits, but a measured **diversification of vulnerability**.

The theme was simple: don't abandon the dollar, but don't depend on it exclusively.

Custodial Risk Becomes Geopolitical Risk
Before 2022, "custodial risk" was a technical term buried in footnotes — a measure of operational exposure in asset management.
After 2022, it became a synonym for **political risk**.

Central banks that once balanced their portfolios on the basis of yield, duration, and liquidity began adding a fourth metric: **jurisdictional distance**.

How far are our assets — legally and physically — from the reach of the G7?
The answer now determined allocation strategy as much as credit rating ever did.

A Shift Measurable in Tons, Not Dollars
By late 2023, the pattern was unmistakable.
The **World Gold Council** reported the largest two-year accumulation of official-sector gold purchases in modern history. Central banks added roughly 2,300 metric tons between 2022 and 2024 — equivalent to the entire annual output of the world's gold mines.

The list of buyers told the story better than any speech:

- **China:** quietly, systematically adding to reserves every month, often through the State Administration of Foreign Exchange rather than the People's Bank to obscure true totals.
- **Turkey:** converting volatile foreign holdings into bullion stored domestically.
- **India, Poland, Singapore, Kazakhstan:** smaller economies aligning their portfolios with a single principle — "If you can touch it, you can trust it."

Gold had become the world's insurance policy against Western discretion.

Why Gold's Shine Returned

Gold's attraction was not return; it was *reliability.*
It has no issuer, no payment system, no password.
In a world of weaponized finance, that simplicity became priceless.

Moreover, gold offered what economists call **non-correlated sovereignty** — the ability to hold value independently of another nation's political cycle.
Unlike dollars or euros, it could not be immobilized by sanctions software.

The shift was not ideological; it was actuarial.
For central bankers, gold's allure was not nostalgia for a pre-digital age, but risk management in a post-neutral one.

The Dollar Share Declines

By 2025, data from the IMF's COFER database confirmed what traders had already sensed: the U.S. dollar's share of disclosed foreign-exchange reserves had slipped to roughly **57 percent**, down from 71 percent two decades earlier.

This erosion was not catastrophic — the dollar remained unmatched in liquidity — but it was steady, structural, and accelerating.
In reserve management circles, people began calling it the **"Russia discount."**

Every new dollar acquired by a non-aligned nation carried a silent premium of anxiety.

The Parallel Strategy: De-linking the Rails

While the first response targeted assets, the second targeted *infrastructure.*
If the West could weaponize custody, then the logical countermeasure was to build **payment rails** beyond its control.

1. **Bilateral Currency Swaps.**
   Nations began to ink direct swap lines — India with the UAE, China with dozens of partners, even Brazil with Argentina — allowing trade to be settled in local currencies rather than converting to dollars first.

2. **Alternative Clearing Systems.**
   China's **Cross-Border Interbank Payment System (CIPS)** gained quiet traction. By mid-2025, over 1,500 financial institutions across 120 countries had some form of connectivity to it. Volumes remained a fraction of SWIFT's, but growth rates were exponential.

3. **Regional Settlement Experiments.**
   The **EAEU** (Eurasian Economic Union) piloted ruble-based trade clearing.
   The **ASEAN+3** bloc revived discussions of an "Asian Monetary Fund," with digital-settlement capacity separate from the IMF's dollar-denominated Special Drawing Rights.

4. **The CBDC Race.**
   Central Bank Digital Currencies, once academic curiosities, became matters of sovereignty.
   China's digital yuan (e-CNY) processed pilot cross-border trades; India's RBI digital rupee began settlement trials with Singapore; and Russia launched a digital ruble architecture designed specifically to bypass Western correspondent banks.

Each initiative shared the same motive: to ensure that trade and reserves could survive an American decision.

From Alternatives to Architecture

What began as small experiments coalesced into a genuine **parallel infrastructure.**
It lacked the depth and efficiency of the dollar system, but it offered something new — *immunity.*

By mid-decade, a new vocabulary entered financial diplomacy:

- **Optionality** replaced **replacement.** No one expected a single rival to dethrone the dollar, but many sought a suite of backups.
- **Multiplicity** replaced **monopoly.** The world no longer needed one dominant rail; it needed many interoperable ones.
- **Resilience** replaced **efficiency.** Faster was no longer better if faster meant more vulnerable.

The post-2022 world wasn't abandoning the dollar; it was **de-risking the dependency.**

Invisible but Irreversible

These shifts did not make headlines because they unfolded below the surface — in memoranda, swap agreements, and settlement code. But when measured in aggregate, they represented a tectonic migration of trust.

A generation earlier, "dollar alternatives" had been political slogans.
Now they were spreadsheets with signatures.

A Technocratic Revolt

What makes this moment historically unique is its character: this is not an ideological rebellion, but a technocratic one.
It is being led not by populists or protesters, but by central bankers, finance ministers, and data engineers.

They are not rejecting globalization; they are **redesigning** it — adjusting the plumbing to ensure that no single valve can shut off global liquidity again.

This is what the world looks like when the Golden Guardrail breaks: a thousand smaller guardrails spring up to replace it.

The Final Break: The End of the Apolitical Dollar

The Moment the Mirror Cracked

For nearly eighty years, the dollar system operated like a one-way mirror.
Every country could see through it — trade, borrow, invest — but could never touch the machinery behind it.
The mirror's reflection was trust: the belief that American financial power was self-restrained.

That illusion shattered not with a default or devaluation, but with a decision — a political act dressed as financial enforcement. When Washington froze the Central Bank of Russia's reserves, it crossed an invisible constitutional line in global finance: it merged the roles of judge, jury, and banker.

For the first time in the modern era, the dollar ceased to be a **universal right** and became a **conditional privilege.**

The Death of the Apolitical Dollar

The dollar's authority rested not just on its size, but on its neutrality. It was the one currency that could exist in the hands of enemies without fear of confiscation.
That neutrality was the psychological spine of globalization — the assurance that commerce could outlive conflict.

Once that neutrality was gone, the dollar's role changed.
It was no longer merely a *reserve asset*; it was a *policy weapon.*
The same Treasury bond that symbolized safety in 2010 symbolized obedience in 2022.

Markets can price risk, but they cannot price ideology.
And once ideology enters the equation, mathematics loses its power.

The Bifurcation of Trust

By 2024, a quiet but profound bifurcation had emerged in the architecture of global reserves.

Every central bank now divided its holdings not only by currency or duration, but by **political access.**

1. **G7 Currency Assets (The Conditional Safe Haven).**
   - Still the most liquid and creditworthy assets in existence.
   - But their accessibility now depends on the geopolitical alignment of the holder.
   - They are *safe to hold*, but not necessarily *safe to use.*
2. **Neutral Assets (The Sovereign Safe Haven).**
   - Gold, strategic commodities, select non-G7 currencies.
   - Harder to transact with, but immune to seizure.
   - They represent not convenience, but autonomy.

This bifurcation marks the birth of a two-tier global financial order — one based on liquidity, the other on liberty.

The One-Way Trade Out of Custody

The reserve system's new logic is simple:

The risk of holding assets in Western custody is no longer financial — it is political.

Every central banker understands that trust, once broken, cannot be printed back into existence.
And while the process of de-dollarization is slow, it is **unidirectional.**

Money may flow back into Treasuries during crises, but the strategic intent of most non-aligned nations has permanently shifted. They no longer see their reserves as mere savings; they see them as potential hostages.

The phrase whispered in policy circles now is **"exposure management."**

Not whether to leave the dollar, but how fast to reduce reliance on it without triggering instability.

This mindset—incremental, cautious, but relentless—is how hegemonies fade: not through revolt, but through quiet optimization.

The Paradox of Endurance

Ironically, the dollar's dominance is now sustained by the very fear that undermines it.
As nations build alternative systems, they still park their liquidity in U.S. assets because there is no substitute — yet.

This creates a strange equilibrium:

- The dollar remains *functionally indispensable* because of its liquidity.
- But it is *psychologically dispensable* because of its conditionality.

Every major sovereign investor now lives in this paradox — needing the dollar but distrusting it.
It is the global equivalent of a marriage held together by convenience rather than love.

The Silent Costs of Weaponization

The decision to weaponize the dollar extracted no immediate financial price; U.S. yields remained low, and markets barely flinched. But its long-term cost is measured in lost optionality — in the shrinking space between economic power and political discretion.

What Washington gained in leverage, it lost in legitimacy.
Each future sanction now carries diminishing impact, as the world adapts to blunt its edge.
Each new financial system built outside the dollar's reach becomes a scar — a reminder that the safe asset can turn hostile.

Empires fall not when they are defeated, but when they overuse the very tools that made them indispensable.

Permanent Consequences

The legacy of the 2022 freeze is not chaos, but **recalibration.**
The dollar will remain the backbone of global finance for years to come.
But it will never again be trusted as the world's apolitical sanctuary.

The change is irreversible because it is psychological.
A central banker who once slept soundly with $200 billion in Treasuries on his balance sheet now keeps part of it in Zurich, part in Shanghai, and part in gold vaults beneath Warsaw or Ankara.

Each ounce of gold, each line of local-currency swap, each investment routed through non-G7 custody is a physical manifestation of lost faith.

From Trust to Leverage — and Back Again

In the long arc of monetary history, the Golden Guardrail was America's greatest invention: a system in which the issuer of money voluntarily submitted to market discipline, and in doing so, earned the world's trust.
That trust became the engine of the modern economy.

By turning the Guardrail into a gate — deciding who may pass — the United States transformed that trust into leverage.
Leverage is powerful, but finite.
Once used, it must be replenished with credibility, or it corrodes the structure it supports.

The future of the dollar, therefore, depends on whether the United States can restore a sense of neutrality — to convince the world that strength need not mean control.

If it fails, the world will not collapse into chaos.
It will simply diversify, hedging not against the fall of the dollar, but against its will.

Chapter 11

The De-Dollarization Narrative and the Commodity Trade

The Energy Foundation of the Dollar Empire

The strength of the U.S. dollar does not come solely from Wall Street or the Federal Reserve. Energy markets have reinforced the dollar's international role for decades, especially because oil has commonly been priced and financed in dollars and because oil exporters have invested large surpluses in global dollar assets. But the dollar's foundation is broader than oil: deep capital markets, legal infrastructure, trade invoicing, and financial network effects all matter.

For half a century, much of internationally traded oil has been priced and financed in U.S. dollars. That practice strengthened transactional demand for dollars and helped generate petrodollar recycling when exporters accumulated large surpluses. It reinforced dollar dominance, but it did not create a universal legal requirement that every barrel be paid for in dollars or that every surplus dollar be invested in U.S. Treasuries.

After the gold window closed in 1971 and the oil shock transformed global payments, the dollar's role evolved rather than acquiring a new commodity backing. Oil invoicing and the recycling of exporter surpluses became important supports for the dollar system, but the post-Bretton Woods dollar remained a fiat currency whose dominance rested on institutions and markets, not an 'energy standard.'

The Collapse That Birthed the Petrodollar

The story begins in 1971, when President Richard Nixon, faced with mounting inflation and dwindling gold reserves, ended the Bretton Woods system by closing the "gold window." Overnight, the dollar was no longer backed by gold. Global confidence teetered. Nations holding dollars wanted to exchange them for metal, not paper.

After the 1973 oil shock, Washington sought a closer economic and strategic relationship with Saudi Arabia, both to stabilize bilateral ties and to manage the enormous flow of oil revenues through the international financial system. That effort mattered—but it was not a secret replacement for Bretton Woods.

Oil's importance made dollar pricing consequential because producers, importers, banks, shippers, and hedgers built contracts and financing around a common unit of account. The advantage was a network effect: the more participants used dollar markets, the cheaper and easier it became for the next participant to use them too.

The 1974 U.S.–Saudi Bargain — What Actually Happened

In 1974, the United States and Saudi Arabia created the U.S.–Saudi Arabian Joint Commission on Economic Cooperation. The arrangement deepened economic ties after the oil embargo, supported Saudi development, expanded opportunities for U.S. goods, services, and technology, and created channels through which oil surpluses could return to international financial markets.

The popular story of a secret OPEC dollars-only pact compresses a more complicated set of security ties, commercial arrangements, market conventions, and capital flows into a single treaty that did not exist.

- **Saudi Arabia's Role:** Maintain a close strategic and economic relationship with the United States while earning large dollar revenues from an oil market already dominated by dollar pricing.
- **The U.S. Role:** Deepen security, economic, and technical cooperation with the Kingdom and provide the world's deepest markets in which dollar surpluses could be invested.

The result was powerful precisely because it did not depend on a single mandatory clause. Security ties, dollar oil pricing, banking relationships, and U.S. capital-market depth reinforced one another.

Oil importers generally needed access to dollar funding because benchmark oil contracts were overwhelmingly dollar-denominated.

But currencies could be converted, and non-dollar settlement remained possible. Dollar dominance was a market convention with strong network effects, not a legal tollbooth.

The system increased transactional demand for dollars and made dollar-based trade finance more convenient. Its larger financial effect came when oil exporters accumulated surpluses and invested them across global assets—many of them denominated in dollars.

The Petrodollar Cycle — How Oil Became a Bond

The petrodollar story is strongest when understood as surplus recycling rather than a secret pricing mandate. During oil booms, exporters accumulated more foreign currency than they could immediately spend at home, and those funds returned to international financial markets.

Here is the mechanism in its more accurate form:

1. **Trade Settlement:** Benchmark oil markets have long been predominantly dollar-priced, although transactions can be settled through other currencies and converted through foreign-exchange markets.
2. **Surplus Accumulation:** When oil revenues exceed domestic spending and imports, exporters accumulate foreign assets, often including large dollar balances.
3. **Recycling into Global Assets:** Exporter surpluses can flow into bank deposits, Treasuries, corporate securities, equities, real estate, and sovereign-wealth portfolios. Treasuries are important because of their scale and liquidity, but they are not the only destination.

The cycle therefore is not a perfect closed circuit. An oil buyer may convert euros, yen, or another currency into dollars; an exporter may then diversify the proceeds across many assets. Repeated use of dollar markets nevertheless reinforces the depth, liquidity, and convenience that keep the dollar at the center of energy finance.

When oil exporters buy U.S. assets, those capital inflows can support U.S. financial markets and, at the margin, reduce financing costs. America's ability to run deficits, however, does not depend mechanically on petrodollar recycling; global demand for U.S. assets is far broader.

The geopolitical effect is real, but it comes from a network of incentives rather than alchemy: energy trade, security relationships, financial-market depth, and dollar liquidity reinforce one another.

The Petrodollar's Invisible Subsidy

The recycling loop performs two essential functions for the United States:

1. **It Can Support Borrowing Conditions.** During periods of large oil surpluses, exporter purchases of dollar assets can add demand for Treasuries and other U.S. securities, helping financing conditions at the margin. That demand is important, but neither permanent nor mechanically guaranteed.
2. **It Recycles External Surpluses.** Oil exporters often reinvest earnings abroad when revenues exceed domestic absorption capacity. Some of those flows return to U.S. markets, but they also move into diversified global portfolios. The mechanism supports dollar finance without automatically absorbing American fiscal deficits.

Every oil boom can therefore generate a second financial current alongside the physical flow of energy: exporter savings searching for liquid, credible assets, many of them in dollars.

The Petrodollar's Global Enforcement Mechanism

The strength of the system lies in network effects rather than compulsion. Because benchmark oil markets have long been predominantly dollar-priced, banks, insurers, shippers, and commodity traders built extensive dollar-denominated contracts, funding lines, and hedging markets around that convention.

- **Banks** must hold dollar reserves for settlements.
- **Corporations** hedge dollar risk through U.S. markets.
- **Governments** hold dollars as reserves to stabilize their currencies.

This network effect turned the dollar from a national currency into a global operating system. And like any operating system, it thrives on lock-in. Once installed, it is nearly impossible to uninstall without breaking everything built on top of it.

The Strategic Logic Behind the U.S.–Saudi Relationship

The architects of the 1970s relationship—including Henry Kissinger and Treasury Secretary William Simon—understood that currency power and security relationships could reinforce one another.

By deepening security ties while dollar oil markets and U.S. capital markets expanded, the two countries strengthened a mutually useful financial relationship. Saudi security ties to Washington and the Kingdom's large external surpluses both mattered, but neither created a legal obligation to recycle every oil dollar into Treasuries.

The arrangement helped place global energy commerce inside a dollar-centered financial ecosystem supported by U.S. banking depth, Treasury-market liquidity, and longstanding security cooperation.

It was not empire by conquest — it was empire by invoice.

The Petrodollar as a Reinforcement of the Golden Guardrail

The petrodollar system also reinforced the Golden Guardrail described in Chapters 1–3. Widespread dollar invoicing in energy increased the value of keeping the currency credible, liquid, and freely usable. It did not force all oil trade into dollars; it strengthened the network advantages of a system already built around them.

Every barrel priced in dollars added another transaction to that network. If U.S. institutions lost credibility, energy markets could diversify settlement and reserve choices over time—one reason monetary and fiscal discipline still matter to dollar leadership.

Thus, the petrodollar was not a new commodity backing for the dollar; it was a powerful post-Bretton Woods network of energy invoicing, capital recycling, and strategic relationships.

The Stakes of De-Dollarization

The current wave of **de-dollarization** — led by BRICS and other non-aligned nations — is not about punishing America; it is about escaping its gravitational pull.
It seeks to unhook global trade from the mandatory dollar circuit and build a parallel energy settlement system in which reserves are held in multiple currencies — or commodities — rather than exclusively in U.S. assets.

If successful, this would not simply reduce U.S. influence; it would dismantle the very circulatory system that finances the American fiscal state.
De-dollarization, in its purest form, is an attempt to turn the *U.S. Treasury bond* from the world's most essential asset into just another investment choice.

The Geopolitical Assault: Sanctions and Strategic Defection

De-dollarization is not a market event. It is a political revolt disguised as financial reform.
While the dollar's supremacy was built through contracts and trust, its challengers emerged from confrontation and coercion.

The campaign to weaken the dollar's monopoly began in boardrooms and ministries — not trading floors. It was led not by traders chasing profit, but by policymakers chasing sovereignty. The trigger was not inflation or interest rates, but the strategic shock of 2022: the weaponization of reserves.

The Russian Catalyst — When Sanctions Became Sovereign

When the United States and its allies froze nearly **$300 billion** in Russian central bank assets in February 2022, it sent an unmistakable message: reserves are no longer neutral.

To the architects of the Western financial order, this was a justified act of deterrence — a moral and strategic necessity following a war of aggression.

But to the rest of the world, it was something more profound: the moment when the dollar revealed its conditional nature.

For decades, nations were told that the dollar system was *rules-based.* Now they saw it was *permission-based.*

The freeze was not a side effect; it was a signal. It declared that participation in the dollar economy was contingent upon political alignment with Washington.

For non-aligned states — India, Indonesia, Brazil, South Africa, even traditional U.S. partners like Saudi Arabia — this triggered a collective awakening. They realized that what had been sold as **security** was also **dependency.**

The Weaponized Clearing System

The most vulnerable point of the global dollar ecosystem was never its currency — it was its **infrastructure.**

All international payments denominated in dollars must pass through a network of correspondent banks and clearing systems located in U.S. or allied jurisdictions. Chief among them is **SWIFT**, the Brussels-based messaging network that connects over 11,000 financial institutions in 200 countries.

In theory, SWIFT is neutral — a simple conduit for communication between banks. In practice, it operates under Western political authority. Disconnecting a country from SWIFT is the financial equivalent of cutting oxygen to its economy.

Russia experienced this firsthand. When several of its largest banks were expelled from the network in 2022, trade finance collapsed overnight. Even countries that wanted to pay Russia for goods suddenly could not.

The lesson was not lost on others. If one of the world's largest energy exporters could be digitally erased from the global banking grid, then no nation was truly sovereign inside the dollar system.

The BRICS Response — Strategic Realignment

The immediate aftermath of the sanctions wave saw an unusual diplomatic acceleration. What had once been symbolic gatherings of the **BRICS** nations — Brazil, Russia, India, China, and South Africa — turned into an active policy forum.

Their common objective was simple, though not unified in execution: **to create financial pathways immune to Western veto.**

The coalition's message to the world was not revolutionary but restorative — a call for *multipolarity*. It appealed especially to middle-income nations that resented being trapped between U.S. sanctions and Chinese debt diplomacy.

By 2024, BRICS had expanded to include Saudi Arabia, the United Arab Emirates, Iran, Egypt, and Argentina. In effect, this reconstituted the 21st-century version of OPEC+, but with a financial mandate.

China's Strategic Blueprint — Yuanization by Design

China quickly became the de facto architect of the de-dollarization movement.

Unlike Russia's reactionary posture, China's approach was

methodical, layered, and deliberately long-term. It did not attack the dollar; it built around it.

1. CIPS — The Chinese Alternative to SWIFT
Launched in 2015, the **Cross-Border Interbank Payment System (CIPS)** was Beijing's quiet answer to SWIFT.
Initially limited to settling trade in Yuan (CNY), by 2025 it had expanded to include more than 1,500 financial institutions across 120 countries.

CIPS remains small — processing less than 5% of global cross-border payments — but its significance is strategic, not quantitative. It provides a **parallel circuit**: a communication and settlement layer that bypasses Western oversight.

CIPS's main advantage is political insulation. While most banks still prefer SWIFT for speed and liquidity, CIPS ensures that trade with China can continue even under sanction. It is the financial equivalent of a diplomatic bunker.

2. Bilateral Swap Lines — The Fabric of an Alternative Network
To support CIPS and Yuan trade, China's central bank — the People's Bank of China (PBoC) — has built the world's largest network of **bilateral currency swap agreements**, exceeding $550 billion in value.

These agreements allow partner countries to exchange their local currency for Yuan directly, settling trade without converting to dollars first.

For resource-rich nations like Indonesia, Nigeria, or Kazakhstan, this provides insulation against dollar volatility and a symbolic expression of independence. For China, it quietly expands the Yuan's global footprint without challenging the dollar head-on.

3. The Energy Front — Yuan for Oil

The more consequential shift has been the willingness of China, Saudi Arabia, and other trading partners to discuss or conduct portions of energy trade outside the dollar. These transactions remain small relative to dollar-based oil markets, but their symbolism is clear: dollar invoicing is dominant by convention and network depth, not by an unbreakable treaty.

The move signaled that even the guardians of the 1974 pact were willing to test the boundaries of U.S. monetary orthodoxy.
Soon after, similar deals followed with the UAE and, in barter-like arrangements, with Russia.

For Beijing, each transaction in Yuan is not just commerce — it is diplomacy.
Every barrel bought in Yuan is a vote for a multipolar reserve future.

Russia's Counteroffensive — Commodities as Collateral

Russia, cut off from Western finance, responded with a brutal kind of innovation.
It began linking its currency, the ruble, to real commodities — natural gas, oil, grain, and gold.

In March 2022, Moscow declared that "unfriendly" nations must pay for gas in rubles. Later, it introduced gold-linked settlement mechanisms for specific export contracts.

Though the ruble's liquidity remains thin, these steps reintroduced a pre-1971 principle into global trade: **a currency backed by things, not promises.**

This approach appealed to many resource-based economies. It offered an ideological contrast to the fiat order dominated by Western finance: *money anchored in matter rather than trust.*

India's Pragmatic Defection

India's approach has been more transactional than revolutionary. As a major energy importer and a member of both BRICS and the U.S.-aligned QUAD, New Delhi plays both sides.

After the sanctions on Russia, India began purchasing discounted Russian oil — paying in rupees through specially designated accounts at domestic banks.
The arrangement effectively created a **rupee–ruble clearing system** that bypassed Western banks entirely.

Though limited in scale, it demonstrated how even democracies aligned with the U.S. could adopt de-dollarized trade mechanisms when strategically convenient.

India's policy mantra is simple: *"We will trade in any currency that reduces our energy cost."*
That pragmatism — not ideology — is what makes the de-dollarization movement resilient.

The Gulf's Strategic Hedging

Perhaps the most consequential shift is occurring in the Middle East — the very birthplace of the petrodollar.
Saudi Arabia, the UAE, and even Qatar have begun diversifying their energy invoicing and sovereign wealth investments.

- **Saudi Arabia** joined BRICS in 2024, signaling openness to Yuan settlement.
- **The UAE** already settles some crude and LNG contracts in non-dollar currencies.
- **Qatar** is exploring Yuan-denominated LNG contracts with China.

These moves are not rejections of the U.S., but recalibrations. The Gulf monarchies still depend on U.S. security guarantees, but they no longer see financial allegiance as the price of protection.

For Washington, this is the strategic equivalent of erosion — not collapse, but the gradual wearing away of monopoly power by a tide of quiet alternatives.

The Structural Limits of De-Dollarization

Despite these political breakthroughs, the new system faces a reality check.
Liquidity, legal credibility, and market depth still overwhelmingly favor the dollar.

The Structural Limits of De-Dollarization — The Safety and Liquidity Chasm

The story of de-dollarization reads, at first glance, like a rebellion destined for success: dozens of nations trading in their own currencies, new payment systems sprouting across continents, and an expanding alliance of resource exporters eager to unshackle themselves from Washington's financial dominance.

Yet beneath this surface momentum lies a stubborn and unavoidable truth: **no currency can replace the dollar until it can replicate its safety, scale, and liquidity.**

The world does not hold dollars because it loves America. It holds dollars because there is no other asset that can perform the same function at the same speed and scale.

This is the heart of the **liquidity paradox** — nations may distrust U.S. power, but they trust U.S. markets.

The Liquidity and Depth Constraint

Global finance runs not on ideology but on plumbing. Every sovereign wealth fund, central bank, insurer, and multinational corporation needs a place to park money — not millions, but trillions — and be certain that it can retrieve that money instantly, at a transparent market price, without causing the market itself to break.

Only one market in the world meets that test: the U.S. Treasury market.

- **Size:** Over $27 trillion in marketable securities.
- **Depth:** Traded daily in volumes exceeding $700 billion.
- **Resiliency:** Even during crises — from 9/11 to COVID-19 — Treasuries remain the global safe haven.

In contrast, no other bond market comes close.

The Euro's Limitation:
Europe has economic scale but no unified fiscal heart. There is no single "Eurobond" representing collective creditworthiness. Instead, there are 20-plus sovereign issuers, each with its own political risk profile. German Bunds are too scarce; Italian BTPs too risky. The euro therefore lacks the singular, scalable anchor that Treasuries provide.

The Yuan's Constraint:
China has ambition but not convertibility. Its bond market may be large on paper, but its **liquidity is trapped behind capital controls**. Investors cannot freely enter or exit positions, and repatriating profits is subject to bureaucratic discretion. No reserve manager can risk holding hundreds of billions under those conditions.

Until a rival can offer the world what the U.S. Treasury offers — infinite scalability without political friction — de-dollarization remains aspiration, not architecture.

Liquidity as a Public Good

The U.S. Treasury market functions as the world's financial oxygen supply — a **public good** provided by a single sovereign. It absorbs panic, anchors interest rates, and provides risk-free collateral for everything from repo loans to derivatives.

The paradox is striking:
The very debt that domestic critics condemn as reckless overspending is precisely what the world demands for safety.

Each new Treasury issuance is not just borrowing; it is the creation of fresh liquidity units for the global economy. This is why efforts by other nations to escape the dollar simultaneously undermine their own financial flexibility. They are rejecting the system that keeps their own markets liquid.

Even Beijing understands this tension. Despite its vocal promotion of the Yuan, China continues to hold roughly **$775 billion in U.S. Treasuries** as of mid-2025. De-dollarization rhetoric is a political weapon; Treasury holdings are an economic necessity.

The Legal and Institutional Guardrail

Beyond liquidity, the dollar system rests on something even harder to duplicate: **trust in law.**

Investors hold U.S. assets because the American legal system is predictable. The rule of law, independent courts, and enforceable contracts create an institutional framework that no other major economy can replicate at scale.

- In New York, a bond contract is enforceable even against the government itself.
- In Shanghai or Moscow, the government is the court.

This difference is existential. For global investors managing pension funds, reserves, and sovereign portfolios, predictability is priceless. It is why Treasuries remain the preferred form of collateral even among America's critics.

The **Golden Guardrail**, as defined earlier in this book, is not merely an economic mechanism — it is a legal covenant. The United States voluntarily binds itself to its creditors through transparent auctions, debt-ceiling debates, and independent monetary policy.

No rival can replicate this openness because none is willing to tolerate that level of external scrutiny.

Capital Controls and the Credibility Deficit

China's capital controls are a perfect case study.
For two decades, Beijing has maintained strict limits on cross-border money movement to protect domestic stability. These controls, while politically rational, are financially fatal to reserve credibility.

A reserve currency cannot have an exit tax. Investors must know they can convert their holdings freely at market value. Without that assurance, even a minor policy shift — a new regulation, a speech from the Politburo, an unexpected intervention — can freeze capital flows and destroy confidence.

This is why the Yuan, despite China's economic scale, remains a **regional currency**, not a global one. It is trusted for settlement, not for savings.

The Psychological Anchor — Faith in Convertibility

The dollar's dominance ultimately rests on psychology — not faith in America's virtue, but faith in its self-interest. The world believes that the United States will never close its markets because doing so would destroy its own wealth.

This mutual dependency between issuer and holder is the quiet genius of the system.
America's debt is the world's asset. America's deficits are the world's surpluses.

The day that equation breaks, the global financial order will unravel.

But for now, even the most defiant actors — Russia, China, and Iran — continue to measure their currencies, their reserves, and their trade flows against the dollar benchmark. It remains the **axis of convertibility**, the universal yardstick of value.

Network Effects: The Invoicing Empire

De-dollarization advocates often focus on reserves, but the real battlefield is *invoicing.*

Roughly **85% of global trade** — including more than 90% of commodity transactions — is denominated in dollars. This dominance extends to:

- **Shipping insurance and maritime law**, which are governed under English or New York jurisdiction.
- **Letters of credit and trade finance**, largely provided by U.S. or European banks.
- **Commodity exchanges**, from Chicago to Singapore, that settle in dollars by default.

This creates an enormous **path dependency**: changing the currency of trade requires rewriting millions of contracts, retraining risk models, and rebuilding trust across entire supply chains.

Even China, which leads de-dollarization rhetoric, still prices most of its exports — from steel to electronics — in dollars. The reason is simple: counterparties trust the pricing transparency and legal enforcement that come with it.

Replacing the dollar in global invoicing is not like switching browsers; it's like rewriting the internet.

Why De-Dollarization Will Be Gradual — and Why That Matters

The forces driving de-dollarization are real and enduring, but their impact will be **evolutionary, not revolutionary.**

The dollar's share of global reserves may slowly decline; more trade may settle in regional currencies; new digital systems may bypass SWIFT.
But each alternative will coexist with, not replace, the dollar system.

The process resembles not the fall of Rome, but the **rise of Byzantium** — a transformation from empire to ecosystem, from dominance to diffusion.

For the United States, this slow adjustment is both a blessing and a warning.
It grants time to reform, to restore fiscal discipline, and to reinforce the credibility of the Golden Guardrail.
But it also tempts complacency — the belief that supremacy is self-renewing.

In truth, the dollar will endure only so long as the U.S. continues to act like the world's most responsible debtor.

The War of Attrition

The struggle over the dollar's future is not a revolution. It is a siege. There will be no collapse, no dramatic dethroning. The empire of green paper will not end with a bang, but with a spreadsheet — a slow, grinding recalibration measured in basis points and barrels, not battleships.

This is the **War of Attrition**: a contest between the U.S. system's structural resilience and the world's political determination to diversify away from it.
Each side fights not through confrontation but through endurance.

Attrition in Motion

Every de-dollarized transaction — every oil contract priced in Yuan, every bilateral swap that bypasses SWIFT, every new reserve allocation into gold — is a small act of rebellion. None of them is lethal alone. But together, over time, they act like water on stone, eroding the monopoly that once seemed eternal.

For the United States, the pain of attrition appears first in the bond market. The demand curve for Treasuries, while still vast, gradually flattens. Marginal buyers — once oil-rich states recycling petrodollars — begin to redirect small fractions of their surpluses elsewhere: sovereign wealth funds diversify into Asian debt, central banks extend gold holdings, and institutional investors seek higher yields abroad.

The result is a **micro-rise** in U.S. borrowing costs — an additional few basis points that seem trivial at first but compound over trillions in debt.

The U.S. Treasury still sells every bond it issues. But each auction now carries a whisper of hesitation, a fraction of the global trust that once made it automatic.

The Economics of Erosion

Consider the math of monetary erosion.
For every 25 basis point increase in average Treasury yields, the U.S. government pays roughly $70 billion more annually in interest — the equivalent of the entire yearly budget of the Department of Education.

A full 1% rise translates to over **$280 billion in new annual costs**. These are not just accounting figures; they are policy constraints. Every extra dollar spent servicing debt is a dollar not spent on defense, infrastructure, or innovation.

De-dollarization, therefore, is not a frontal assault on the U.S. — it is a campaign to make its dominance more expensive to maintain.

The Weaponization of Patience

America's challengers have learned that time is the only currency the dollar cannot print.
China, Russia, and their allies are not trying to destroy the dollar; they are trying to **outlast** it.

Each small defection from the dollar system — each new swap line, gold purchase, or regional payment rail — is a trench dug in a long geopolitical campaign. The objective is not replacement, but **irreversibility**: to create enough parallel infrastructure that the world never again depends entirely on Washington's good graces.

This slow strategy exploits America's greatest strength — the liquidity of its markets — as its Achilles' heel. The deeper the world's integration into the dollar system, the greater the cost to defend it from political backlash.

It is not the strength of rivals that weakens empires, but the friction of holding power too long.

The Shifting Composition of Power

In this war, every side adapts. The battlefield is invisible, its weapons intangible.

- **The U.S.** uses sanctions, Treasury auctions, and rate policy to preserve the dollar's primacy.
- **China** uses trade, swap lines, and CIPS to build a financial perimeter.
- **The Gulf States** use diversification as leverage, balancing American protection against Chinese demand.
- **Europe** speaks the language of autonomy but still clears most of its trade in dollars.

No one wants to destroy the system; everyone wants to **redefine their terms within it.**

This creates a dynamic equilibrium — a multipolar dependency where no power can fully dominate but none can fully withdraw. It is globalization reconfigured as a balance of distrust.

Interest Rates as the New Battlefield

The front line of this attrition war lies in interest rates — the price America pays for its privilege.

Each incremental loss of foreign demand for Treasuries shifts the supply-demand balance, forcing the Federal Reserve to choose between two painful paths:

1. Allow rates to rise, tightening fiscal pressure.
2. Intervene more aggressively, risking the appearance of monetizing debt.

Either option erodes the moral foundation of the Golden Guardrail: the image of the U.S. as a disciplined borrower bound by market constraints.

The paradox is cruel. The more the Fed intervenes to stabilize the bond market, the more it resembles the state-directed central banks it once lectured — and the less the dollar looks apolitical.

In this sense, de-dollarization is not only about the rest of the world. It is about America's ability to restrain itself.

The Illusion of Invincibility

The danger for Washington is not imminent collapse but complacency.
Empires do not fall when rivals attack them; they fall when they stop believing their own rules apply.

Every time Congress toys with the debt ceiling, every time partisan brinkmanship threatens default, every time fiscal discipline gives way to political expedience, it chips away at the very credibility that underpins global trust in the dollar.

For foreign observers, these domestic dramas are more damaging than any BRICS summit. They are reminders that the dollar's reliability depends on the same political system that now routinely flirts with dysfunction.

De-dollarization may be driven by foreign actors, but its fuel is American hubris.

The Endurance of Scale

And yet — the dollar endures.
Its network is too vast, its liquidity too essential, its legal framework too robust to replace quickly. Even as rivals chip away, the dollar's gravitational pull keeps global finance in orbit.

The War of Attrition does not mean the fall of the dollar; it means the end of its effortless supremacy. The world is learning to live with partial dependency — to treat the dollar not as destiny, but as a choice.

That shift in mindset is irreversible. Once nations discover alternatives, even imperfect ones, trust never returns to monopoly.

America's challenge in the coming decades will not be defending the dollar from collapse — it will be justifying why the world should continue to pay for the privilege of using it.

Next, we bridge to *Part IV: The Policy Path Forward*, examining how the United States can preserve the Dollar Paradox not through coercion or complacency, but through renewed discipline — proving that credibility, not control, remains the ultimate reserve asset.

The Policy Choice for Supremacy

By 2025, the contest over the dollar's future no longer looks like ideology versus economics; it looks like management versus drift. The world is not waiting for the dollar to collapse. It is waiting to see whether the United States still deserves the privilege of issuing it.

The paradox has never been clearer: America can keep its supremacy only by acting like a country that could lose it.

The Three Fronts of the Credibility War

In Washington, the debate over the "dollar threat" usually divides along party lines — hawks blame deficits, doves blame geopolitics — but the truth cuts across ideology. The defense of the dollar is fought on three interlocking fronts: **fiscal discipline, productive strength, and institutional integrity.**

1. **Fiscal Discipline — The Price of Trust.**
   The dollar's power begins with confidence that U.S. debt will always be honored, not inflated away. Yet the same Congress that lectures the world on responsibility now toys with default every election cycle.
   Each debt-ceiling crisis is a self-inflicted crack in the foundation. Markets no longer fear American insolvency; they

fear American dysfunction.
The fix is not austerity but **predictability**: credible budgets, transparent borrowing, and a long-term debt path that convinces investors the pain of repayment will be managed, not postponed.

2. **Productive Strength — Earning the Privilege.**
The dollar's reserve status endures because U.S. markets generate the highest-quality assets on earth — from technology to Treasuries.
But fiscal credibility alone cannot sustain supremacy if the real economy stagnates. Innovation, energy independence, and manufacturing resilience are not side shows; they are the supply chain of confidence.
A reserve currency must be backed by a society that still makes things the world needs. Otherwise, it becomes a hollow claim on nostalgia.

3. **Institutional Integrity — The Golden Guardrail at Home.**
The rest of the world watches not America's speeches but its procedures: whether its courts enforce contracts, whether its central bank resists politics, whether data are transparent.
The Federal Reserve's independence is now as geopolitically valuable as an aircraft carrier. The moment Congress dictates interest rates, the moment the Fed becomes a partisan arm, the Golden Guardrail breaks from within.

The Discipline Dividend

Restoring credibility pays immediate dividends.
Every 10-basis-point drop in Treasury yields saves roughly **$28 billion a year** in interest. That saving is not theoretical; it compounds. It is the real fiscal dividend of being trusted.

In the same way that reckless policy quietly raises the cost of power, restraint quietly finances it.

Trust, once regained, becomes self-funding. Investors reward consistency with cheaper money, and cheaper money underwrites strategic freedom — from defense spending to social investment.

The U.S. does not need to outproduce China in factories or out-mine Russia in resources. It needs to remain the world's most predictable debtor. That is the secret of supremacy.

Re-Anchoring the Golden Guardrail

The original architects of America's financial order — from Hamilton to Volcker — understood that credibility is not a moral virtue; it is an engineering choice. The Guardrail must be serviced, not mythologized.

Re-anchoring it for the twenty-first century means codifying limits that outlast political cycles:

- **Automatic Debt Stabilizers:** Budget rules that force Congress to offset new spending with new revenue, except during officially declared emergencies.
- **Independent Debt Commission:** A standing body that issues non-partisan assessments of the federal balance sheet, akin to the Congressional Budget Office but insulated from appropriation politics.
- **Institutional Sanctity:** Legal reinforcement of the Federal Reserve's independence and the inviolability of Treasury payments — making default or politicized monetization legally impossible without a supermajority override.

These are not glamorous reforms. They are guardrail maintenance — the boring work that keeps a superpower solvent.

Soft Power Through Predictability

The global contest for currency dominance is not about who shouts loudest but who shows up on time.
When emerging markets hold U.S. assets, they are buying

predictability — the confidence that rules will be applied tomorrow exactly as they are today.

Every country that has tried to weaponize its currency — from Britain in the 1950s to Russia today — eventually learns that control breeds fragility.
The dollar's miracle has always been the opposite: voluntary restraint as strategy.

If Washington can preserve that restraint while modernizing its fiscal machinery, it will convert political humility into strategic advantage.
Predictability is the new soft power.

A New Metric of Leadership

The next era of supremacy will not be measured by GDP share or aircraft carriers. It will be measured by **trust velocity** — how quickly the world believes the United States when it speaks through its markets.

- When Congress passes a budget, yields will move.
- When the Fed signals a rate change, currencies will realign.
- When a U.S. court enforces a foreign judgment, capital will flow back.

Every small act of credibility amplifies America's voice more effectively than any sanction or summit.

The Choice Before Washington

The U.S. faces a simple but fateful decision:
Continue borrowing credibility from the past, or start earning it again.

If it re-commits to fiscal transparency, renews industrial capacity, and protects institutional independence, the dollar will remain the world's gravity center — not by force, but by function.

If it treats the privilege as permanent, the attrition described in earlier sections will accelerate until supremacy becomes nostalgia.

The final paradox is this: **America can print dollars, but not trust.**
The nation that understands that difference will own the future.

The End of Monopoly: From the Petrodollar to the Polycurrency World

Every financial empire ends the same way—not necessarily with defeat, but with dilution. The dollar-centered energy system, once far more dominant, is sharing space with a growing set of settlement and reserve alternatives. None alone can replace it; together they can weaken its network advantage.

The world that once cleared every transaction through New York now hums with parallel circuits: CIPS in Shanghai, rupee-ruble accounts in Delhi, regional clearing banks in Dubai. Each is small. Each is imperfect. But each reduces the singular dependence that once defined global finance.

In this new order, there will be no single "next dollar." There will be **many smaller ones** — currencies that coexist, overlap, and compete, bound not by ideology but by necessity.

The age of monopoly finance is ending; the age of **polycurrency pragmatism** has begun.

The Quiet Rebalancing of Power

The power of the dollar was never just about exchange; it was about hierarchy.
The U.S. set the price of money, and the rest of the world paid the conversion fee. Every trade settlement, every loan, every oil cargo invoiced in dollars reinforced an invisible pyramid with Washington at the top.

That pyramid is flattening.

A company in Malaysia can now pay for Chinese components in Yuan, settle freight in Singapore dollars, and hedge exposure in rupees — all without touching the dollar once.
A Russian gas exporter can accept payment in rubles, gold, or crypto-linked accounts in Dubai.
A Nigerian refinery can settle crude imports in a mixture of euros and digital Yuan.

The global economy is fragmenting not into chaos, but into **modular networks** — each small, self-sufficient, and insulated from sanctions. The new rule is not alignment, but optionality.

The Petrodollar's Slow Sunset

The petrodollar system is not collapsing; it is aging. The U.S.–Saudi economic and security relationship that reinforced dollar-centered oil finance now coexists with symbolic yuan settlements, local-currency arrangements, and more diversified sovereign portfolios.

Even Saudi Aramco, long the custodian of the dollar's commodity throne, now prices select shipments in multiple currencies. The change is incremental but irreversible.

Just as the British pound did not vanish overnight after losing reserve status, the dollar will linger as the world's financial lingua franca long after it stops being its single source of truth.

Reserve status fades not when alternatives triumph, but when confidence stops compounding. The world still uses dollars, but it no longer trusts that the system will never turn on its users.

That psychological break is permanent.

The Dollar's Paradoxical Strength

And yet, for all the talk of decline, the dollar remains the center of gravity.
It anchors interest-rate models, collateral frameworks, and valuation benchmarks across every market on earth. Even the systems designed

to bypass it — like CIPS or India's rupee corridors — quietly peg their internal pricing to Treasury yields.

The irony of de-dollarization is that it cannot escape the dollar's math.
The world is not rejecting the dollar's function — only the politics surrounding it.

As long as America keeps the Guardrail intact — borrowing, not printing; stabilizing, not coercing — the dollar will outlast the rhetoric of its critics. Its strength lies not in purity, but in permanence: it has been the least bad option for seventy-five years.

The Trust That Outlived Gold

When the U.S. left the gold standard, skeptics predicted collapse. Instead, trust replaced metal. Faith in America's institutions became the new reserve asset — a belief that contracts would hold, markets would stay open, and power would restrain itself.

That faith has survived wars, recessions, and political chaos because, despite everything, the system still works. Payments clear. Courts enforce. The bond market breathes.

De-dollarization cannot yet recreate that architecture of reliability.
It can only imitate fragments of it.

The real risk, therefore, does not come from foreign rivals but from within — from the temptation to weaponize trust faster than it can be rebuilt.

The Lessons of Empire

History suggests that great monetary powers fall for one of two reasons: they either **inflate** their currency into irrelevance or **politicize** it into fragility.
The United States, to its credit, has so far avoided both extremes — but it has begun to flirt with the second.

The weaponization of finance — the freezing of reserves, the overreach of sanctions — may win short-term victories but loses the long-term peace. Each time Washington uses the dollar as a sword, it dulls its edge as a shield.

Empires that learn restraint endure. Empires that mistake dominance for immunity do not.

The Coming World of Managed Multipolarity

The next phase of the global system will not be a cold war between currencies, but a **managed multipolarity**:

- The dollar will remain the central operating system.
- The euro, Yuan, and digital currencies will function as regional layers.
- Gold and commodities will serve as the backup batteries of trust.

In this configuration, the U.S. still leads — but it leads by **coordination**, not by command. The new diplomacy of money will be about interoperability, not obedience.

This is the environment the Federal Reserve and Treasury must now design for: a world where every rival currency is also a partner in preventing collapse. The paradox of leadership is that it survives only when shared.

The Bridge to the Digital Era

The digitalization of money will complete the transformation. Central Bank Digital Currencies (CBDCs) — programmable, traceable, instantaneous — will bring efficiency and transparency, but also surveillance and fragility.

In Chapter 12, we will explore how these digital architectures could either strengthen the Guardrail — by enforcing discipline through code — or destroy it — by merging the Spender and Printer once again, this time through software.

The next battle for the dollar will not be fought in deserts or debt auctions, but in data centers.

The Price of the Paradox

The United States can no longer assume that its debts are the world's dreams.

The era of automatic trust is over. What remains is the paradox itself — a nation that must borrow to lead, and lead by showing that it borrows honestly.

The final measure of supremacy will not be the number of dollars in circulation, but the number of nations still willing to hold them without fear.

That faith, once again, will be earned the hard way — through credibility, transparency, and the discipline of restraint.

Because in the end, money — like power — belongs to whoever the world believes will use it wisely.

Chapter 12

The Digital Challenge: Central Bank Digital Currencies (CBDCs)

The New Battlefield of Finance

Every empire finds its next challenger not on the battlefield, but in the ledger.
For the United States, the dollar's real war is now being fought in code.

While headlines focus on inflation, elections, and interest rates, the deeper shift is unfolding in the invisible infrastructure that moves value around the globe. It is here—inside digital payment rails, cryptographic protocols, and central bank data centers—that the future of monetary sovereignty is being redrawn.

The weapon is not a missile or tariff; it's a **Central Bank Digital Currency (CBDC)**—a digital version of national money issued directly by a country's central bank.

A CBDC is not Bitcoin. It is a digital liability of a central bank, denominated in the sovereign currency. Features such as programmability, identity rules, transaction limits, offline use, or privacy are design choices layered onto that core definition—not unavoidable properties of every CBDC.

For the first time since the invention of paper money, governments are redesigning the very operating system of money itself.

Why It Matters

If the twentieth century belonged to the printing press, the twenty-first belongs to the algorithm. The question is no longer who controls the mint, but who controls the *protocol.*

A cross-border CBDC platform can reduce reliance on correspondent banks, clearing chains, and traditional dollar settlement rails. Depending on its design, commercial banks may still play an intermediary role. The strategic significance is not that every CBDC bypasses banks, but that new settlement architecture can create routes that do not require the same dollar plumbing.

China moved quickly. By 2025, U.S. policy rejected a retail CBDC and favored regulated dollar-backed stablecoins.

The Catalyst: When Trust Was Weaponized

The digital money revolution was not born in Silicon Valley; it was born in Washington—by accident.

When the U.S. and its allies froze roughly $300 billion in Russian central-bank reserves after the 2022 invasion of Ukraine, they proved that the dollar system could be turned off like a switch.

That act, justified geopolitically, detonated financially. For decades, central banks believed that their U.S. Treasury holdings were sacrosanct—politically neutral, immune from seizure. The freeze shattered that assumption. It signaled to every finance minister from Riyadh to Jakarta that **the world's safest asset could now be politicized**.

What the Pentagon calls deterrence, the rest of the world saw as exposure. Within months, a quiet revolution began: engineers, economists, and central bankers set out to build payment systems that could survive outside Washington's reach.

The Dollar Paradox Meets the Digital Age

Everything established in Parts I and II—America's decision to borrow instead of print, the global addiction to its debt, the Captive Customer loop—depends on friction.

Every cross-border dollar transaction travels through a maze of correspondent banks, compliance checks, and settlement lags. That friction is what grants the U.S. its jurisdictional leverage.

CBDCs threaten to remove it entirely.

A digital-currency transaction between, say, the United Arab Emirates and China could clear in seconds through a shared blockchain ledger, without ever touching a U.S. bank, a SWIFT message, or a Treasury regulator. The geopolitical "off-switch" disappears.

The paradox flips: the very efficiency that once made the dollar indispensable now becomes its vulnerability.

Bypassing the Plumbing

For fifty years, every major global transaction has run through the same metallic arteries—SWIFT in Brussels, Fedwire in New York, CHIPS in Jersey City. Together, they form the nervous system of the dollar empire.

A CBDC rewrites that circuitry.

1. **Atomic Settlement.**
   CBDCs settle trades instantly. There is no waiting for banks to reconcile ledgers or for intermediaries to clear payments. Once both central banks' digital ledgers confirm the transaction, value moves—irreversibly, simultaneously, and without human approval.
2. **Jurisdictional Escape.**
   When payments occur entirely on a non-dollar network—say, China's e-CNY or the mBridge platform—U.S. sanctions law no longer applies. Control shifts from jurisdiction to protocol. The world's most powerful compliance system loses its sockets.
3. **Collateral Damage to Influence.**
   The United States still issues the world's reserve currency, but if its enforcement tools can no longer reach the rails of trade, monetary power becomes symbolic. The system remains admired—but no longer feared.

The Erosion of Captive Demand

The second strike is subtler but far more dangerous: CBDCs attack the *recycling loop* that has kept U.S. debt cheap for generations.

Under the traditional dollar-centered model, a country that earned large dollar trade surpluses had strong incentives to hold liquid dollar assets, including U.S. Treasuries. The loop was powerful but never automatic: trade in dollars generated dollar balances, and deep U.S. markets made those balances convenient to invest.

But if trade settles in digital Yuan, rupees, or multi-CBDC tokens, the compulsion disappears. Nations can now store value in the same digital currency they used to settle trade, never touching a Treasury bond.

That shift doesn't spark a crisis; it creates a slow leak. Over time, the captive bid that suppressed America's borrowing costs evaporates. The U.S. must then compete for buyers—offering higher yields, paying more interest, and transferring ever-greater sums from taxpayers to creditors.

The Exorbitant Privilege becomes an *Expensive Necessity*.

CASE STUDY:
Project mBridge — A Parallel Highway

If Bretton Woods built the interstate of global money, **Project mBridge** is its bypass.

Launched in 2021 by the People's Bank of China (PBOC) and the Bank for International Settlements, joined by the central banks of Thailand, Hong Kong, and the UAE, the project pilots a shared blockchain platform for cross-border settlement among multiple digital currencies.

Its architecture is deliberately inclusive: each central bank issues its own tokens, but the ledger links them through a common bridge. No single country controls the system, yet China's technological lead ensures it sets the speed limit.

In early pilots, transactions that once took two days cleared in two seconds. The test volume was small—tens of millions, not trillions—but the proof was existential. A functioning, non-dollar payment highway now exists.

And unlike Bitcoin, it comes with central-bank legitimacy.

Strategic Implications

Project mBridge does not aim to dethrone the dollar; it aims to **route around it**.

Its genius lies in subtlety: it presents itself as a neutral efficiency upgrade, not a geopolitical revolt. But every transaction that clears on mBridge is one less that depends on New York's pipes.

If a meaningful share of Gulf-Asia energy trade eventually settles on non-dollar rails, one channel that historically supported dollar balances and dollar-asset demand could weaken. That would not automatically drain Treasury demand, but it would widen the menu of settlement and reserve choices.

China doesn't have to convince the world to trust the Yuan. It only has to convince it to *use* it.

The Federal Reserve's Dilemma

Meanwhile, in Washington, the digital-dollar debate plays out like a family argument at a dinner table no one wants to leave.

Should the U.S. modernize its currency to compete—or preserve the old guardrail to protect its banks?

The Institutional Risk:

Critics warn that a retail CBDC would let citizens hold money directly at the Fed, draining deposits from private banks in a crisis. A digital bank run could happen in minutes, not days, crashing the credit system before regulators could react.

The Privacy Backlash:

Civil libertarians fear a surveillance state with perfect financial vision—a digital dollar that records every coffee, every donation, every dissent. The idea cuts against the American grain: a nation founded on private enterprise and suspicion of central power.

The Defensive Imperative:

Yet delay carries its own peril. If the digital future belongs to China's e-CNY or to cross-border platforms like mBridge, the dollar's infrastructure advantage evaporates. The cost of hesitation is relevance.

The Paradox Reborn

The United States now faces a mirrored version of its own paradox: Should it risk **destabilizing its domestic banking system** to preserve **its global dominance**?
Or maintain stability at home and watch its international influence erode?

Either path carries pain—the difference is who pays first.

The Blueprint of Digital Money

To understand why Central Bank Digital Currencies could reorder global finance, one must separate what is inherent from what is optional. A CBDC is digital central-bank money. Programmability, identity requirements, transaction limits, offline functionality, and privacy rules depend on design and law.

Cash can provide a high degree of practical anonymity. Digital central-bank money generally creates electronic records, but who can see those records and under what circumstances depends on the architecture. A CBDC can be designed with intermediaries and privacy protections rather than a single central bank watching every retail transaction.

Behind the sleek dashboards and smartphone apps lies an invisible power shift: **from market intermediaries to the monetary sovereign itself.** Every transaction becomes a line of code in a centralized database maintained by the state.

This is not merely evolution; it is re-architecture — the state reclaiming its monetary infrastructure from private banks.

The Plumbing of Power

Imagine the entire banking system compressed into a single, programmable spreadsheet.
That's a CBDC ledger.

At the top sits the central bank — the ultimate node. Every citizen or institution granted access holds an account on this national ledger, and every transaction is validated directly by the monetary authority's servers. There are no correspondent banks, no clearinghouses, no SWIFT messages drifting through cyberspace.

The architecture comes in two possible forms:

1. **Retail CBDC (Direct Model):**
   The public holds accounts directly with the central bank. This is the purest version — simple, efficient, and politically explosive. It bypasses commercial banks entirely, giving citizens risk-free access to the ultimate balance sheet of the nation.

2. **Wholesale CBDC (Two-Tier Model):**
   Commercial banks retain their intermediary role, but the settlement layer beneath them becomes programmable and instantaneous. The Fed or PBOC doesn't handle every transaction; it supervises the code that does.

Both systems promise speed and precision. Both quietly redefine sovereignty.

Programmable Money: The Power of Conditions

One potentially revolutionary feature is programmability. A CBDC system can be designed so that rules or conditions are attached to transactions, but programmability is a policy choice rather than an inherent requirement of digital central-bank money.

Digital ledgers can retain transaction information. The degree of traceability, however, depends on the system's privacy model, the role of intermediaries, and the legal rules governing access to data.

Each unit can be coded with rules: where it can be spent, when it expires, or even what it can buy. A government could issue stimulus funds that self-destruct after 90 days, ensuring immediate consumption. It could target subsidies only to approved merchants or restrict certain purchases entirely.

For policymakers, this is a dream: monetary policy becomes surgical. For citizens, it is a Faustian bargain — efficiency traded for autonomy.

The same code that enables instant, precise relief can also enforce instant, precise control.

The Surveillance Dilemma

In Beijing's design labs, engineers frame the **e-CNY** not as a tool of repression but of modernization. Its white papers read like an instruction manual for technocratic utopia: reduced corruption, perfect audit trails, real-time economic data.

But to the rest of the world, the implication is clear: a monetary panopticon.

Every transaction, down to the morning coffee, becomes a data point in a state-owned database. Officials can trace, tax, or terminate any flow of funds in real time.

This is not a conspiracy theory; it is a technical feature. The People's Bank of China has publicly described its dual-layer architecture — anonymity for small payments, traceability for large ones — as "controllable privacy."

Controllable by whom is the question that divides democracies from autocracies.

The Global Experiment

Over one hundred central banks are now experimenting with digital currencies. Each pilot reveals a philosophy of governance hidden in code.

- **China's e-CNY:** Centralized and state-supervised, designed to replace cash and undercut Alipay and WeChat Pay's private duopoly.
- **Europe's Digital Euro:** The European project has emphasized privacy protections and a two-tier distribution model in which supervised intermediaries would continue to serve users. The precise privacy and holding rules remain matters of design and legislation.
- **Nigeria's e-Naira:** A case study in overreach — launched quickly, adopted reluctantly. Citizens preferred cash, viewing the e-Naira as surveillance disguised as innovation.
- **Bahamas' Sand Dollar:** The first fully deployed CBDC, created to extend banking access across scattered islands. Its scale is tiny, but its symbolism vast: the future of money began not in Beijing or Washington, but in Nassau.

The common thread across all these pilots is ambition — and anxiety.
Every government wants the efficiency. None want the backlash.

The Technological Decoupling

What makes CBDCs geopolitically explosive is not the technology itself, but *where* that technology runs.

Each national ledger becomes its own closed circuit. When these systems interconnect, the question becomes whose standards define the bridge.

- If the bridge runs through Beijing's servers, Chinese engineers control the protocol.
- If it runs through Basel, the BIS governs the rules.
- If it never touches U.S. soil, Washington's sanctions lose reach.

Project mBridge—developed with participating central banks and the BIS Innovation Hub—reached its minimum viable product stage in 2024. In October 2024, the BIS Innovation Hub handed the project over to the participating central banks. Its continued significance lies in demonstrating how cross-border settlement can occur on shared digital infrastructure outside traditional correspondent-banking chains.

It is not defection; it is diversification. But for the U.S., every diversified node is one less guarantee of dollar dominance.

The Code Is the Contract

In traditional finance, contracts are enforced by law. In the world of CBDCs, they are enforced by software. Once written into the code, rules execute automatically.

This automation removes the need for trust — and therefore removes the need for intermediaries like correspondent banks or international courts.

But it also removes recourse. If a CBDC transaction is frozen by algorithm, there is no appeal.
The code becomes both judge and executor.

For nations seeking freedom from U.S. jurisdiction, that is the appeal.
For democracies that prize checks and balances, it is the danger.

The Invisible Competition

To the average American, the debate over CBDCs feels remote, even irrelevant. Most people already use digital money daily — Venmo, PayPal, credit cards, Apple Pay. Why does it matter who runs the back end?

Because **infrastructure is power**.

The network that clears a nation's payments determines who can be excluded, who can be monitored, and who can be saved. The race for CBDC dominance is the 21st-century equivalent of building global railroads in the 19th. Whoever lays the tracks controls the routes of commerce for decades.

China is building railroads. The U.S. is holding town halls about track safety.

From Payment to Policy

CBDCs are not just payment tools; they are policy instruments. Imagine a central bank adjusting interest rates not by signaling markets but by literally changing the code of money in circulation — altering the yield or velocity of specific digital wallets.

This is monetary policy at the level of the individual — precision engineered and instantly deployable.
In the hands of a responsible democracy, it could revolutionize crisis response.
In the hands of a populist autocrat, it could erase financial freedom overnight.

The line between innovation and control has never been thinner.

The American Divergence

By late 2025, Washington's debate had moved beyond a simple choice between launching a Digital Dollar and doing nothing. The United States had chosen a different digital-money strategy from many CBDC experiments abroad.

The policy question was how to preserve dollar leadership through private and bank-based digital rails while keeping a retail central-bank currency out of ordinary consumer accounts.

That shift matters because it changes the strategic contest: the United States is modernizing the dollar without making a retail Federal Reserve CBDC its active implementation path.

The 2025 Policy Turn

On January 23, 2025, the White House ordered federal agencies not to establish, issue, or promote a U.S. CBDC and directed ongoing agency plans or initiatives aimed at creating one to be terminated, except where required by law.

The same executive order explicitly supported lawful dollar-backed stablecoins as a means of protecting and promoting U.S. dollar sovereignty. By the book's November 18, 2025 publication date, that was the federal executive branch's stated policy.

The Federal Reserve's position was narrower but compatible with that reality: it had made no decision to issue a CBDC and had said it would proceed only with authorizing legislation. Earlier research remained informative, but it was not an active retail-CBDC launch program.

1. **Bank Disintermediation:** A direct retail CBDC could shift transactional balances away from commercial banks, particularly in stress. An intermediated design can reduce that risk, but moving a large share of deposits toward central-bank money could still alter bank funding and credit creation.

2. **Two-Tier Banking:** U.S. policy has long relied on private banks and payment firms to serve customers while the Federal Reserve supplies the monetary base and settlement infrastructure. The 2025 policy turn preserves that distinction rather than placing universal retail accounts at the Fed.

3. **Mission Creep:** Any retail public-money platform would require clear statutory limits on data access, account restrictions, and the central bank's role. The concern is not that surveillance is technically inevitable, but that digital infrastructure can expand state capability if governance does not constrain it.

Under current U.S. policy, those concerns prevailed at the federal executive level. The country is attempting to modernize the dollar without placing a universal retail ledger inside the Federal Reserve.

The Stablecoin Strategy

Congress moved in the opposite direction from a retail Fed CBDC. The GENIUS Act became law on July 18, 2025, establishing a federal statutory framework for payment stablecoins.

The emerging U.S. strategy is therefore to extend dollar use through regulated private liabilities and modern payment rails rather than through a new retail liability of the Federal Reserve.

1. **The Technological Arms Race:** China's e-CNY and participation in cross-border projects such as mBridge give Beijing experience with sovereign digital settlement. That does not make the yuan a free-floating global reserve currency, but it can reduce payment friction with partners and expand China's influence over technical standards.

2. **Sanctions Slippage:** The dollar's enforcement power depends partly on jurisdiction over financial institutions and payment rails. As alternative networks proliferate, some

transactions may become harder to reach through U.S. correspondent banking, even though sanctions can still operate through asset jurisdiction, trade controls, and other legal tools.

3. **Defensive Dollarization:** Regulated dollar-backed stablecoins can carry the dollar onto new digital rails without giving retail users direct claims on the Federal Reserve. If credible and redeemable, they can extend dollar network effects into markets that might otherwise migrate toward non-dollar settlement.

The strategic question is therefore not whether digital money will matter, but whether the dollar remains the preferred unit of account, reserve asset, and settlement reference as the rails diversify.

Why a Retail CBDC Became Politically Toxic

At the heart of U.S. resistance lies an old American instinct: distrust of concentrated government power. Critics argue that a direct retail CBDC could place far more financial activity inside a government-operated system than Americans are accustomed to.

The feared scenarios are technically possible in some designs, but they are governance choices rather than unavoidable properties of CBDCs:

- What if an administration freezes the accounts of protesters under national security pretexts?
- What if stimulus money becomes conditional—restricted to "approved" expenditures?
- What if financial censorship replaces due process?

The technology may be neutral, but power never is.

To many Americans, a retail Digital Dollar therefore sounds less like a neutral technology project than a constitutional question about how much financial infrastructure the state should control.

From Project Hamilton to Policy Reversal

The Boston Fed and MIT completed Project Hamilton in December 2022. It was a technical research project into potential CBDC architecture—not a decision to issue a Digital Dollar and not an ongoing deployment program.

By January 2025, the executive branch had moved from exploration to explicit prohibition of agency work to establish, issue, or promote a CBDC, absent a change in law.

The Federal Reserve's public position remained that it had made no decision to issue a CBDC and would proceed only with authorizing legislation. Technical research could still inform payment policy, but a U.S. retail CBDC was not the government's active implementation path.

In practical terms, the retail Digital Dollar project was dormant under current federal policy while private dollar digitization accelerated.

The United States had not abandoned digital-dollar leadership; it had chosen to pursue it primarily through regulated private instruments and bank-based payment infrastructure.

Congressional Choice

Congress's decisive 2025 action was not a CBDC statute but the GENIUS Act, signed into law on July 18, 2025. It created a federal framework for permitted payment-stablecoin issuers, reserve backing, supervision, and redemption standards.

- The framework treats stablecoins as private payment liabilities rather than central-bank money. That preserves the distinction between the dollar as sovereign unit of account and the private institutions that distribute digital claims denominated in it.
- Supporters see that structure as a way to extend dollar use without creating universal Fed accounts. Critics still worry

about private concentration, run risk, surveillance by intermediaries, and the regulatory perimeter.

- The policy choice does not end the liberty-versus-control debate; it relocates much of it from the central bank to regulated private issuers, banks, payment firms, and the rules governing them.

The result is divergence, not paralysis: Europe continues toward a potential digital euro, China expands e-CNY experimentation, and the United States is betting that a regulated private-sector digital dollar ecosystem can preserve leadership without a retail CBDC.

The Private Sector's Countermove

Private stablecoins had already become a major part of digital-dollar activity by 2025. Tether, USDC, and other dollar-backed tokens provide rapid digital settlement without being central-bank liabilities.

They can strengthen the dollar's international reach while shifting important questions of reserves, redemption, compliance, and privacy to regulated private issuers rather than the Federal Reserve.

In that sense, much of the world is already using digital representations of the dollar—just not a retail CBDC issued by the United States.

Between Liberty and Leadership

The Digital Dollar debate is not about code; it is about conviction. It asks whether the U.S. can modernize without compromising the principles that made its money trusted in the first place.

America's greatest strength has always been the voluntary nature of its power. Nations hold U.S. debt because they choose to, not because they are forced to. Citizens use the dollar because they believe in the system's fairness, not its surveillance.

If the digital transformation of money turns trust into a function of software, then the U.S. must decide what its code stands for.

Efficiency or freedom.
Control or confidence.
Leadership or restraint.

The paradox remains: the dollar can lead the world, but only if it still deserves to.

The Quiet Race for Digital Territory

Globalization once meant convergence — supply chains linking continents, currencies settling through common channels, capital flowing like water.
CBDCs are reversing that story.

Instead of a single, interoperable financial web, the world is now building digital fortresses — national networks stitched together by politics, not efficiency.

Every government experimenting with digital currency insists it's doing so for domestic modernization. Yet beneath the surface, a deeper reality is taking shape: **money is becoming geopolitical again**.

The invisible lines that once separated East from West are being redrawn in code.

The East: The Architecture of Control

China's digital currency project, the **e-CNY**, is the world's largest live pilot for programmable, sovereign money. It already circulates among millions of users, embedded in mobile apps, used to pay transit fares, salaries, and even government subsidies.

But the genius of the e-CNY lies not in its domestic reach — it lies in its export potential.

China has no intention of turning the Yuan into a free-floating reserve currency in the traditional sense. Instead, it is **building infrastructure — not ideology**. Through partnerships under the Belt and Road Initiative, Chinese engineers are embedding payment software into the financial systems of Asia, Africa, and the Middle East.

Each time a partner nation adopts Chinese-built payment rails, it inherits Beijing's standards of compliance, cryptography, and—subtly—its influence. The result is a sprawling digital sphere of economic alignment, one that bypasses SWIFT entirely.

Call it *digital mercantilism.* China provides the code, the cloud, and the connectivity — in exchange for loyalty to its protocols.

The West: The Architecture of Consent

The Western bloc, led by the U.S. and the European Union, frames its approach differently.
It emphasizes "trust," "transparency," and "data protection." But beneath the democratic language lies the same strategic goal: preserve the dollar- and euro-based clearing systems as the global default.

The European Central Bank continues work toward a potential Digital Euro with privacy protections and intermediated distribution under debate. The United States has chosen a different path: as of November 2025, federal executive policy rejects a U.S. CBDC while Congress has created a framework for regulated private dollar-backed stablecoins.

In practice, both sides are racing toward the same finish line — *whoever writes the code rules the system.*

The difference is philosophical.

- China builds compliance into the money itself.
- The U.S. builds compliance into the institutions that move the money.

Both paths lead to control. One is explicit; the other, procedural.

The Middle Bloc: The Architecture of Options

Between these digital empires lies a restless coalition — the **non-aligned economies** of the Global South, the BRICS+, and the resource-rich middle powers that supply the world's commodities.

For them, CBDCs are not ideology but insurance.

They remember what happened to Russia's reserves in 2022. They saw dollar access weaponized. And they've drawn a sober conclusion: dependence on any single system is a structural risk.

Thus, they are building redundancy.

- India experiments with **digital Rupee trade settlements** with the UAE and Singapore.
- Saudi Arabia and the Gulf states explore **multi-CBDC oil payments**.
- Brazil and South Africa test interoperability frameworks designed to clear trade in either Western or Eastern systems.

Their motto is pragmatic: *Never again be frozen out.*

The Digital Iron Curtain

In the analog Cold War, the world split into two military blocs. In the digital monetary war, it is splitting into **two networks of trust**.

1. **The Western System:** anchored by the dollar, governed by open-market principles, but administered by private banks subject to U.S. law.
2. **The Eastern System:** anchored by the e-CNY and related technologies, governed by state-led digital infrastructure, insulated from U.S. sanctions.

Every nation is now choosing — or hedging — between them.

The dividing line is no longer ideology. It's **infrastructure**. A country can vote with its bandwidth, not its ballot.

The Fragmentation of Global Finance

Until recently, finance was the one truly globalized system. A dollar cleared in New York was the same dollar used in Singapore, Frankfurt, or Lagos. This universality made the dollar not just money, but the operating system of capitalism.

CBDCs threaten that universality.

Once money becomes software, interoperability depends on politics. Each national blockchain sets its own parameters for access, compliance, and reversibility. These parameters are not compatible by default — they must be negotiated.

The cost of mistrust becomes latency. The new inefficiency is political friction.

We are entering an era where **the world's money no longer speaks a common language**.

The BIS Balancing Act

The **Bank for International Settlements (BIS)**—the central bank of central banks—recognizes this danger. Its labs in Basel are working on cross-border frameworks designed to keep the system from splintering completely.

BIS Innovation Hub projects such as mBridge and Icebreaker explored ways for multiple central-bank digital currencies to transact across borders. mBridge reached a minimum viable product stage and was handed over to its participating central banks in October 2024, so it should no longer be described as an ongoing BIS-led project.

But neutrality has limits. The BIS can design the bridge; it cannot guarantee who controls the toll booth. As geopolitical polarization deepens, even shared platforms risk being politicized by design.

The Weaponization of Standards

In global finance, *standards* are power.
Whoever defines the protocol defines the future.

Think of it as the "USB problem."
If every computer port is different, every cable must adapt.
If one standard becomes universal, the company that controls it controls the entire ecosystem.

China's goal is not to make the world love the Yuan.
It is to make the world dependent on **Yuan-compatible protocols** — the payment equivalent of USB-C. Once those rails are entrenched, switching back to dollar systems becomes costly and cumbersome.

In this new world, dominance is not measured in currency share, but in **default settings**.

The Erosion of the Dollar's Invisible Empire

The United States won the 20th century not because it printed the most dollars, but because it controlled the most **infrastructure of trust** — the courts, the contracts, the clearinghouses, the reputational capital.

That infrastructure is now being duplicated in code.

Each CBDC platform, each cross-border payment network, each blockchain standard represents a new jurisdiction — an alternate source of truth. The dollar remains strong, but its monopoly on *trust* is being unbundled.

What began as modernization is ending as fragmentation.
And for the first time in living memory, the world's financial architecture is no longer a single cathedral — it is becoming a constellation of competing temples.

From Faith to Code

Every monetary system is built on a single, invisible foundation: belief.
For centuries, markets have operated on trust—trust in signatures, in reputations, in the rule of law. The digital transformation of money is rewriting that foundation in machine language.

CBDCs replace *belief* with *verification.*
Every transaction is authenticated by code; every balance validated by cryptography. The motto of the new financial order might as well be:

"In algorithms we trust."

To technocrats, this is progress.
To historians, it is heresy.

The shift from institutional trust to technological verification is not merely a financial evolution—it is a civilizational pivot. The world that once ran on promises will soon run on proofs.

The Death of the Signature

In the analog age, signatures were sacred. A signed contract, a bond certificate, a stamped seal—all symbols that reputation stood behind the transaction.

In the digital age, signatures are replaced by keys—long strings of numbers known only to machines. A cryptographic hash now guarantees what character once did.

This change seems technical, but its implications are profound. A contract enforced by trust invites forgiveness, discretion, and diplomacy. A contract enforced by code has none.

When the payment is automated, the penalty is instant.
When the ledger is incorruptible, so is the consequence.

The system becomes fairer—and colder.

The Rise of Algorithmic Sovereignty

As CBDCs proliferate, nations are discovering that monetary sovereignty no longer depends solely on who issues the currency, but on *who controls the verification process.*

Each country must decide where its digital ledger resides:

- **Domestically**—under its own servers and cybersecurity standards.
- **Regionally**—within a cooperative platform such as mBridge or Icebreaker.
- **Globally**—on cloud infrastructures that may be owned by rival powers.

Whichever path they choose defines their new sovereignty.

In this world, power migrates from treasuries to technologists. The most important officials in tomorrow's finance ministries may not be economists but software architects—keepers of the national code.

The money supply is no longer limited by metal, paper, or even politics, but by *protocol.*

The Transparency Trap

CBDCs promise to eliminate fraud, corruption, and tax evasion through total traceability. Every payment leaves a trail; every ledger can be audited in real time.

But transparency cuts both ways.

When everyone is visible, no one feels safe.
Citizens begin to self-censor financially, curbing donations, purchases, or associations that might be misinterpreted by an algorithm. Economists call this *monetary chilling*: when fear of observation changes behavior before any law is even enforced.

The paradox is brutal: perfect transparency erodes the very trust it was meant to restore.

The Market Without Mystique

The digitalization of money also changes how markets perceive risk. In a world of programmable liquidity, information asymmetry disappears. Every participant sees the same data in real time. Price discovery becomes mechanical.

Speculation—the art of anticipating human behavior—shrinks. Arbitrage fades. Volatility declines, then resurges in catastrophic bursts when algorithms misread each other's signals.

Finance loses its human texture.
Traders stop reading the room and start reading the code.

The market becomes a mirror—reflecting not psychology, but protocol.

The New Hierarchy of Trust

In the analog world, the hierarchy of trust ran through institutions: Governments → Central Banks → Commercial Banks → Citizens.

In the digital world, that pyramid flattens into a network. Each node—individual, merchant, or machine—can transact directly with the central bank.

This direct connection sounds democratic, but it also eliminates buffers.
If the state decides to freeze accounts or change monetary parameters, there are no intermediaries to slow or soften the blow.

Speed becomes absolute. So does control.

The most powerful lever in modern economics—the interest rate—could one day be adjusted not for banks, but for individuals. Imagine a world where your personal wallet earns or loses yield based on your spending behavior or carbon footprint.

The macro becomes micro. Monetary policy becomes moral policy.

The Global Shift: Trust as a Premium Asset

As verification replaces faith, *trust itself* becomes scarce—and therefore valuable.

Private systems that can guarantee privacy, neutrality, and redemption will command a premium.
Gold, decentralized cryptocurrencies, and even old-fashioned cash will trade not for their yield but for their autonomy.

In effect, the global economy will bifurcate:

- **Verified Wealth:** assets existing inside traceable, programmable systems—efficient, compliant, and controllable.
- **Trusted Wealth:** assets existing outside them—inefficient, opaque, and free.

The richer the verification network grows, the more people will pay for the luxury of discretion.

The New Paradox

The Dollar Paradox was born from a voluntary act of restraint: America's decision to borrow, not print.
The Digital Paradox will be born from a voluntary act of exposure: the world's decision to replace trust with total transparency.

Both paradoxes share the same moral center—discipline as strength.
But where the first rewarded institutional credibility, the second demands technological credibility.

The empire of trust is giving way to the empire of code.

The Coming Monetary Reckoning

Every financial revolution ends with the same question: *who disciplines the power that disciplines the world?*
When money was paper, restraint came from scarcity. When it became credit, restraint came from law. In the digital age, restraint must come from design.

The arrival of CBDCs will test whether humanity can encode humility.

For the United States, the stakes are existential. The dollar's supremacy has never been purely technological—it has been moral. It thrived because it embodied a promise that no algorithm can replicate: the commitment to fair dealing even when unfairness is easy.

That is the essence of the Golden Guardrail. It is not a line drawn by code or law; it is a culture of self-control.

Designing Digital Restraint

If a Digital Dollar is to preserve the credibility of its paper ancestor, it must be built with constraint baked in.
The architecture must refuse temptation by design.

1. **Separation of Powers in Code**
   The same principle that divided the Spender from the Printer must divide the *Issuer* from the *Overseer.*
   - The Federal Reserve should operate the technical ledger.
   - The Treasury should set policy on issuance and redemption.
   - Neither should be able to alter the system's records unilaterally.

In essence, the Iron Law must be rewritten in software.

2. **Programmable Privacy**
   Absolute transparency breeds fear; total secrecy breeds corruption.
   The solution lies in *programmable privacy*: thresholds that preserve anonymity for small transactions but demand disclosure for systemic ones. Such calibration is the digital counterpart of the banknote—trusted because it hides only what must be hidden.

3. **Hard Limits on Monetary Manipulation**
   To maintain confidence, a Digital Dollar must include circuit breakers against arbitrary devaluation or targeted interest rates. Money must remain a medium, not a message.

The Fed's New Mission

The central bank of the future will no longer merely regulate liquidity; it will regulate *legitimacy*.
Its credibility will depend on how well it can balance the paradox of visibility and independence.

A Fed that monitors everything risks becoming omnipotent.
A Fed that refuses modernization risks irrelevance.

The narrow path forward is radical transparency about the system's code but radical restraint in its use. The more citizens can inspect the machinery, the less they will fear its abuse.

In this sense, open-source principles—once the domain of idealistic programmers—may become the constitutional foundation of the next monetary era.

The Digital Dollar as a Public Utility

The U.S. must approach the Digital Dollar not as a surveillance tool or a profit engine but as **infrastructure**—a public good akin to highways or electricity.

It should:

- Guarantee universal access but never mandate use.
- Compete with private innovation rather than crush it.
- Strengthen the dollar's role as *the world's trust platform*, not as a monopoly.

If built this way, the Digital Dollar could become the modern extension of the Golden Guardrail itself—a system that enforces discipline on its issuer before imposing it on the world.

The Return of Pain

Every generation forgets why pain matters.
The Great Depression taught discipline. The 1970s taught inflation. The 2008 crisis taught humility. The digital age will teach accountability.

The ease of printing digital money—the ability to click rather than mint—will tempt governments to mistake convenience for control. But the market will still demand proof of restraint. If dollars can be created with keystrokes, then *credibility* must be earned with behavior.

In a programmable economy, the true scarcity will be trust.

The Human Factor

Technology cannot save a society from moral decay.
A CBDC may automate honesty, but it cannot automate virtue. The long-term survival of any monetary system still depends on people who believe in fairness more than expedience.

That is why the U.S. cannot simply build faster payment rails; it must rebuild *confidence*—domestically, politically, and institutionally. The digital architecture must reflect not just efficiency but character.

As the world transitions from analog wealth to algorithmic credit, America's greatest export must remain what it has always been: faith in the integrity of its promise.

The Final Lesson of the Digital Paradox

The first paradox of the dollar was that America borrowed when it could print.
The next paradox will be that it must show restraint when it could program control.

If the United States succeeds in encoding discipline into its digital money, it will not just preserve the Golden Guardrail—it will reinvent it for the twenty-first century.

If it fails, the Guardrail will dissolve into a thousand competing protocols, and the empire of trust will fragment into empires of code.

The choice is no longer between paper and pixel.
It is between *power and credibility.*

PART IV

The Policy Choice for Sustaining Supremacy

Chapter 13

The Policy Trap: The Myth of Austerity and the Political Pathologies

The Moralization of Money

Every great nation invents a story to justify its discomfort.
For the United States, that story is **austerity** — the conviction that virtue lies in financial pain, that balancing the federal budget is not an economic necessity but a moral crusade.

From the earliest political sermons about "living within our means" to the Sunday-morning talk-show refrain that "Washington should tighten its belt like any family," the same parable repeats. Debt is sin. Discipline is salvation. Austerity is repentance.

This belief survives every data point that disproves it because it is not an argument; it is a faith.
And faith is immune to arithmetic.

The Household Illusion

The most powerful metaphor in politics is the kitchen table.
Politicians frame the nation's finances as if they were a family budget:

"If you or I ran our household like Washington, we'd be bankrupt."

It sounds plausible. It is economically illiterate.

A family is a **currency user**.
It must earn dollars before it spends them. When it borrows, it promises to repay in a currency it cannot create.
A sovereign nation that issues its own money is a **currency issuer**. It spends first, then taxes and borrows later to regulate demand and interest rates. Its solvency is denominated in its own promises.

To conflate the two is to confuse physics with morality.
Yet that confusion drives entire platforms, elections, and crises.

When a household runs a deficit, it faces bankruptcy.
When a sovereign runs a deficit, it creates the very dollars the household uses to pay its bills.

The same policy that would ruin a family — spending more than income — is what sustains a modern economy. Austerity in that context is not prudence; it is self-harm dressed as virtue.

The Politics of Pain

Why, then, does austerity retain such emotional power?
Because it flatters the voter's sense of discipline and punishes an invisible villain.

Cutting "waste" and "fat" sounds noble when the victims of those cuts are abstract. Balanced budgets evoke the Protestant ethic: salvation through suffering. The phrase "fiscal responsibility" polls like sainthood because it implies character rather than competence.

For decades, politicians have sold restraint as morality while quietly expanding spending through back doors — tax expenditures, emergency authorizations, or unvoted entitlements. The performance of pain substitutes for the practice of policy.

The irony is almost tragic: the harder America tries to appear fiscally righteous, the more recklessly it behaves in practice. Austerity has become the political camouflage of indulgence.

When Virtue Becomes Vice

The danger of moralizing economics is that it converts prudence into pathology.
In 1937, Franklin Roosevelt, haunted by deficit critics after the New Deal, abruptly slashed federal spending to prove discipline. The result was swift and brutal: industrial production collapsed 33 percent, unemployment surged again, and the recovery from the Great Depression reversed overnight.

Historians call it "the recession within the Depression." Economists call it proof that you cannot cut your way to confidence.

Eight decades later, the Eurozone repeated the experiment. Greece, Spain, and Italy embraced austerity under the banner of responsibility. GDPs shrank, youth unemployment exceeded 50 percent, and populism filled the vacuum.

The lesson is universal: when governments starve an economy to feed ideology, trust dies before debt does.

The Debt That Holds the World Together

Austerity's moral blindness extends beyond national borders.
The United States is not merely a borrower; it is the **issuer of the world's collateral**. Every Treasury bond retired in the name of virtue removes a building block from the global credit system.

In Washington, "paying down the debt" sounds like heroism. In Basel and Beijing, it sounds like **deflation**.

The dollar system relies on abundance of safe assets, not scarcity. Each bond the Treasury issues is a promise the world believes in; each bond it destroys is trust withdrawn from circulation. Austerity shrinks not just spending but stability.

Faith vs. Function

If the debt is the rent America pays for its empire of trust, austerity is the vandalism that threatens to burn it down.
The Golden Guardrail — the separation between the political Spender and the monetary Printer — requires constant, visible borrowing to prove restraint. Remove the borrowing, and the proof disappears.

Yet the cult of austerity persists because pain is easy to preach and complexity is hard to explain. "Cut spending" fits on a bumper sticker; "maintain the global collateral base" does not.

And so, the richest country in history continues to debate its finances in the language of self-denial, not self-awareness.

The Road Ahead

The challenge for policymakers is not to abandon discipline but to redefine it.

True fiscal integrity is not measured by the absence of debt, but by the *capacity to service it without strangling growth.*

Only by confronting the psychology of pain can America rediscover the economics of purpose.

The Paradox of Prudence

Austerity's greatest illusion is that debt reduction is always safe. To the political imagination, paying off debt conjures serenity: tidy balance sheets, quiet markets, moral applause. In reality, it is the fiscal equivalent of draining the blood from a living body to prove you are healthy.

The global financial system does not merely tolerate U.S. debt — it **depends** on it. Every Treasury bond retired in the name of prudence removes a heartbeat from the world's circulatory system. The paradox is cruelly simple: what looks like virtue in Congress is catastrophe in Basel.

The World's Operating Collateral

At the core of modern finance sits a quiet, unglamorous object: the U.S. Treasury security. It is more than a loan to the government; it is the lubricant that keeps every gear turning.

- **In Banks:** Treasuries are used as collateral for overnight borrowing through the repo market — the invisible market that clears trillions every day.
- **In Central Banks:** They are reserves, insurance policies, and benchmarks for risk-free returns.
- **In Derivatives:** They anchor the valuation of complex instruments, providing the baseline "safe" yield used to price every asset from mortgages to emerging-market bonds.

Without Treasuries, the financial system doesn't merely shrink. It seizes.

The 2019 Warning Shot

In September 2019, the world briefly glimpsed what collateral scarcity looks like.
A routine mismatch between Treasury issuance and corporate tax withdrawals triggered a liquidity crunch in the overnight repo market. Overnight borrowing rates — normally around 2 percent — exploded to nearly 10 percent. Banks that had more than enough capital suddenly couldn't find enough **Treasuries** to pledge.

The Federal Reserve intervened within hours, flooding the system with hundreds of billions in emergency liquidity.
What caused the panic was not excess debt, but the **temporary absence** of it.

This episode was a live-fire demonstration of the Global Collateral Constraint: too little Treasury supply and the world's credit markets suffocate.

The Austerity Fallacy

Imagine, then, what would happen if the United States — bowing to political pressure — embarked on an aggressive program to "pay down" the national debt.

1. **Collateral Collapse:** Fewer Treasuries mean fewer instruments for banks to use in repo transactions. The cost of short-term funding would spike, strangling credit creation.

2. **Liquidity Freeze:** Central banks and sovereign funds would scramble to replace lost reserves, pushing up the price of remaining Treasuries and driving yields down in destabilizing bursts.

3. **Asset Bubbles Everywhere Else:** Trillions in global savings would be forced into riskier assets — corporate bonds, equities, real estate — inflating bubbles detached from fundamentals.

The result would not be a stronger dollar but a global financial migraine. Prudence, weaponized, becomes chaos.

The Savings Sink

Treasury debt serves another vital, often misunderstood function: it is the **savings sink** of the planet.

Every surplus nation — from Germany to Japan to Saudi Arabia — must park its excess capital somewhere safe, liquid, and legal. There is only one pool deep enough to absorb it: the U.S. Treasury market.

When Washington issues more debt, it provides a home for the world's savings. When it issues less, that savings must go elsewhere — into speculative instruments or unstable currencies.

Austerity, by shrinking that pool, doesn't cleanse global finance; it contaminates it with volatility. The world needs U.S. debt for the same reason an engine needs oil: without it, friction turns to fire.

The Engine Analogy

The Repo Market, described in Chapter 8, is the engine room of modern liquidity.
Each Treasury bond functions as a piston: reliable, interchangeable, infinitely reusable. Remove enough pistons, and the engine still turns — but it begins to rattle, overheat, and finally stall.

Austerity is the decision to remove the pistons while the machine is still running.

Politicians celebrate the smaller engine as "leaner government." The markets hear the metallic screech of an impending stall.

The Structural Role of U.S. Debt

It is easy to forget how deliberately the system was built.
After World War II, the U.S. designed a global order in which its debt would be the foundation of trust. The Bretton Woods

architecture, the Eurodollar market, and the modern repo system all presuppose a steady, expanding supply of American sovereign debt.

This was not carelessness; it was statecraft. Debt became the **infrastructure of leadership**.

To dismantle it now in pursuit of ideological purity would be to unravel the architecture of global confidence that has taken eight decades to construct.

The Illusion of "Paying It Off"

When policymakers talk about "reducing the debt," they imply an endpoint — a hypothetical moment when the ledger reads zero. But a zero-debt America is a contradiction in terms. The global economy's risk-free benchmark cannot be extinguished without extinguishing the system that uses it.

A world without U.S. Treasuries would look less like paradise and more like the 19th-century gold standard: chronic deflation, capital shortages, and violent boom-bust cycles.

In that world, austerity wouldn't cleanse; it would condemn.

The Political Mirage

Still, austerity sells. It offers politicians the illusion of control. "Balancing the budget" is a line that fits neatly in a campaign speech; "maintaining adequate global collateral supply" is not.

The average voter cannot see the repo market; they can, however, see a national debt clock ticking like a time bomb. So the political system performs fiscal hygiene while the financial system quietly prays for incontinence.

The Real Discipline

The Golden Guardrail was never about eliminating debt; it was about enforcing **painful transparency** — forcing the government to borrow in public, at market prices, under the gaze of investors.

The true test of fiscal virtue is not how much the U.S. owes, but whether it can continue to borrow at a price that affirms trust.

Austerity confuses punishment with discipline.
The market prefers the latter.

The Mathematics of Misery

Austerity always begins with good intentions. The slogans sound responsible: "tighten the belt," "live within our means," "restore confidence."
But economies are not families, and confidence is not a moral reward — it is a function of demand.

When governments slash spending in pursuit of virtue, they remove the single largest engine of demand in existence. Every dollar cut from the federal budget is a dollar subtracted from someone's paycheck, someone's order book, someone's tax revenue.

The result is not efficiency but entropy. Revenues fall, unemployment rises, social spending automatically increases, and the deficit — the very evil austerity was meant to destroy — widens again.

That is the **Fiscal Death Spiral**: contraction feeding on itself, virtue punished by arithmetic.

The Roosevelt Reversal

History's clearest warning came in 1937.
After four years of New Deal expansion, the U.S. economy was finally recovering from the Great Depression. Industrial production had soared, unemployment had halved, and confidence was returning. Then came the political backlash.

Critics in Congress accused Roosevelt of fiscal irresponsibility, demanding balanced budgets and smaller government. Bowing to pressure, the administration slashed public spending by nearly 20 percent and raised taxes to prove discipline.

Within months, the recovery collapsed.

- Industrial output fell **33 percent**.
- The stock market lost half its value.
- Unemployment surged back above **19 percent**.

Roosevelt's retreat into austerity erased four years of progress in less than one. Economists still study that episode as proof that a sovereign can **cut its way into recession** far faster than it can spend its way out.

Europe's Lost Decade

The same script replayed in Europe after 2010.
In the wake of the global financial crisis, leaders across the Eurozone vowed to restore "fiscal sanity." The result was synchronized austerity — budget cuts across nations that could not print their own money.

Greece slashed pensions and wages. Spain raised taxes amid 25 percent unemployment. Britain imposed the harshest spending contraction since World War II.

The outcome was predictable and devastating:

- GDP across southern Europe stagnated for nearly a decade.
- Youth unemployment exceeded **50 percent** in several countries.
- Public debt ratios **rose**, not fell, because GDP collapsed faster than budgets shrank.

Austerity did not rescue Europe; it hollowed it out. The real growth went not to the disciplined but to the daring — nations like the U.S. and China, which kept stimulating demand while others preached abstinence.

The Political Cost of Pain

Economic contraction rarely stays economic. It becomes political. When jobs vanish and living standards fall, voters seek scapegoats. Austerity breeds resentment, and resentment breeds populism.

In Greece, austerity gave rise to Syriza. In Italy, it fueled Five Star. In the U.K., it culminated in Brexit.
Each movement was framed as rebellion against elites, but the deeper grievance was stagnation — the feeling that the pain was moralized rather than managed.

The irony is stark: policies sold as fiscal responsibility end up destabilizing the very institutions that sustain creditworthiness. Markets crave predictability; populism thrives on outrage. Austerity manufactures the latter at the expense of the former.

The American Echo

The United States is not immune to the same pathology.
After the 2008 crisis, Congress pivoted to deficit reduction far earlier than history warranted. The result: the weakest recovery in postwar history. Between 2010 and 2016, GDP growth averaged barely 2 percent, even as the Fed held interest rates near zero. Fiscal restraint forced monetary policy to shoulder the entire burden of recovery, inflating asset prices while wages stagnated.

The top 10 percent recovered; the middle class treaded water. Political polarization deepened. The populist wave that followed — culminating in the 2016 election — was not born of ideology; it was the political offspring of economic fatigue.

Austerity, again, had rewritten democracy's script.

The Mechanism of Collapse

The Fiscal Death Spiral follows a grim but predictable sequence:

1. **Fiscal Retrenchment:** Spending cuts reduce public investment and social transfers.

2. **Demand Shock:** Private sector income falls; consumption contracts.
3. **Revenue Decline:** Lower incomes reduce tax receipts.
4. **Automatic Stabilizers Activate:** Unemployment benefits rise; the deficit widens again.
5. **Renewed Austerity:** Policymakers misread the deficit as overspending and tighten further.

Each cycle digs the hole deeper, turning political virtue into mathematical failure.

In technical terms, austerity reduces the denominator of fiscal sustainability — GDP — faster than it reduces the numerator — debt. The ratio that truly matters, **debt-to-GDP**, worsens even as spending shrinks.

When Confidence Becomes Fear

Markets, far from rewarding austerity, often punish it. Investors know that contraction today means weaker tax capacity tomorrow. Bondholders demand higher yields to compensate for slower growth — the exact opposite of the intended outcome.

Confidence, the holy grail of austerity advocates, cannot be commanded; it must be earned through competence. The bond market respects credible growth more than performative thrift.

The Paradox of Political Theater

Why, then, does every fiscal debate return to the same destructive ritual — the debt-ceiling standoffs, the shutdown threats, the televised brinkmanship?
Because austerity is easier to dramatize than discipline is to explain.

Telling voters that debt is dangerous wins headlines; explaining that debt is collateral wins no applause. Cutting spending makes noise; maintaining liquidity makes peace.

Washington's addiction to fiscal theater turns the global reserve currency into a stage prop. Each crisis, however narrowly averted, chips away at the perception that U.S. governance is rational.

The danger is not that America will default. It is that the world will stop believing its leaders know what they are doing.

The Exit from the Spiral

Escaping the Fiscal Death Spiral requires the courage to violate austerity's moral code. It means replacing virtue signaling with productive investment — spending not less, but **smarter**.

Infrastructure, research, education, and clean-energy transitions are not indulgences; they are productivity engines. They expand GDP — the denominator of the debt ratio — and thereby make existing debt more affordable.

The pain of the debt must remain visible, but it must be purposeful. The only sustainable path is one that grows the base faster than it grows the burden.

That is not irresponsibility. It is the true art of fiscal discipline.

The Theater of Virtue

The national debt is the only crisis in Washington that gets worse every time someone tries to fix it.
It exists less as a number and more as a stage — a place where politicians rehearse morality while avoiding arithmetic.

Every few years, the same actors return:

- A Congress promising fiscal virtue.
- A Treasury pleading for solvency.
- A public watching in confusion as the richest country on Earth threatens to default on itself.

It is a performance that terrifies the markets, excites the media, and changes nothing.

The reason is simple: America's debt debate is not about economics. It is about blame.

Pathology 1: The Misdirection of Blame

When the deficit rises, Washington's first instinct is to moralize, not measure.

Politicians decry "reckless spending" and "bloated bureaucracy" — a narrative that focuses attention on the **discretionary budget**, the tiny slice of federal spending that funds things people can actually see: parks, science, education, diplomacy.

In reality, over two-thirds of the federal budget is **mandatory** — locked in by law, not annual vote. Social Security, Medicare, Medicaid, and defense spending are the true engines of the long-term deficit.

But cutting these programs is political suicide, so leaders aim the fire hose elsewhere. They scapegoat the visible and protect the sacred.

A $5 billion program for public broadcasting becomes a talking point; a $900 billion entitlement system remains untouchable. The result is a political illusion — the spectacle of fiscal cleansing that leaves the real debt dynamics untouched.

The U.S. doesn't suffer from a lack of discipline; it suffers from a surplus of denial.

The Budget Mirage

The federal budget process reinforces this pathology by design. Every spring, Congress debates the *discretionary* budget — roughly one dollar in every seven the government spends — while the rest flows automatically.

Cable news covers these debates as if the entire solvency of the Republic depends on the outcome. In truth, they are moral pageants, not financial events.

By the time the fiscal year ends, the numbers barely move, but the soundbites live forever.
The deficit becomes the political equivalent of original sin — invoked endlessly, absolved never.

Pathology 2: The False Economy of the Debt Ceiling

Of all Washington's rituals, none is more perverse than the debt ceiling.
It is a law that limits how much the Treasury can borrow to pay for spending Congress has already approved. In practice, it is a hostage note Congress writes to itself.

Each time the ceiling approaches, the same drama unfolds. The Treasury warns of default; Congress threatens to "stand firm." Markets tremble as the world wonders whether the United States — issuer of the global safe asset — might willfully torch its own credibility.

The crisis always ends the same way: with a last-minute deal, a sigh of relief, and billions in unnecessary cost.

In 2011, during one such showdown, the U.S. lost its **AAA credit rating** for the first time in history. The irony was exquisite: the government had not defaulted on a single bond, yet the mere *threat* of self-inflicted chaos was enough to make investors question its sanity.

The debt ceiling is not a fiscal brake. It is a demolition switch wired to credibility itself.

The Constitutional Absurdity

The U.S. Constitution grants Congress the power to spend and the power to tax.
The debt ceiling creates a third, contradictory power: the power to renege.

By refusing to raise the ceiling after authorizing spending, Congress essentially tells the Treasury to perform an impossible act

— to pay bills without paying. It is legislative schizophrenia masquerading as accountability.

Economists from across the political spectrum agree that the ceiling serves no functional purpose. Yet abolishing it is politically taboo, because it eliminates the illusion of restraint. The ceiling allows politicians to posture as fiscal guardians without ever cutting a dollar of actual spending.

It is austerity's ultimate theater trick: a self-imposed cliff that Congress approaches every few years just to prove it fears heights.

Pathology 3: The Obsession with "Funding" Social Security and Medicare

The most persistent myth in American politics is that Social Security and Medicare are "going bankrupt."
Every election season, candidates cite a year — 2034, 2035 — as the moment when the trust funds will "run out." The phrasing is apocalyptic; the economics are misleading.

The U.S. government cannot "run out" of dollars in programs it funds in dollars. It can only mismanage the real resources — doctors, nurses, caregivers, and goods — that those dollars buy.

The **true constraint** on these programs is demographic, not fiscal.
As the population ages, the ratio of workers to retirees falls. Fewer workers producing goods and services means fewer real resources to meet the consumption needs of the retired. The challenge is productivity, not solvency.

Yet the political debate treats this as an accounting problem rather than a generational one.
The solution, therefore, is misplaced: instead of reforming benefits or raising payroll caps, lawmakers debate whether to "borrow less" or "cut spending."

The trust fund myth endures because it is emotionally potent — it tells citizens that their benefits depend on moral stewardship rather than political courage.

The Hidden Cost of Fear

These three pathologies share a common purpose: they redirect accountability.

- By blaming discretionary spending, Congress avoids structural reform.
- By weaponizing the debt ceiling, it transforms dysfunction into spectacle.
- By invoking insolvency myths, it replaces policy with panic.

Each pathology converts complexity into emotion — and emotion into inertia.

Meanwhile, the true fiscal danger grows quietly: the rising **interest cost** of the national debt, the real "taxpayer's burden."

While Washington debates morality, the math compounds.

The Voter's Dilemma

Ordinary citizens, trapped between alarmism and abstraction, respond predictably: they disengage.
Polls show that most Americans believe the national debt is a major problem, yet almost none can describe what it actually is. The political conversation has replaced literacy with liturgy.

Every crisis is presented as an apocalypse narrowly averted. Every compromise is sold as statesmanship. Yet nothing fundamental changes.

In this environment, cynicism becomes the most rational emotion. And cynicism, once normalized, corrodes the very trust that makes the U.S. bond market function.

The Institutional Irony

The Golden Guardrail was designed to enforce discipline through markets, not morality. Its power lies in transparency — in forcing politicians to borrow publicly, at market rates.
But the modern debate reverses that principle: it uses opacity as virtue.

Leaders now pursue moral optics rather than mathematical coherence. They perform restraint while practicing delay. The result is a political class addicted to crisis and a public desensitized to dysfunction.

The world still buys U.S. debt, but not because it believes in American politics — it believes in American law. That is the final margin of trust.

If the politics ever become as unstable as the rhetoric, that margin will evaporate.

The Way Out

Repairing this pathology requires an act of political humility: ending the theatrics and accepting that debt, properly managed, is not a moral failing but an instrument of policy.

The U.S. can no longer afford fiscal debates that trade in metaphors and panic. It needs a compass, not a stage — a measurable rule for when debt becomes dangerous and when it remains sustainable.

From Morality to Measurement

Every great civilization reaches a moment when morality becomes a poor substitute for math.
The United States has reached that point in its debt debate.

The language of "prudence" and "belt-tightening" once served a purpose — it curbed excess when money was scarce. But in a fiat world where the sovereign issues its own currency, discipline must come not from metaphors but from metrics.

The correct question is no longer *"How much do we owe?"* but *"How expensive is the debt relative to what we produce?"*

That simple shift — from moral arithmetic to economic proportion — reframes the entire conversation.

The True Fiscal Metric: Debt Service Cost-to-GDP

The absolute size of the national debt — $35 trillion, $40 trillion, or more — is politically dramatic but economically meaningless. The number that actually governs sustainability is the **Debt Service Cost-to-GDP Ratio**:

$$\text{Debt Service Ratio} = \frac{\text{Interest Payments on Debt}}{\text{Gross Domestic Product}}$$

This ratio tells us how much of the nation's productive capacity is consumed each year by interest — the rent paid on past political decisions.

- When the ratio is low and stable, debt is sustainable.
- When it rises faster than growth, the treadmill begins.

Think of it as the country's vital sign. You don't judge health by a person's weight alone, but by how hard their heart works to maintain it.

The Historical Benchmark

Since the 1960s, the U.S. Debt Service Ratio has averaged between **1.5 % and 3 % of GDP**.

During the Volcker years, when interest rates exceeded 15 %, it briefly spiked to 3.3 %, only to fall again as rates normalized.

By 2023, after years of near-zero rates, the ratio hovered around **2.5 %** — manageable but rising quickly as the Fed tightened policy. A sustained level above 4 % would mark the threshold of pain, where debt service begins crowding out discretionary spending and constraining fiscal flexibility.

This ratio — not the national debt clock in Times Square — should be the anchor of every fiscal conversation in Washington.

The Discipline Hidden in the Ratio

Focusing on the cost-to-GDP ratio does not mean abandoning restraint.
It means enforcing it through math rather than morality.

The ratio automatically punishes irresponsibility:

- If growth stagnates while borrowing accelerates, the numerator (interest cost) grows faster than the denominator (GDP).
- Markets respond by demanding higher yields, further increasing the cost.

This feedback loop enforces the Golden Guardrail far more effectively than self-imposed austerity or debt ceilings. It is discipline without the theatrics — pain without panic.

Policy Lever 1: Grow the Denominator

The first way to stabilize the ratio is to expand GDP — not through consumption bubbles but through **productive investment**.

Public spending is not inherently inflationary or wasteful; it depends on what it buys.
Spending that increases the economy's capacity to produce — infrastructure, education, technology, clean energy — lowers the debt ratio by enlarging the base of output.

Each new bridge, port, or microchip factory is not just a cost; it is an interest-reduction device disguised as national development.

When productivity rises, every borrowed dollar earns its keep.

Policy Lever 2: Manage the Numerator

The second lever is to manage the cost of debt — the numerator — by maintaining market trust.

That trust is earned through **predictability, transparency, and competence**, not through arbitrary pain.

The U.S. Treasury's credibility allows it to borrow trillions at lower yields than almost any nation in history. Preserving that advantage means avoiding self-inflicted crises — the shutdowns, the debt-ceiling brinkmanship, the budget showdowns that signal dysfunction.

Each manufactured crisis adds a few basis points to Treasury yields. Each basis point costs taxpayers billions.

Fiscal credibility, like credit, is cumulative — earned slowly, lost suddenly.

Policy Lever 3: Tax Policy as a Counter-Cycle Tool
Taxes are not the punishment side of the ledger; they are the stabilizer.
The goal of taxation is not simply revenue collection but **cycle management** — cooling demand during booms, supporting it during busts, and maintaining long-term fiscal balance.

The proper test of tax policy is not ideological — high or low — but functional: does it stabilize the cost-to-GDP ratio without suppressing growth?

A system that automatically collects more during expansions and less during contractions — progressive yet predictable — functions as an economic shock absorber.

This is how fiscal policy and monetary policy align rather than conflict: one controls the cost of money, the other controls the pace of spending.

The Narrative Advantage

The beauty of the cost-to-GDP compass is rhetorical as well as mathematical.
It allows policymakers to explain fiscal discipline in language the public can grasp:

"We are not aiming for zero debt. We are ensuring that the cost of our debt never exceeds the growth of our nation."

This framing converts austerity's guilt into accountability. It communicates balance without invoking scarcity.

The debate shifts from panic to proportion — from a moral struggle to a management question.

The Real Danger Zone

The danger is not that the U.S. will one day be "unable to borrow." The danger is that the **interest cost** consumes so much of the budget that every crisis — pandemic, war, recession — requires new borrowing at higher rates, triggering a debt-service spiral.

When the interest bill itself becomes the largest line item in the federal budget, the paradox collapses. The world's safest asset turns into its most expensive.

Avoiding that future requires vigilance, not virtue — active management of cost and growth, not ritual denunciations of debt.

The Compass as Policy Doctrine

In practice, this means Congress and the Treasury should adopt the cost-to-GDP ratio as an explicit fiscal anchor — a target to guide policy much like the Federal Reserve's inflation target.

- Keep the ratio **below 4 %** in normal times.
- Allow temporary rises during recessions or wars.
- Commit to reversing them once growth returns.

Such a framework would transform the national conversation from one of partisan accusation to one of measurable accountability. It would replace the moral theater of debt with the mathematical clarity of stewardship.

The Modern Definition of Fiscal Responsibility

Fiscal responsibility, in this light, is no longer about refusing to borrow.
It is about borrowing **intelligently** — issuing debt for investments that raise the economy's capacity to pay its own interest in the future.

The United States became the world's financial superpower not by eliminating debt, but by using it to build the institutions, infrastructure, and innovations that made it indispensable.

The lesson of the dollar paradox is not abstinence. It is mastery.

The Illusion of Escape

Every generation believes it can outwit arithmetic.
Some do it with ideology — "cut spending, save the nation."
Others do it with optimism — "growth will pay for everything."
Both are wrong in the same way: they mistake motion for control.

The United States cannot cut its way out of its debt, nor can it grow without discipline. The only sustainable path is equilibrium — the continuous, visible management of cost and capacity.

Fiscal mastery is not a finish line. It is a permanent act of navigation.

The Two Dangers: Panic and Complacency

The next decade will test whether the country can resist both extremes.

Panic tempts policymakers to lunge toward austerity when deficits widen.
This creates the contractionary spiral that history already condemned — the Roosevelt Reversal, Europe's Lost Decade, the manufactured crises of the debt ceiling era.

Complacency, its mirror opposite, tempts leaders to ignore the interest bill altogether, trusting that the world will forever subsidize American excess.

Both impulses violate the same law: the Golden Guardrail requires pain to remain credible. The world must see the U.S. pay a price for its privilege — not ruinous pain, but the visible cost of responsibility.

The Discipline of Transparency

The surest way to sustain that credibility is not austerity but transparency.
Markets forgive debt; they do not forgive deception.

Every bond buyer understands that the U.S. will always borrow more. What they watch is *how* it borrows:

- Is the process transparent?
- Are the auctions orderly?
- Are policy decisions predictable?

When Congress turns fiscal management into theater — shutdowns, brinkmanship, and last-minute rescues — it replaces transparency with spectacle.
Spectacle is expensive. Each episode widens the spread between U.S. Treasuries and perfect trust.

The cost of dysfunction is not theoretical; it is calculated daily in basis points.

The Political Cost of Clarity

A society that confuses clarity for cruelty soon loses both.
Real fiscal transparency means telling voters truths that politicians hate to speak aloud:

- That taxes must rise when demographics demand it.
- That defense spending cannot remain infinite.
- That entitlement reform is arithmetic, not ideology.

The irony is that honesty about limits is not weakness — it is the ultimate display of strength. Nations collapse not from debt itself, but from the refusal to explain it.

The Global Mirror

Abroad, America's choices are studied not for imitation but for calibration.
When Washington governs by crisis, other capitals hedge their bets — diversifying reserves, seeking alternate payment rails, experimenting with digital systems that reduce their exposure to U.S. jurisdiction.

The weaponization of trust (Chapter 10) made diversification rational. The spectacle of dysfunction makes it urgent.

Every act of domestic fiscal theater thus doubles as foreign policy. Each time Congress toys with default, Beijing gains another argument for mBridge. Each time the U.S. blames debt instead of managing it, it tells the world that political stability is the dollar's weakest link.

The True Nature of Power

The lesson of the Dollar Paradox has always been simple:
The world's most powerful nation must behave as if it is accountable to the world's smallest investor.

That accountability is not altruism; it is strategy. The trust of others is the cheapest capital the U.S. will ever raise. Lose it, and no amount of military dominance or GDP growth can replace it.

Empires fall not when they run out of money, but when they run out of credibility.

The Moral of Pain

The Golden Guardrail was never meant to make debt pleasant. It was meant to make it honest.
Every interest payment, every auction, every yield curve inversion is a

public confession of restraint. It says: *we will borrow, but we will do so under supervision — yours.*

This ritual of visible pain is the price of trust.
It separates the United States from the kingdoms, juntas, and populist regimes that print until collapse.

If America ever loses the will to pay that price — to face its debt in daylight — the paradox will end not with hyperinflation or default, but with irrelevance. The dollar will not die; it will simply cease to matter.

The Road Ahead

The path forward is not austerity and not indulgence. It is **discipline without delusion** — the ability to accept cost as the currency of trust.

The United States must commit to three permanent rules:

1. **Never Print to Spend.** Preserve the Iron Law of Separation. Pain must precede liquidity.
2. **Never Borrow in Darkness.** Maintain transparency in debt issuance and policy.
3. **Never Moralize Debt.** Replace blame with measurement — the cost-to-GDP ratio as the compass of policy.

Together, these rules preserve the paradox rather than destroy it. They ensure that America's debt remains the foundation of global stability, not the symptom of its decline.

Chapter 14

The Necessary Pain: Using the Golden Guardrail for Economic Stability

The Debt as the Counter-Cyclical Shock Absorber

Every economic boom contains the seeds of its own reversal. A speculative wave builds, the credit cycle turns, confidence shatters—and then the question arises: who catches the falling body?
For the United States, the answer is not the private sector or even the Federal Reserve. It is the national debt itself.

The Mountain of Debt is often portrayed as a moral failing, but in practice it is the nation's built-in airbag. When the economy contracts, that debt expands automatically, cushioning the fall before politics even wakes up. It is not waste; it is reflex. The very feature that pundits call "irresponsible borrowing" is the structural mechanism that prevents capitalism from eating itself alive.

1. Automatic Stabilizers in Action

Modern fiscal design allows Washington to respond to a downturn without a single vote being cast. Economists call these devices *automatic stabilizers*—pre-programmed valves in the federal budget that open the instant growth stalls.

- **Tax receipts fall.** When profits and wages shrink, income- and corporate-tax collections plunge.
- **Safety-net spending rises.** Unemployment benefits, Medicaid, and nutrition programs surge by law, not by legislation.

Those twin forces instantly widen the federal deficit. To fund it, the Treasury must issue new debt. Investors, simultaneously fleeing risk, line up to buy it. Fear on one side becomes fuel on the other. The panic finances its own containment.

During the **Great Recession of 2008**, the system performed exactly as engineered. Federal receipts collapsed by roughly 16 percent in a single fiscal year while outlays crossed $3 trillion for the first time. The deficit nearly tripled. Yet instead of a 1930s-style depression, credit markets stabilized and GDP began recovering within twelve months. The "red ink" on Washington's ledger was the visible scar tissue of a healed wound.

A decade later, in **2020**, the same stabilizers scaled to unprecedented size. Within weeks of the COVID-19 lockdowns, the economy lost twenty million jobs. Automatic spending programs detonated; tax inflows evaporated; and the deficit quadrupled. Treasury issuance surged by $3 trillion in half a year—an amount so vast it could have spooked global markets. Instead, investors from Tokyo to Zurich fought for the new paper, driving yields below 1 percent. The greater the fear, the cheaper the borrowing. The mechanism worked flawlessly: liquidity poured into the system precisely when confidence had vanished.

Had austerity prevailed—had Washington "tightened its belt" in the name of discipline—the result would have been catastrophe. Every dollar of spending cut by government would have been a dollar of income lost by someone else, deepening layoffs, shrinking tax revenue further, and forcing still more cuts. That downward spiral is the **fiscal death loop** that turned the 1930s crash into the Great Depression. The post-COVID recovery, by contrast, became the shortest recession in American history. The difference was not luck; it was design.

2. Debt as the Balance-Sheet Record of Rescue

Each crisis leaves behind a numerical monument: a higher national-debt figure that politicians brandish as evidence of failure. Economists read it differently. Those trillions are the price tag of survival—the accounting proof that the stabilizers fired, liquidity flowed, and collapse was averted.

Between 2008 and 2013, gross federal debt rose by about $5 trillion. During the same period, household net worth rebounded above its pre-crisis peak, banks were recapitalized, and unemployment fell by half. The government absorbed the pain so the private sector could heal. The red ink on the public balance sheet was the mirror image of black ink on the household one.

Debt, in this sense, functions like **national insurance**. The premium—the interest the Treasury pays—is the recurring cost of maintaining that insurance even in good times. Refuse to pay it, and the next shock arrives uninsured.

3. Why Pain Is the Proof

The paradox of the Golden Guardrail is that its discipline looks like indulgence. The world sees the U.S. borrowing freely and assumes recklessness; what it misses is that every dollar borrowed must still face the market's judgment. Each Treasury auction is a test of faith in American solvency. The pain—the interest cost—is that faith priced in real time.

When recessions strike, the United States can act fast because it has already earned credibility through decades of honoring that pain. Investors know the ritual: the government will borrow massively, the Fed will provide liquidity, and the system will stabilize. They buy not out of charity but out of trust in the architecture itself.

The resulting expansion of debt is not a moral hazard but a macroeconomic necessity. It is the physical manifestation of counter-cyclical power—the ability to create money responsibly because the market believes you will not abuse it.

In this way, debt becomes the Republic's shock absorber and its proof of discipline at once. Each new issuance during crisis is the world's confirmation that America still understands the most painful truth in finance: credibility costs money, and someone must pay the premium.

The Debt as the Inflation Anchor

Every modern economy wrestles with the same invisible enemy: excess capital with nowhere to go.
Profits accumulate faster than new opportunities appear; savings swell faster than productive investments can absorb them. If left uncontained, those idle trillions hunt for yield, flooding into housing markets, commodity speculation, or fragile emerging economies—

and prices begin to climb. Inflation, in the twenty-first century, is not born of scarcity; it is born of abundance.

In this environment, U.S. government debt performs a role that no private asset can: it absorbs the overflow. The Treasury market is not just a funding mechanism; it is a global drainage system. Every time Washington issues another bond, it gives the world's investors a pressure valve for their own excess liquidity.

1. The Global Safe-Asset Gap

Across continents, pension funds, insurance companies, and central banks face a structural dilemma: they must hold assets that will not disappear when the next crisis hits.

The supply of those assets—the truly risk-free, instantly tradable ones—is chronically insufficient. Economists call this the **Global Safe-Asset Gap**, and for decades, the only institution capable of closing it has been the U.S. Treasury.

A Treasury bond is more than an IOU. It is a piece of institutional architecture: standardized, deep, and continuously priced. Its yield is the reference point for every other instrument on Earth. A 10-year Treasury is worth holding not only because it pays interest, but because it will always find a buyer—at any hour, in any market, under any administration. That guarantee of liquidity is what gives the world's wealth its resting place.

This is why the U.S. debt is paradoxically deflationary in its long-term effect. By supplying trillions of safe bonds, the government soaks up capital that might otherwise chase scarce goods or risky assets, cooling speculative fever before it ignites. In effect, Treasury issuance transforms raw liquidity into trust.

Between 2009 and 2019, as federal debt doubled, global inflation remained subdued. Investors bought roughly $10 trillion in new Treasuries during a decade when average U.S. consumer-price growth hovered near 1.8 percent. The government's borrowing did not cause inflation—it contained it.

2. The Debt as the World's Monetary Sponge

Each Treasury auction is an act of macroeconomic housekeeping. Capital inflows from exporters, energy producers, and surplus nations pour into U.S. debt because no other market offers the same scale, safety, or transparency. Those inflows remove trillions of dollars of purchasing power from circulation and park it in sterile, interest-bearing form.

To critics, this looks like addiction—the United States borrowing endlessly to fund its consumption. But the truth is almost the opposite: America's deficits are the world's savings, recycled and sterilized through the Golden Guardrail.

When China sells goods to U.S. consumers and receives dollars, those dollars must end up somewhere. Chinese firms deposit them at local banks; the banks swap them for yuan at the People's Bank of China; and the central bank invests the dollars in U.S. Treasuries. Each step converts private income into public debt, neutralizing what would otherwise be inflationary pressure in both economies. The same cycle repeats with oil exporters, European pension funds, and Japanese insurers.

The irony of this system is that it works best when the debt grows. The greater the supply of Treasuries, the smoother the plumbing of global finance becomes. A shortage of U.S. debt would be far more dangerous than an excess, because it would leave no anchor for the sea of private liquidity that constantly expands around it.

3. Liquidity as a Public Good

Liquidity—the ability to buy or sell an asset instantly without distorting its price—is often taken for granted. Yet it is one of the most precious public goods in modern capitalism, and it exists only because the Treasury market is vast and continuous.

The Federal Reserve relies on that liquidity to conduct monetary policy. Each open-market operation, each change in the policy rate, transmits through Treasury prices into every other corner of finance—from mortgage rates in Des Moines to corporate loans in Frankfurt. If that market were shallow or fragmented, the Fed's control of inflation would be erratic, its signals misread.

Instead, the sheer depth of the Treasury market produces a clean, readable yield curve—a real-time measure of what investors believe about future inflation and growth. The Fed reads that curve as a physician reads a pulse. It is not the act of borrowing that creates stability; it is the precision with which borrowing can be measured and managed.

When economists describe Treasuries as the "benchmark risk-free asset," what they really mean is that the U.S. has built the only monetary instrument large enough to keep the global system predictable. In this sense, debt is not a drag on growth; it is the infrastructure of foresight.

4. The Inflation Anchor in Practice

The best way to see the anchor at work is to imagine its absence. If the world suddenly lacked a safe, liquid store for surplus capital, that money would rush toward tangible assets—land, housing, food, metals. Prices would soar not because people were wealthier, but because their wealth had nowhere safe to rest. Every boom would end in a bubble, every bubble in a crash.

The U.S. debt prevents that cycle by offering a near-infinite container for trust. In moments of panic, it deepens; in moments of exuberance, it steadies. It is not the problem to be solved but the ballast that keeps the ship from capsizing.

5. The Hidden Logic of Pain

The interest paid on that debt—the "Taxpayer's Real Burden" described in Chapter 13—is the maintenance fee for global equilibrium. Those payments circulate back into the same financial system that depends on them. Pension funds collect them as income;

central banks record them as reserves; private investors treat them as the floor of the yield spectrum.

The pain is not arbitrary—it is design. Without the visible cost of carrying the debt, there would be no credibility in its promise. The world trusts the dollar not because it is free of pain, but because the United States chooses to pay it.

The Interest Rate Mechanism: Enforcing Foresight

Nothing in the global economy is more misunderstood than the interest rate on U.S. debt.
To the casual observer, it is a penalty — a toll extracted by creditors from a reckless borrower. In reality, it is the most important instrument of accountability ever built into a democracy.

The rate the United States pays on its debt is not imposed by foreign creditors or political fiat; it is discovered, in real time, by the market's collective judgment. Each Treasury auction is a referendum on the nation's credibility — a recurring vote of confidence in whether Washington's promises are worth the paper they're printed on. The price of money is the price of trust.

1. The Cost Signal That Never Lies

Every few days, the Treasury enters the market to sell new debt. Investors bid, the yields adjust, and in that process, the nation receives something no legislature or committee could ever produce: an unvarnished signal about the future.

If Congress spends recklessly, or the Federal Reserve loses control of inflation, the bond market responds instantly. The yield curve steepens, interest costs rise, and the pain becomes visible — not years later, but immediately.

This is the **Cost Signal** function of the Golden Guardrail: a dynamic feedback loop that prices political irresponsibility in real time.

- **Short-term pleasure, long-term price:** A politician can vote today for a popular, unfunded tax cut. But within days, the Treasury's next auction will price in the risk, raising yields and locking in higher interest payments that last for a decade.
- **Accountability by arithmetic:** The higher the rate, the greater the share of future tax revenue that must be diverted to interest rather than services or investment. The political reward of instant gratification comes packaged with the economic punishment of higher debt service.

This is why the interest rate is the ultimate self-correcting mechanism in fiscal policy. It forces every administration — Republican or Democrat, conservative or progressive — to reckon with the market's verdict on its credibility. In a sense, it is democracy's second ballot box: one that cannot be gerrymandered, bought, or spun.

2. The Interest Rate as Political Memory

In Washington, political time is short. Presidents think in four-year cycles; legislators think in two. The market does not. It thinks in decades, sometimes centuries.

When yields rise, they outlive the politicians who caused them. A ten-year Treasury issued today will still be paying interest when two elections have come and gone. Each careless fiscal choice is thus memorialized in the coupon rate printed on the bond. Those numbers do not forget.

This is the cruel genius of the Golden Guardrail. It transforms ephemeral political decisions into long-lived financial obligations. Even the most short-sighted populist cannot escape the compounding math of the bond market. By turning bad policy into enduring cost, the system disciplines behavior not by ideology but by interest.

The Necessary Pain of those higher yields is not a malfunction; it is the immune response of a healthy financial organism. The market demands higher compensation for higher risk — and in doing so, forces the political class to confront the consequences of its own rhetoric.

3. The Fed's Partner in Discipline

The same feedback loop that keeps Congress honest also gives the Federal Reserve its teeth. When the Fed raises its policy rate to combat inflation, it relies on the Treasury market to transmit that pain through every layer of the economy.

Each Treasury security acts like a node in a vast neural network of global finance. When short-term yields rise, investors reprice every asset that references them — mortgages, corporate bonds, municipal debt, even foreign sovereign loans. The signal spreads instantly, contracting credit, cooling demand, and bringing prices back down.

This is why the national debt is not an obstacle to monetary policy but its delivery system. The debt is the *medium* through which the Fed exercises control. Every open-market operation — buying or selling Treasuries to add or drain liquidity — requires a vast, deep pool of existing bonds to function. Without that ocean of debt, the Fed's instruments would be blunt and imprecise, its influence on inflation haphazard.

The irony is profound: the same politicians who decry "too much debt" are the ones whose economic survival depends on its abundance. Without a massive, liquid Treasury market, there would be no stable mortgage rates, no predictable credit curves, no reliable transmission of monetary policy at all. The mountain of debt is the scaffolding that holds the economy steady.

4. Market Pain as Preventive Medicine

Interest, in the end, is a form of economic medicine. It stings, but it heals. The pain of higher borrowing costs discourages future recklessness and restores discipline before catastrophe.

When investors demand higher yields, it does not mean the United States is on the brink of default; it means the immune system is working. The market is injecting caution into the bloodstream of policy, forcing sober reflection where hubris once reigned.

The great fiscal collapses of history — from Weimar Germany to modern Argentina — occurred precisely when that pain was denied. Governments that tried to abolish the cost of borrowing by printing their own currency destroyed the credibility that made their money worth anything. Once pain is outlawed, inflation becomes lawless.

In the U.S. system, the opposite principle prevails: the price of pain is the price of power. The willingness to endure it is what keeps the dollar supreme.

5. The Democratic Discipline

Democracy is a short-memory system. Politicians come and go; promises multiply faster than revenues. The Golden Guardrail — the market's discipline enforced through the interest rate — is the one institution that cannot be bribed, distracted, or replaced.

Every auction is a reminder that the system still believes in accountability. Every coupon payment is the cost of that belief. The United States remains the anchor of global finance not because it avoids mistakes, but because it allows the consequences of those mistakes to be priced transparently and paid in full.

That, ultimately, is the paradox's moral center: pain is not a symptom of dysfunction; it is the proof of integrity.

Debt as the Transmission Mechanism of Monetary Policy

Every lever the Federal Reserve pulls begins and ends with the U.S. Treasury market.

When the Fed raises or lowers interest rates, it does not flip a single master switch. It moves the price of money by altering the yields on the only asset that every financial system in the world must hold: U.S. government debt.

The Treasury market is the circulatory system through which monetary policy travels. Without it, the Fed's power would be theoretical—a speech, a statement, a gesture with no transmission mechanism. Debt, paradoxically, is what gives the central bank its strength.

1. The Mechanics of Transmission

Every monetary decision the Fed makes ultimately passes through one instrument: the Federal Funds Rate—the overnight lending rate between banks.

But this microscopic rate matters only because it cascades outward. Banks and investors extrapolate it to price every other financial product: the 2-year note, the 10-year bond, the 30-year mortgage.

When the Fed tightens—raising its target rate—it sells Treasuries from its portfolio to drain liquidity from the system. That sale pushes bond prices down and yields up, signaling to the entire economy that credit will now cost more. Conversely, when it loosens policy, it buys Treasuries, injecting liquidity and lowering yields.

Each purchase or sale ripples instantly through global markets. The Treasury market's depth and liquidity make it the perfect transmission wire: trillions of dollars can change hands daily without jamming the circuit.

The Treasury market is to the Fed what a bloodstream is to a heart. The pump's rhythm means nothing without open arteries.

2. The Fed's Balance Sheet: Power Built on Debt

Every Treasury security on the Fed's balance sheet is a tool of control. These bonds are not passive holdings—they are active instruments of policy.

When the Fed buys a Treasury, it credits the selling bank's reserve account with newly created dollars. Those reserves expand the money supply, easing financial conditions. When the Fed sells, the reverse occurs—reserves shrink, tightening conditions.

The entire system of open market operations depends on a continuous, abundant supply of government debt. Without it, the Fed could not modulate liquidity smoothly. Its operations would be clumsy, restricted, and potentially destabilizing.

This is why fears of "too much debt" misunderstand the architecture. The Treasury issues; the Fed circulates. One manufactures the instruments of stability, the other adjusts their price. The more efficient their coordination, the steadier the global economy.

In moments of stress—2008, 2020, 2023—the Fed's purchases of Treasuries (so-called *quantitative easing*) prevented financial collapse not by printing money recklessly, but by ensuring that the system's safest asset remained liquid. The Fed's credibility depends on the existence of a deep, continuous Treasury market it can enter at will.

3. The Yield Curve as the Market's Compass

The yield curve—the line connecting short- and long-term Treasury rates—is the single most informative picture in finance.
When it is steep, investors expect future growth and inflation; when it flattens or inverts, they expect slowdown or recession. The curve's shape dictates the behavior of lenders, borrowers, and central banks alike.

The Fed uses that curve like a stethoscope. It listens to the heartbeat of the economy through the yields on 2-, 5-, and 10-year bonds.

- **If long-term yields rise sharply:** markets fear inflation or fiscal excess; the Fed tightens policy.
- **If they collapse:** markets expect contraction; the Fed loosens to reintroduce liquidity.

But this feedback loop works only because the Treasury market is enormous and continuous. The curve is smooth because there are buyers and sellers for every maturity, every day.

Shrink the supply of debt too much, and the curve becomes jagged and unreliable. Monetary policy would turn from science into guesswork.

The Treasury market, in other words, is not the byproduct of monetary policy—it is its *instrument panel.*

4. Debt as the Anchor of Global Pricing

Every asset class in the world—stocks, bonds, commodities, currencies—ultimately prices itself against the U.S. yield curve. When the Fed raises short-term Treasury yields, it indirectly reprices the entire global menu of risk. Corporations must offer higher returns to attract capital. Mortgage rates rise, cooling real estate. Even gold, oil, and crypto adjust to the new opportunity cost of holding dollars.

The Treasury yield is the gravitational center of capitalism. Remove it, and orbits decay.

In this sense, the U.S. national debt is not merely domestic bookkeeping—it is the *reference price of time itself.* It tells the world what the future is worth in dollars. The more credible the issuer, the more stable the price of time. That credibility is what separates an orderly slowdown from a currency crisis, and a disciplined democracy from a desperate one.

5. Why the Fed Needs the Debt to Be Big

A common fallacy imagines that if the U.S. government paid off its debt entirely, the Fed would be stronger. The truth is the opposite. If there were no Treasury securities to buy or sell, the Fed would lose its steering wheel. It could no longer conduct open-market operations or manage interest rates through asset purchases. Monetary policy would become a blunt instrument limited to reserve requirements or capital controls—methods more suited to fragile, authoritarian economies than to the world's leading democracy.

The Fed's precision depends on abundance. It must have trillions of safe assets to trade daily, across maturities, to fine-tune liquidity and signal expectations. The Treasury provides that raw material. The system works because both institutions—one political, one technocratic—are locked into mutual dependence, neither able to dominate the other.

That interdependence is not weakness; it is the architecture of trust. The Printer cannot exist without the Spender's debt, and the Spender cannot act without the Printer's price discipline. Together they enforce the paradox: the United States maintains global order not by avoiding pain, but by managing it with mathematical grace.

6. The Golden Guardrail in Motion

Each Treasury auction, each shift in the Fed's policy rate, activates the Golden Guardrail in real time. The market tests the credibility of policy; the Fed tests the resilience of markets; and the interest rate—the system's pulse—keeps both honest.

It is not a static institution but a living organism of incentives, constantly adjusting to shocks, absorbing risk, and translating fear into price. Every time investors buy a Treasury bond, they reaffirm their belief that the pain of borrowing will always be preferable to the chaos of printing. That belief is what keeps the world safe for capitalism.

The pain, therefore, is not accidental; it is engineered. It is the deliberate cost of having a system that can correct itself without collapsing. In a global economy addicted to quick fixes, that design is the rarest form of stability.

Debt as a Public Good: The Paradox of Supply and the Price of Stability

The word *debt* carries moral weight.
It implies failure, irresponsibility, excess — a promise broken or deferred. In political speeches, it's treated like sin. But in global finance, U.S. government debt occupies a very different moral category. It is the one liability that functions as everyone else's asset. It is the foundation stone of modern capitalism.

This is the final twist in the Dollar Paradox: the U.S. national debt, often condemned as proof of weakness, is the very reason the system holds together. Its continuous expansion is not a bug in the code; it is the code itself.

1. The Paradox of Supply: The More It Grows, the Safer It Becomes

In most markets, scarcity creates value. The rarer a commodity, the higher its price.

Treasury debt breaks that rule. The more of it the United States issues, the more valuable it becomes—not because its yield rises, but because its liquidity deepens. Abundance, not scarcity, is what makes it precious.

Each new Treasury bond adds to a global web of collateral that underpins everything from money-market funds to mortgage securities. Every additional trillion in debt makes it easier for banks to meet regulatory capital requirements, for pension funds to hedge liabilities, and for central banks to settle cross-border payments.

If the Treasury were to suddenly *reduce* issuance to "balance the budget," it would not restore fiscal health—it would suffocate the financial system's lungs. The Repo Market would seize up, short-term lending would freeze, and liquidity would evaporate. The system needs constant replenishment of this safe collateral, just as the body needs oxygen.

This is the paradox of supply: stability demands abundance. What appears to be a mountain of debt from one perspective is, from another, the scaffolding of trust that holds the global economy upright.

2. The Debt as Infrastructure

To think of the national debt as "borrowing" is to miss its true nature.

It is infrastructure — invisible, but as essential as the interstate highway system or the electric grid.

Each Treasury bond is a node in a vast network of transactions: it can be pledged, rehypothecated, or traded billions of times before it matures. Banks use Treasuries as collateral for short-term borrowing. Money-market funds use them as backing for deposits. Foreign central banks use them as reserve insurance against volatility.

Destroy that infrastructure, and modern finance collapses. That's why global regulators, after the 2008 financial crisis, required banks to hold more Treasuries, not fewer. The lesson of that collapse was not that there was too much U.S. debt in the world, but that there was too little liquidity when panic struck. The financial system nearly drowned not in debt, but in its absence.

When the United States issues debt, it is not just funding government programs; it is maintaining the plumbing of capitalism.

3. The Interest Payment as Maintenance Fee

The annual interest on the national debt—what Chapter 13 called the *Taxpayer's Real Burden*—is not deadweight. It is the maintenance cost of running the world's financial infrastructure.

That payment circulates through the same ecosystem that demands it:

- Foreign central banks earn interest on their reserves, strengthening their currencies and stabilizing trade.
- Pension funds receive predictable income to match their long-term liabilities.
- U.S. banks use the Treasury yield curve as a benchmark to price every other loan they extend.

When viewed this way, the interest payment is not tribute to creditors; it is service rendered to the system that sustains the dollar's supremacy. The United States pays interest not to survive, but to preserve stability. The pain is proof that the system is functioning as designed.

Without that visible cost, the credibility of the entire structure would collapse. Pain is the signal that the rules still apply.

4. The Deb as Global Public Good

Economists often speak of *public goods* — things like clean air or national defense that benefit everyone and cannot be privately produced at scale.

U.S. Treasury debt is a financial public good. It provides liquidity, stability, and safety that no private market can replicate.

The global system's need for that public good is so vast that it has become self-reinforcing:

- **Central banks** hold Treasuries because they are universally accepted collateral.
- **Private institutions** hold them because they are required for regulatory capital.
- **Investors** hold them because every portfolio needs a risk-free benchmark.

This collective dependency ensures that the demand for Treasuries remains insatiable, even when political rhetoric at home turns hostile. It is why every fiscal standoff in Washington—the debt-ceiling crises, the government shutdown threats—provokes not a run from Treasuries, but a rush *into* them. The rest of the world treats American dysfunction as a buying opportunity, because no alternative exists.

That is the ultimate irony of the Dollar Paradox: the perception of political risk strengthens the financial system built on the very debt those politics produce.

5. The Moral Reversal: From Shame to Stewardship

The great moral inversion of the modern era is that America's debt is not a symbol of decay but of trust.

Every coupon payment is a public act of credibility. Every bond auction is a ceremony of stability.

To "reduce the debt" in the abstract would be to destroy the very mechanism that prevents global chaos. What the United States must manage is not the size of its debt, but its credibility — its willingness to keep paying, keep borrowing, and keep honoring the discipline of the market.

This is what separates the United States from empires that collapsed under their own currency: not moral superiority, but institutional transparency. The Golden Guardrail—the visible pain of interest, the ritual of borrowing, the self-enforcing honesty of the auction—turns debt from weakness into governance.

The United States has built the only empire in history whose power depends on its willingness to owe, and to pay, forever. That is the price of global stability—and the privilege of leading it.

Chapter 15

The True Policy Path: Growth over Austerity

The Growth Solvent: Why America Must Outgrow Its Debt

The policy debate in Washington has long confused morality with arithmetic. Politicians preach that virtue lies in paying down the debt, as though the nation could atone its way back to prosperity through fiscal abstinence. But the math of sovereignty does not work like the math of a household. For a nation that issues its own currency, the goal is not to *repay* the debt but to *outgrow* it.

Every empire in history has tried austerity. None have thrived on it. The ones that survived built something far more powerful: growth so large, so self-sustaining, that their debt shrank in comparison. The debt did not disappear—it was simply dwarfed by the scale of what followed. That is the true lesson of post-war America, and the true policy path forward.

1. The Arithmetic of Credibility

For a sovereign issuer of the world's reserve currency, fiscal responsibility is not defined by the *size* of the debt but by the relationship between two numbers:
the growth rate of the economy (g) and **the cost of the debt (r).**

If the economy expands faster than the interest it pays, the debt becomes lighter every year, even if its nominal size grows. If the reverse happens—if borrowing costs rise faster than national income—the debt becomes a treadmill, demanding ever more energy just to stay in place.

Economists call this relationship the golden inequality: **g > r.** It is deceptively simple, yet it captures the entire strategy of sustainable power. When growth outpaces interest, debt serves as leverage; when interest outpaces growth, it becomes a trap.

The United States has lived both sides of that equation. After World War II, federal debt stood at 119 percent of GDP, higher than today's level. Yet by the 1970s, that ratio had fallen below 35 percent—not because Washington "paid down" the debt, but because the denominator exploded. A wave of industrial expansion, suburbanization, and innovation made the wartime debt look small against the backdrop of an economy that had doubled and redoubled in size.

By contrast, the early 1980s and mid-1990s saw bouts where **r > g**, driven by high real interest rates and sluggish productivity. Each episode triggered fiscal panic and political calls for austerity—but the real cure was not budget cuts; it was renewed investment that restored growth.

2. The Virtuous Cycle

When **g > r**, the fiscal math turns elegant.

Even with modest primary deficits—when the government spends slightly more than it collects in taxes—the debt-to-GDP ratio falls naturally. The economy's expanding output outpaces the accumulation of interest, and the Taxpayer's Real Burden (the share of national income devoted to interest) shrinks without any dramatic spending cuts.

This is the **Virtuous Cycle**: prosperity makes debt sustainable, and debt finances the investments that fuel prosperity. It is the self-reinforcing rhythm of a confident sovereign system. The post-war boom, the 1990s internet expansion, even the recovery from COVID-19 all followed this logic. Borrowing was high, but growth was higher.

3. The Vicious Cycle

When the inequality reverses—when **r > g**—the same logic becomes merciless.

Even a balanced budget cannot stop the debt ratio from rising, because interest compounds faster than the economy grows. The government must borrow just to service previous borrowing, and interest payments consume an ever-larger share of fiscal capacity. This is the **Taxpayer Treadmill** introduced in Chapter 13: motion without progress.

The only escape from that treadmill is to push the growth rate back above the interest rate. Austerity—cutting spending across the board—cannot achieve this. It may reduce nominal outlays, but it also throttles demand and investment, lowering growth further and deepening the inequality. Fiscal contraction raises the very burden it seeks to ease.

That is why the **True Policy Path** rejects austerity as a moral illusion. The goal is not to erase the Mountain of Debt; it is to expand the base of the mountain until the slope no longer feels steep.

4. The Growth Agenda: Turning the Inequality in Our Favor
The Growth Agenda is not a slogan; it is a deliberate policy design aimed at maximizing the nation's productive capacity. It asks a simple question: Which investments make the future bigger than the bill?

Pillar 1: Infrastructure and Logistics
Productive infrastructure—roads, ports, broadband, power grids—is the plumbing of prosperity. Every bottleneck removed multiplies the efficiency of private enterprise.

- **Multiplier Effect:** Studies from the Congressional Budget Office and the IMF consistently show that a well-targeted dollar of infrastructure spending yields between $1.40 and $2.50 in GDP over the medium term.
- **Historical Proof:** The Interstate Highway System, financed through debt in the 1950s, generated returns that dwarfed its cost. The highways did not burden the budget; they became the arteries of a continental economy.

When debt finances assets that endure for decades and reduce the cost of doing business, it is not a liability; it is a transfer from the future to itself.

Pillar 2: Human Capital and R&D
No investment yields compound returns like education and innovation. Basic research funded by the public sector laid the

foundation for entire industries—the semiconductor, the microchip, the internet.

Every generation of American dominance has begun in a laboratory the private sector considered too risky to fund.

- **Public Research:** Agencies such as the NSF, NIH, and DARPA have historically produced the breakthroughs that later built trillion-dollar markets.
- **Human Capital:** Early-childhood education, vocational training, and affordable higher education increase labor productivity—the true driver of GDP growth. A worker who is twice as productive justifies twice the wage and pays twice the taxes without raising rates.

Human capital converts fiscal spending into an engine of compounding returns. It is how a debt-financed stimulus becomes a generational dividend.

Pillar 3: Energy Transition and Climate Resilience

Energy policy is economic policy. A nation dependent on volatile fossil-fuel markets cannot control its inflation or its trade balance.

Investment in renewable energy, grid modernization, and climate resilience lowers systemic risk and creates durable industries.

The cost of inaction is measurable: every climate-driven disaster wipes billions off GDP and forces emergency spending that produces no lasting asset. Preventing that damage—through resilient infrastructure, clean-tech innovation, and energy independence—is the most fiscally conservative act imaginable.

5. The Political Challenge: Distinguishing Spending from Investment

The obstacle to this strategy is not economics; it is perception. Voters, steeped in the household analogy, see no difference between borrowing for consumption and borrowing for construction. A fighter jet that depreciates in 10 years and a power grid that endures 50 years both appear as identical line items in the budget.

The distinction is existential:

- **Consumption Spending** funds the present and dies with it.
- **Investment Spending** funds the future and pays for itself through growth.

True fiscal discipline requires raising taxes to pay for the former while borrowing to finance the latter. A nation that blurs this line sabotages itself—under-taxing consumption and under-investing in productivity.

6. The Fed's Role: The Hidden Partner in Growth

The Federal Reserve cannot legislate fiscal policy, but it shapes the environment in which **g > r** can persist. Its task is not to make borrowing free, but to make the cost of capital predictable.

- **Stable Inflation:** By anchoring inflation expectations, the Fed allows investors to plan decades ahead. Stability breeds risk-taking; volatility breeds paralysis.
- **Market Liquidity:** Through open-market operations, the Fed ensures that Treasury securities remain the most liquid asset in existence. This liquidity keeps long-term borrowing costs low, enabling productive public investment without crowding out private enterprise.

In effect, the Fed manages the *r* side of the equation while Congress and the private sector manage the *g* side. The Dollar Paradox survives only when both fulfill their roles without encroachment—the Printer keeping rates credible, the Spender deploying debt for productive ends.

7. Growth as Discipline

The True Policy Path demands more rigor than austerity ever did. Cutting budgets is easy; building growth is hard. It requires prioritization, evidence, and patience—the willingness to fund what will not pay off for years. Yet this is the only form of fiscal virtue that matters.

The debt is the cost of membership in a system that has kept the world stable for nearly a century. Growth is what keeps that membership affordable.
The aim is not to eliminate the Mountain of Debt, but to keep climbing faster than it rises—to ensure that the price of credibility never exceeds the nation's capacity to earn it.

Strategic Public Investment: The Three Pillars of Growth

Every generation of American prosperity has begun with a public bet — a moment when Washington decided to borrow not to survive, but to build. The New Deal built the dams and roads that industrialized a continent. The Cold War built the research base that put a man on the moon. The 1990s built the digital architecture that now defines the global economy.

Each of those moments was financed through deficit spending. Each looked reckless at the time. And each, within a decade, was revealed as the foundation of a new age of growth.

The path forward is no different. To sustain the Dollar Paradox—to keep the Mountain of Debt as the world's most valuable asset—the United States must use its borrowing power not for consumption, but for construction. The difference between waste and wealth is not the size of the deficit, but what it purchases.

1. Pillar One: Infrastructure and Logistics — The Arteries of Growth

The most basic function of debt is to build assets that last longer than the loan.
Infrastructure fits that definition perfectly. Roads, bridges, airports, power grids, broadband networks—these are not expenses; they are multipliers. They reduce the friction of commerce, shorten the

distance between buyers and sellers, and expand the real productive capacity of the private sector.

The United States once understood this instinctively. In 1956, President Eisenhower signed the Federal-Aid Highway Act, authorizing $25 billion—then the largest infrastructure investment in world history. Critics called it reckless. Yet within twenty years, that network of asphalt and concrete had cut logistics costs by half, doubled suburban housing markets, and created entire industries—from fast food to long-haul trucking—that did not exist before. The debt that financed the highways was dwarfed by the GDP it unleashed.

Today's infrastructure deficit is the mirror image of that success. The American Society of Civil Engineers estimates that outdated transport and energy systems cost the economy nearly $1.5 trillion in lost productivity every decade. That is the hidden tax of decay—the price of underinvestment disguised as fiscal prudence.

Borrowing to rebuild that foundation is not "spending"; it is deferred maintenance on the nation's competitiveness. The Treasury that funds the next Interstate, or the next digital backbone, is not adding to the debt problem—it is buying down the future cost of stagnation.

2. Pillar Two: Human Capital and R&D — The Engine of Productivity

If infrastructure is the skeleton of growth, human capital and research are the brain.
No force in economic history has proven as powerful as the combination of public research and private application. Every major leap in productivity—from the steam engine to the smartphone—began with a state-sponsored risk no private investor would take.

The United States perfected this model. The Defense Advanced Research Projects Agency (DARPA) created the protocols that became the internet. NASA's space-race technologies became the

building blocks of the modern computer industry. The National Institutes of Health funded the genomic research that underpins today's pharmaceutical breakthroughs.
Each dollar of public R&D generated a cascade of private innovation worth hundreds more.

The debt that finances research is not consumption; it is capital formation in its purest form. It converts taxpayer dollars into collective intellectual property—an asset that compounds forever.

The Education Dividend

Human capital investment multiplies this effect. A child who graduates from a high-quality school earns more, pays more in taxes, and is less dependent on social programs. A nation that underfunds education is not saving money; it is borrowing from its future workforce.

Yet the U.S. continues to spend more on tax subsidies for capital gains than on early education. That imbalance reveals the short-term bias of the political cycle: policymakers reward accumulated wealth instead of cultivating the next generation of creators.

An effective Growth Agenda reverses that. It treats education, training, and research not as "social spending" but as national defense—the defense of long-term productivity. The only credible form of fiscal conservatism is one that maximizes the earning power of its citizens.

3. Pillar Three: Energy Transition and Climate Resilience — The Industrial Revolution of the 21st Century

The third pillar of the Growth Agenda is energy transformation—the most ambitious industrial project since the electrification of America. The energy transition is not a moral crusade; it is an economic necessity. The current system, built on fossil volatility, exposes the U.S. to inflationary shocks, supply disruptions, and climate costs that dwarf the investment required to prevent them.

Energy as Fiscal Policy

Energy drives every price in the economy—from food to freight to finance.

When oil prices spike, inflation rises, the Fed tightens, and borrowing costs climb. The result is slower growth and a weaker "g > r" balance.

A stable, domestic, renewable energy system is therefore not environmental policy—it is anti-inflation policy.

Investment in solar, wind, nuclear, and grid modernization directly stabilizes the dollar by insulating it from geopolitical oil shocks.

Each solar field built in Nevada or offshore wind project in New England adds a fraction of a percentage point to the nation's resilience index—a silent form of fiscal insurance.

The Global Competitiveness Dividend

The U.S. currently imports more green technology than it exports. That imbalance is both an industrial and geopolitical vulnerability.

By investing in advanced battery production, rare-earth mineral processing, and next-generation nuclear technology, the U.S. can reclaim leadership in the industries that will define the 21st century.

Every dollar of climate adaptation and clean-tech investment is a dollar spent on future trade supremacy. The global shift to low-carbon production is inevitable. The only question is who manufactures it. A country that lags in the transition will not only lose jobs; it will lose the pricing power that anchors its currency's dominance.

Climate Resilience as Economic Continuity

The economic costs of climate inaction are not abstract.

The Congressional Budget Office projects that weather-related disasters could reduce U.S. GDP by up to 3 percent annually by 2050 if left unchecked. That is the equivalent of a permanent recession, priced into the calendar.

Borrowing to prevent that loss is the cheapest debt imaginable. When the Treasury funds coastal defenses or wildfire prevention, it is not "spending money we don't have." It is protecting the assets we already own.

4. Investment vs. Consumption: The Political Fault Line

Every fiscal crisis in modern U.S. history has shared the same root problem: the failure to distinguish investment from consumption.

Tax cuts funded by debt, defense projects with no long-term return, and politically motivated subsidies all masquerade as economic stimulus but deliver none of the compounding effects of productive investment. They inflate **r** (the cost side) without improving **g** (the growth side).

The challenge is conceptual, not technical. The budget process treats all outlays as equal, even though their effects diverge dramatically over time. A bridge that carries freight for fifty years and a tax credit that expires next spring both increase the deficit, but only one pays itself back.

The Growth Agenda demands a new fiscal language—one that distinguishes *productive borrowing* from *political borrowing.*

- **Productive Borrowing:** Funds durable assets, raises productivity, lowers future costs.
- **Political Borrowing:** Buys votes, lowers taxes temporarily, raises future costs.

Without that distinction, fiscal debates will continue to swing between reckless spending and reckless restraint—between sugar highs and starvation diets.

5. Growth as Governance

Growth is not a side effect of good governance; it is its measure. The ability to expand the economic base faster than the debt burden is what makes a superpower sustainable. It keeps the debt credible, the currency strong, and the system legitimate.

The paradox is that the U.S., which owns the world's most flexible financial system, often governs it with the least strategic foresight. Every political cycle treats the debt as a scandal instead of as a tool. The Growth Agenda reclaims it as the sovereign instrument it was designed to be.

If austerity is fear disguised as virtue, growth is courage disguised as work.
The challenge of the next decade is not whether America can afford to invest—it is whether it can afford not to.

The Political Challenge, the Federal Reserve, and the Growth Mandate

For all its mathematical simplicity, the equation $g > r$ collides with the hardest obstacle in American governance: politics.
Economists may agree that growth is the solvent, but politicians are rewarded for drama, not arithmetic.
The most destructive illusion in Washington is that all spending is equal and all debt is bad. That illusion turns every budget cycle into a morality play—one that ends, inevitably, in paralysis.

1. The Political Challenge — Why Democracy Fears the Future

Democracy's short-term memory is its defining weakness.
Elected officials live inside two-year or four-year feedback loops; the economy lives inside decades. Borrowing for long-term productivity looks like waste when measured by the next election poll.

The result is fiscal schizophrenia.
In recessions, Congress panics about deficits and cuts investment just when borrowing is cheapest.
In booms, it showers tax breaks on voters and donors, overheating the cycle.
Both instincts are self-defeating: fear in downturns starves recovery, and indulgence in expansions fuels inflation.

The deeper problem is semantic.
When politicians promise to "live within our means," they mean the government's means, not the nation's.
But the government's deficit is the private sector's surplus. When Washington saves, Main Street bleeds.
Cutting federal investment in the name of prudence removes the oxygen that businesses and workers depend on.

A democracy that cannot explain that relationship ends up performing austerity as theater—a performance that reassures voters but quietly corrodes their prosperity.

2. The Need to Differentiate Spending — Consumption vs. Construction

Fiscal sanity begins with vocabulary.
The public must learn to distinguish **consumption spending** from **investment spending**—not morally, but functionally.

- **Consumption spending** pays for the present: salaries, subsidies, tax rebates, and defense outlays that expire the moment they're spent.
  These should be financed, wherever possible, with current revenue.

- **Investment spending** builds the future: infrastructure, education, research, and clean-energy systems that increase productive capacity.
  These deserve to be financed through long-term debt, because they deliver long-term returns.

The United States already understands this principle in private life.
No homeowner pays cash for a house; no company funds a factory out of last quarter's profits. They borrow because the asset endures.
Yet when the federal government does the same—borrows to build—the conversation turns moralistic.

The Growth Agenda demands a new fiscal rule: **tax consumption, borrow for construction.**
That single distinction would transform the debt debate from ideology to strategy.

A balanced budget should apply to the operating account—the year-to-year flow of consumption.
The capital account—the investment portfolio of the nation—should remain open and dynamic, expanding whenever a project's return exceeds its cost of capital.
This is how every successful corporation on Earth manages its balance sheet. A sovereign should do no less.

3. The Role of the Federal Reserve — The Invisible Partner in Growth

While Congress controls the fiscal wheel, the Federal Reserve determines the slope of the road.
Its control over the real interest rate (*r*) defines the environment in which growth must operate.
When the Fed raises rates, it tightens the future; when it cuts them, it extends the runway.

Monetary Credibility and the Iron Law

The Fed's first responsibility is to maintain credibility—the Iron Law of Separation that keeps monetary policy independent from political temptation.
Without that independence, inflation expectations unmoor and *r* rises permanently, choking investment.
A government that manipulates its central bank to keep rates artificially low gains short-term relief but loses the market's trust—the ultimate inflation tax.

The Fed as liquidity Architect

The Fed's second task is structural: to ensure that Treasury markets remain liquid enough for productive borrowing.
Its open-market operations guarantee that Treasuries can be traded

instantly, in any volume, at transparent prices.
That liquidity is the bloodstream of capitalism. It keeps financing costs low for households and businesses, translating public credibility into private confidence.

When the Fed manages liquidity well, it allows Congress to pursue the Growth Agenda without crowding out private credit.
A stable, predictable Treasury market gives entrepreneurs the courage to borrow, invest, and hire.
Thus, the Fed enforces discipline not through punishment but through design—it keeps the cost of debt honest, and the supply of credit continuous.

4. Growth as the True Fiscal Discipline

For decades, "fiscal discipline" has meant cutting programs, freezing wages, and preaching thrift.
But true discipline is not about smaller numbers; it's about smarter leverage.
A nation disciplined in its investments produces more than it spends.
A nation disciplined only in its cuts eventually spends everything repairing what it destroyed.

When growth leads interest, time becomes an ally.
Each year of compounding output makes yesterday's borrowing easier to bear.
The debt-to-GDP ratio falls quietly, invisibly, through expansion, not sacrifice.

The simplest test of a nation's fiscal health is not how much it owes, but how quickly it can make those obligations feel light.
That, not austerity, is sustainability.

5. Institutional Design for the Growth Age

If the United States is to institutionalize the Growth Agenda, it must rebuild its fiscal machinery around performance, not politics.

A National Investment Board

Create a non-partisan body, modeled on the Congressional Budget Office, charged with scoring federal projects not by their cost but by their expected rate of return.

This board would separate capital spending from consumption spending, allowing Congress to issue long-term bonds only for projects that demonstrably raise productivity.

It would transform borrowing from a political scandal into an engineering decision.

A Debt Target Based on Service Cost

Abandon the obsession with the absolute debt figure and replace it with a target ratio: **interest payments as a share of GDP.**

As long as that cost remains stable—say, under 3 percent—the debt is sustainable regardless of its nominal size.

This metric ties fiscal discipline to reality: the ability to pay, not the fear of owing.

Automatic Stabilizer Enhancement

Strengthen the fiscal shock absorbers that already work. Unemployment insurance, Medicaid, and food assistance automatically expand during recessions and contract during booms. Rather than trimming these programs, Congress should streamline their triggers, ensuring that aid flows instantly when indicators flash red.

Automaticity is apolitical; it replaces panic with protocol.

6. Why Austerity Is the True Irresponsibility

Every attempt to slash deficits in the name of virtue has ended in deeper debt.

Britain's post-2010 austerity left infrastructure rotting and productivity stagnant.

Southern Europe's budget purges prolonged the euro crisis by a decade.

In each case, the cost of stagnation exceeded the savings from restraint.

The United States flirted with the same mistake in 1937, when Roosevelt, fearing deficits, cut spending too soon. The economy collapsed again within months, erasing four years of recovery. History's verdict is clear: austerity is not discipline—it is deferred damage.

A nation that issues the world's reserve currency cannot balance its books the way a household balances a checkbook.
Its credibility is earned not by scarcity but by performance—by the relentless demonstration that it can transform borrowed dollars into lasting wealth.
That credibility is the most valuable asset the U.S. owns, and the only one that cannot be borrowed.

7. The Growth Mandate — Sustaining the Dollar Paradox
The Dollar Paradox endures only when America's debt continues to be viewed as the safest, most productive investment on Earth.
That perception rests on one question: does the United States still know how to grow?

The debt is the admission ticket; growth is the show.
If growth falters, the ticket loses its value.
If growth accelerates, investors will line up to pay any price of admission.

This is the ultimate equilibrium: the U.S. borrows not to consume, but to maintain the stage on which the world performs its commerce.
Its debt is the scaffolding of global trust.
The Necessary Pain—the interest bill that politicians bemoan—is the proof of life, the signal that the guardrail still holds.
A country that pays its creditors while building its future is not declining; it is compounding.

8. From Fear to Foresight
The debate over the national debt has always been framed in fear: fear of default, fear of inflation, fear of tomorrow.

But the real danger is the absence of foresight.
A society that fears its own currency cannot lead the world that depends on it.

The path of growth is harder because it demands faith—faith that investment will yield progress, and that discipline can coexist with ambition.
But that faith is precisely what built the American century.
The post-war architects of the global order borrowed at 2 percent to grow at 5 percent, and the world followed.

To preserve that legacy, the United States must remember what it once knew: pain is not the enemy; stagnation is.
The Mountain of Debt is not a curse to be repaid—it is the monument of a system that still works.
And the true measure of its success is not how small the mountain becomes, but how high the nation climbs upon it.

Chapter 16

The Future of the Paradox: Sustaining Supremacy in a Multi-Polar World

The Dollar Paradox was never designed to be eternal.
It was designed to be *earned.*
Every generation of American policymakers inherits a system whose power depends not on conquest, but on credibility — a currency empire sustained not by armies or borders, but by the world's collective faith in the discipline of its issuer.

For nearly eighty years, that faith held without serious challenge. The dollar became the oxygen of global commerce, the reference point for every balance sheet and the settlement mechanism for every major trade. It reigned not because it was flawless, but because every alternative was worse.

Now, that unipolar order has expired. The post–Cold War era, which granted America a near-monopoly on financial trust, is giving way to something harder, more dynamic, and more dangerous: *Competitive Coexistence.*

This is the new equilibrium of the 21st century — a world where multiple powers can issue currencies, build payment networks, and shape financial norms, but where only one system retains the institutional gravity that everything else orbits. The United States no longer dominates by default; it must lead by design.

1. The End of Easy Power

For three decades after the Soviet Union's collapse, the dollar's supremacy seemed self-reinforcing. Every global shock — from the Asian Financial Crisis to the Global Financial Crisis to COVID-19 — sent investors running not from the dollar, but *to* it. Each emergency made the U.S. Treasury market deeper, the dollar's network broader, and the myth of its inevitability stronger.

But myths have half-lives.
Part III of this book chronicled the rise of new challenges: China's digital currency experiments, the growing appetite for trade settlement in non-dollar terms, and the slow erosion of trust caused

by U.S. political dysfunction. These forces mark the end of *unipolar complacency*.

The next era will not be defined by collapse, but by contest. America's currency will share the stage with rivals. What determines its survival is not exclusivity, but indispensability.

The goal of U.S. policy should no longer be to crush competition, but to remain the *one currency no system can live without.* That requires two things: a renewal of institutional discipline at home and a recognition that global dominance is now an act of maintenance, not momentum.

2. The Institutional Stickiness of Collateral

The United States retains one unmatched advantage: *the stickiness of its collateral.*

No matter how loud the rhetoric of de-dollarization becomes, global markets still hinge on a single fact — there is no other asset on Earth that can replicate the liquidity, safety, and legal reliability of a U.S. Treasury bond.

Depth and Liquidity as a Global Utility

Every trading day, trillions of dollars in U.S. debt change hands. This is not mere volume — it is infrastructure. The Treasury market is the global clearinghouse of trust. It allows a Japanese insurer, a German pension fund, or a Brazilian central bank to sell massive positions and convert them to cash within seconds without shaking the price. That capacity for frictionless exchange is the purest form of confidence capitalism has ever invented.

Other markets can grow in size, but not in *depth*.

The U.S. system's scale is self-reinforcing: every buyer adds liquidity, every trade tightens the spread, every participant makes it safer for the next.

This is why even America's fiercest critics continue to hold its bonds — not out of love for its politics, but out of dependence on its predictability.

A Treasury security is more than a loan to the U.S. government; it is a license to function in the modern economy.

Institutional Trust as the Ultimate Moat

What protects this system is not military power or GDP alone — it is *institutional credibility*. The Golden Guardrail described in Chapter 1 and the Iron Law of Separation from Chapter 3 are not abstract theories; they are the living proof that the United States can be trusted to restrain itself.

Foreign investors buy Treasuries because they believe that:

1. Contracts will be honored.
2. The Federal Reserve will remain politically independent.
3. Property rights will survive electoral cycles.

These are not financial assumptions — they are constitutional virtues.
The world does not invest in America's wealth; it invests in America's *process.*
That process, fragile as it appears, is the moat no autocracy can cross.

3. The Two Necessary Vows

If the United States intends to sustain the Dollar Paradox in this new competitive age, it must renew two vows — one of restraint and one of ambition. Together they form the covenant that underpins global power.

The First Vow: Non-Politicization

The first vow is the promise that the U.S. will not weaponize its own financial plumbing.
This is the essence of the Golden Guardrail — the firewall between fiscal politics and monetary execution. The Federal Reserve must remain an independent institution, and the Treasury market must remain sacrosanct.

Nothing damages American credibility faster than the Debt Ceiling spectacle — a uniquely self-inflicted ritual in which Congress threatens to default on its own obligations to score domestic points. Each episode, watched by foreign central banks and finance ministries in real time, is a televised erosion of faith.

No external adversary could design a better propaganda campaign against the dollar than America's own politicians dangling its creditworthiness for applause lines.

To sustain the paradox, the United States must prove that it can govern its money as carefully as it governs its military. Fiscal debate belongs before the borrowing, not during it. Once the bond is sold, payment must be as automatic as sunrise.

A sovereign that threatens not to pay its own bills is not exercising freedom; it is experimenting with suicide.

The Second Vow: Growth

The second vow is the pledge to grow — to treat the $g > r$ principle not as a macroeconomic curiosity but as a national creed.
Debt must serve productivity, not procrastination. Borrowing for consumption is self-defeat; borrowing for innovation is sovereignty.

The U.S. must direct its deficits toward the engines of expansion: education, research, infrastructure, and energy transformation. Every dollar that lifts long-term GDP growth lightens the weight of past borrowing. Every dollar that funds short-term political theater deepens it.

The Growth Vow is therefore both economic and moral.
It requires humility — the recognition that America's power comes not from what it consumes, but from what it builds.
The paradox survives only when the nation keeps enlarging the denominator of its debt equation: a bigger, smarter, more productive economy that makes the Mountain of Debt look smaller every year.

4. The New Competitive Landscape

Even if the U.S. keeps both vows, it must still navigate a world that is rapidly innovating around it.
The threats ahead are structural, not ideological — they come not from revolutions, but from software.

The Digital Currency Challenge

Central Bank Digital Currencies are the new frontier of monetary competition. China's digital yuan is not designed to replace the dollar in size, but to bypass it in function — to allow trade and settlement between nations without ever touching a U.S. bank.

That innovation exposes the dollar's single greatest weakness: friction.
A global transaction in dollars still moves through a century-old pipeline — correspondent banks, SWIFT codes, multi-day settlements. In a world where data moves instantly, waiting forty-eight hours for a payment to clear feels prehistoric.

The solution is not panic-building a "digital dollar" but *modernizing the rails* of the existing system.
Instant settlement technologies, real-time gross payment systems, and next-generation clearing mechanisms can make the dollar as fast as its rivals while keeping the safety of its legal ecosystem.

The dollar does not need to reinvent itself as code; it needs to become *frictionless credibility.*
If global finance must choose between speed and trust, it will still choose trust — but only as long as trust doesn't lag behind technology.

5. The Weaponization Dilemma

The dollar's dominance has also become its temptation. Every time Washington uses the global financial system as an instrument of punishment, it proves the power of the empire — and exposes the fragility of its legitimacy.

Sanctions as a Double-Edged Sword

Financial sanctions can paralyze an adversary's economy faster than any army, but their overuse corrodes the neutrality that makes the dollar indispensable.
Each new sanction teaches the world the same lesson: dependency is risk.
Allies may applaud the first strike; they quietly prepare after the fifth.

Russia's reserve freeze in 2022 was the most dramatic case — justified morally, catastrophic structurally. It told every other nation that dollar assets are safe only for friends.
From that day forward, diversification was not ideology; it was insurance.

The Recalibration of Power

The answer is not abstinence but restraint.
Sanctions should be surgical, multilateral, and rare — the equivalent of a constitutional emergency, not a routine executive order.
The credibility of the dollar depends on its perceived neutrality as a *public good.*
The more it is weaponized, the more it becomes ordinary politics — and ordinary politics cannot sustain extraordinary privilege.

The paradox here is cruel but clear: the U.S. must sometimes sacrifice its immediate leverage to preserve its long-term hegemony. Power restrained is power renewed.

6. The Ultimate Test: Political Will

The Mountain of Debt is more than an accounting figure; it is the monument of America's institutional endurance. Every Treasury bond in existence is a receipt of trust — proof that the world continues to believe in the country's ability to govern itself through discipline, not decree.

The dollar's supremacy will not end when another country invents a better currency. It will end when the United States forgets why its own still works.

The greatest danger to the system is not China, not digital disruption, not de-dollarization. It is Congress. It is the temptation to treat the world's most valuable asset — institutional trust — as a disposable campaign issue.

The paradox demands pain. The interest bill, the constant scrutiny, the limits imposed by the global market — these are not signs of decline; they are the maintenance costs of leadership. The dollar is strong precisely because it is never free.

The empire of trust can endure indefinitely — but only if the republic behind it remembers that the rent for global power is never negotiable.

The Dollar Paradox ends where it began — with a contradiction too costly to resolve and too essential to abandon.
The United States remains the only nation on Earth that can borrow in its own currency without limit, yet still pays a visible price for doing so. That visible price — the interest, the scrutiny, the constant exposure to market judgment — is not a flaw in the system. It *is* the system.

The debt is not a sign of weakness but of accountability. The United States owes because the world still trusts it enough to lend. That trust, though invisible, is the most valuable export America has ever produced.

The Empire of Trust

The true American empire was never territorial; it was contractual. It was built not through conquest but through confidence — the shared assumption that a U.S. Treasury bond is worth its face value everywhere, always, under any political weather.

That assumption made the dollar not just a currency but a constitution — an unwritten agreement among nations that global commerce would flow through a single, dependable channel. The strength of that channel has defined the modern age of peace and prosperity.

Every era of empire is defined by its organizing principle. Rome had law, Britain had trade, and America has *trust.*
That trust is not sentimental; it is mechanical. It lives in the plumbing of the global financial system — the clearinghouses, repo markets, and custody ledgers that make every other transaction possible. The entire world economy balances on the belief that the dollar will remain redeemable, liquid, and politically neutral.

The empire of trust, however, has one fatal vulnerability: it cannot defend itself by force. Its shield is credibility, and credibility cannot be imposed — it must be *maintained.*
Every debt auction, every interest payment, every transparent act of governance is a small renewal of that empire's charter.

The High Cost of Stability

Global stability is not cheap.
The Mountain of Debt — now roughly $38 trillion and climbing — is the operating budget of the world's financial peace. Each Treasury bond is both a promise and a policy: a promise that the U.S. will always honor its obligations, and a policy that guarantees every nation on Earth can find a safe place to store its savings.

Critics see that mountain as an impending collapse; historians will see it as the price of order.
The debt is the tax America pays to prevent chaos. Every coupon payment sent to a pension fund in Europe, a central bank in Asia, or an insurance company in South America is a dividend on global stability.

The paradox is that the same interest payment that American taxpayers resent is the very mechanism by which the rest of the world continues to believe in the United States.
The U.S. does not buy loyalty; it leases trust — and the rent is due every quarter.

The Cycle of Self-Sabotage

The danger, as always, lies within.
The greatest threat to the Dollar Paradox is not inflation or competition but *political forgetfulness*. The more the U.S. benefits from the system, the more it takes that system for granted.

Every debt-ceiling crisis, every government shutdown, every partisan performance that treats default as a rhetorical weapon chips away at the foundation that makes the empire possible.
When lawmakers turn the Treasury market into a stage prop, they are not debating policy — they are rehearsing decline.

The world does not fear a U.S. that borrows; it fears a U.S. that stops understanding what its borrowing means.
The paradox survives only when humility outlasts hubris — when the issuer of the world's currency remembers that it is also its caretaker.

The Lessons of Empire

Every great power collapses for the same reason: it forgets the source of its strength.
Empires fall when they mistake privilege for permanence — when they believe the rules that govern others no longer apply to them.

The British pound ruled the 19th century under the same illusion that now tempts the dollar. It financed railroads, trade, and empire — until the cost of two world wars and the loss of institutional discipline shattered its credibility. The pound did not die because its economy collapsed; it died because its government tried to maintain power through printing instead of through pain.

The dollar's supremacy endures precisely because it has so far resisted that temptation.
The U.S. accepts the pain — the borrowing ritual, the public auctions, the mandatory exposure to market discipline. Every bond sale is a voluntary trial by fire, a moment when the global market passes judgment on the republic.

The price of that ritual is high. The alternative is extinction.

The Path Forward — Reforging the Golden Guardrail

The next century will test not the dollar's dominance but the nation's ability to maintain the discipline that made it dominant.
Sustaining that discipline requires three reforms — not revolutionary, but restorative — that return the system to its founding principles.

1. Make Credibility Automatic

The debt ceiling must end.
The idea that the United States can authorize spending and then later threaten not to pay for it is not fiscal conservatism — it is constitutional vandalism.
The U.S. must codify payment as an automatic function of its sovereignty, as self-evident as the collection of taxes.
The Borrowing Ritual must remain public, painful, and priced by the market — but it must never again be interrupted by politics.

2. Separate Consumption from Construction

Congress must distinguish clearly between short-term spending and long-term investment.
The first should be paid through taxes; the second through debt.
A nation that borrows for bridges, schools, and research is investing; a nation that borrows for subsidies and consumption is decaying.
This distinction should be written into budget law — a fiscal firewall that forces the government to defend every dollar of new debt as either productive or parasitic.

3. Institutionalize the Growth Mandate

The principle of $g > r$ must be elevated from theory to policy.
The Office of Management and Budget, the Congressional Budget Office, and the Federal Reserve should coordinate forecasts and targets explicitly linking fiscal planning to expected GDP growth.
The goal should be clear: every deficit must be justified by its contribution to future productivity. Borrowing that grows the

denominator of the debt equation is sustainable; borrowing that does not is self-defeating.

These are not ideological reforms. They are engineering adjustments — restoring the machine of credibility that the world depends on.

The Dollar's Last Advantage — The Rule of Law

Amid all the complexity of financial systems and macroeconomic equations, one truth still separates the dollar from its rivals: **law**.
The United States, for all its dysfunction, remains the only global power where the rule of law consistently outranks the rule of men. Contracts are enforced. Courts are independent. The central bank is insulated from political command.
No digital platform, no basket of currencies, no authoritarian alternative can reproduce that framework of predictable justice.

The final defense of the dollar is not the yield curve or the repo market; it is the U.S. Constitution itself — the legal architecture that guarantees that money and power remain separated.
The rest of the world does not buy Treasuries because it loves America; it buys them because it trusts the one thing America still does better than anyone else: obey its own laws.

The Endurance Test

The Dollar Paradox will never resolve; it will only renew.
Each generation of Americans must decide anew whether it is willing to pay the price of stability — not just in taxes, but in discipline.

The world has no shortage of currencies; what it lacks is restraint. The dollar's value lies not in its abundance, but in the integrity of the system that backs it.
If America forgets that, the empire of trust will crumble not with a bang, but with a shrug — a slow, silent migration of confidence elsewhere.

Yet history still leans toward continuity.
The same system that survived Vietnam, stagflation, Watergate, and the Great Recession continues to produce the deepest markets, the freest capital, and the most consistent rule set. The paradox endures because, for all its chaos, the United States continues to choose order.

The Final Reckoning: The Price of Privilege

At the heart of this book lies a single proposition: the United States is rich because it is trusted, and it is trusted because it endures pain in public.
Every interest payment, every debt auction, every public debate over deficits is a confession of accountability — proof that the U.S. still submits to the discipline of the market and the limits of democracy.

That pain is not something to be solved; it is something to be preserved.
It is the scar tissue of a system that works.

The empire of trust does not end when others rise; it ends when America stops deserving it.
The dollar will remain king not because it is omnipotent, but because it remains *honest* — the rare currency backed not by gold, but by governance.

As long as the world believes that, the paradox will hold.
And the rent of global power — that eternal interest bill — will continue to be the best investment humanity ever made.

Chapter 17

The Paradox's Policy Conflict: Trade Deficits vs. Tariffs

The Financial Logic of the Deficit

The Dollar Paradox rests on an awkward truth that no political slogan can erase:
America's global power depends on its willingness to live in deficit. The world needs dollars to trade, invest, and save; those dollars must come from somewhere. They enter circulation only when the United States buys more from the world than the world buys from it. The trade deficit is not a symptom of failure; it is the bloodstream of the system.

For half a century, every container ship docking at Los Angeles, every iPhone assembled in Shenzhen, every German sedan imported through Newark has carried more than goods. Each transaction exports trust—the paper promise that keeps global finance alive.

The paradox is that the same imbalance that populists call weakness is the mechanism that makes the U.S. strong. The deficit is the price of the privilege.

1. The Financial Imperative for Low *r*

Every global system requires a lubricant. The lubricant of the modern economy is the U.S. Treasury bond—the one asset everyone believes will still be money tomorrow.
The supply of that asset depends directly on the flow of dollars outward.

The Exorbitant Privilege Loop

1. **Dollar Supply.** U.S. consumers import far more than they export, flooding the world with dollars.
2. **Debt Demand.** Foreign exporters and their central banks reinvest those earnings in Treasuries—the safest, deepest market available.
3. **Low Cost of Debt.** Their steady demand keeps yields low, subsidizing both U.S. taxpayers and borrowers worldwide.

This cycle—consumption, reinvestment, cheap credit—is the circulatory system of the global economy.
Break it, and the cost of money rises for everyone.

The irony is profound: the trade deficit, condemned as evidence of decline, is what keeps interest rates—the vital *r* in our equation—affordably low.
When foreigners hold trillions in Treasuries, they are not exploiting America; they are underwriting it.

2. The Tariff Shock — Starving the Treasury Market

Tariffs promise to fix what they cannot fix. They are sold as tools to "restore balance," yet balance is precisely what the Dollar Paradox cannot tolerate.
By taxing imports, tariffs restrict the very inflow of goods that generates the outflow of dollars—and therefore the demand for U.S. debt.

A. The Chain Reaction

When imports fall, exporters abroad earn fewer dollars. Fewer dollars mean fewer Treasury purchases.
The world's safest bond suddenly has fewer natural buyers. The Treasury must court a different class of investor: domestic funds that demand higher yields.
Bond prices fall; *r* rises. What began as an industrial policy morphs into a fiscal problem.

B. The Yield Curve Effect

Foreign central banks are price-insensitive; they buy for liquidity, not profit. When they retreat, markets lose the one participant that never blinks.
To replace them, Washington must pay up. Each percentage-point increase in average borrowing cost adds hundreds of billions to the annual interest bill.

Tariffs, then, are not free revenue—they are a disguised rate hike.

3. The Tariff Revenue Mirage

Every administration touts the billions collected at the customs gate as proof that tariffs "pay for themselves."
They don't.

A. The Scale Mismatch

Tariff income is measured in billions; interest expense in trillions.
A single year of higher yields can erase a decade of tariff collections.
What the Treasury gains at the port, it loses at the auction.

B. The Hidden Tax

Tariffs are inflationary by design.
Importers pass costs to retailers, retailers pass them to consumers, and consumers absorb them in higher prices.
The policy that promises to help the worker quietly taxes his paycheck. Inflation erodes real wages, forcing the Federal Reserve to tighten policy—raising *r* still further.
Protectionism, in practice, protects nothing but the upward slope of the yield curve.

4. The Strategic Rationale — Paying for Resilience

And yet, tariffs persist.
If they are financially costly, their survival must serve a purpose beyond accounting. That purpose is security.

The 21st-century argument for protectionism is not mercantilism but resilience—the belief that the nation cannot depend indefinitely on rival powers for the materials of its prosperity.

A. Reshoring as Insurance

The pandemic shattered faith in just-in-time globalization. A microchip shortage can now ground an air force; a supply interruption can paralyze a hospital.
Tariffs and industrial subsidies function as an insurance premium—a deliberate inefficiency paid to guarantee supply in crisis.

By tilting the economics of production, Washington hopes to pull critical manufacturing—semiconductors, rare-earths, pharmaceuticals—back within friendly borders. The immediate cost is higher prices; the long-term reward is strategic autonomy.

B. Technological Dominance

Tariffs also serve as a defense of innovation. Shielding nascent industries buys time for learning curves to steepen.
The objective is not permanent protection, but momentum—to push new sectors past infancy until they can compete on merit.
If successful, the payoff is structural: higher productivity, better wages, and a rising growth rate (*g*).

The question is whether those gains can arrive before the financial cost compounds.

5. The Taxpayer Feedback Loop — Building *g*

When reshoring works, it creates a self-reinforcing loop between productivity, income, and public finance.

1. **Higher Wages.** Advanced manufacturing and engineering jobs replace low-wage service work, lifting median income.
2. **Broader Tax Base.** Stronger payrolls and property values expand revenue at every level of government.
3. **Reduced Transfer Spending.** Fewer citizens rely on welfare and emergency support, freeing fiscal space.
4. **Reinvestment Multiplier.** Government can redirect savings into infrastructure and R&D, further raising potential *g*.

If the multiplier effect holds, the growth rate can accelerate enough to outpace the rise in *r*.
That is the only circumstance under which tariffs make sense within the paradox: when the short-term pain of higher borrowing costs buys a permanent lift in national productivity.

6. The Leakage Risk

But policy rarely runs as planned.
Tariffs can fail quietly, leaking their intended benefits into unintended pockets.

- **Corporate Pass-Through.** Large firms may simply raise prices, keeping margins intact while consumers foot the bill.
- **Complacency Trap.** Industries shielded from competition may innovate less, producing costlier goods with no quality gain.
- **Inflation Spillover.** Rising input costs cascade through supply chains, forcing the Fed to tighten further, erasing the growth dividend.

A policy meant to raise *g* can therefore end up raising only *r*.
The challenge is to design protection that protects competition, not privilege—to turn defense spending into an investment rather than a subsidy.

7. Quantifying the Trade-Off — The *g vs. r* Equation

The tariff debate is ultimately a wager between present cost and future capacity.
Policymakers are saying, in effect:

"We are willing to accept a higher *r* today—more expensive debt, slower dollar recycling, and a diminished global privilege—in exchange for a structurally higher *g* tomorrow."

That trade-off is the modern face of the Dollar Paradox.
For most of the post-war era, America maximized efficiency: open trade, cheap imports, global liquidity. Now it seeks durability: secure supply, national self-reliance, resilient growth.

Both cannot coexist perfectly. The system that keeps interest rates low also exports jobs; the system that brings jobs home raises interest rates.

The equilibrium will depend on whether the productivity of the new domestic economy can grow fast enough to offset the financial friction of reduced foreign demand.

If $g > r$, the strategy succeeds. If $r > g$, the empire pays twice—once in higher yields and again in slower growth.

8. The Strategic Limit of the Privilege

This is the final lesson of the Dollar Paradox: every privilege has a price, and every advantage contains its undoing.

The trade deficit is both the symbol and the substance of America's financial power. To shrink it is to cut off oxygen to the very market that keeps U.S. borrowing affordable.

Tariffs are the political expression of discomfort with that dependence—a declaration that perpetual consumption cannot be the foundation of national strength.

But the numbers do not yield to pride. The math of trust is immutable: the world cannot hold dollars unless America spends them.

In the end, the question is not whether the U.S. can eliminate its deficit, but whether it can transform it—from a passive channel of consumption into an active engine of growth.

If the goods America imports are matched by the ideas, technologies, and capital it exports, the paradox resolves into harmony: the world still gets its dollars, and the U.S. gets richer producing the things those dollars buy.

That is the frontier beyond privilege—the moment when the empire of trust becomes an economy of purpose.

The choice is not between global dominance and national resilience. It is between managing the contradiction or letting it manage us.

The New Arithmetic of Empire

The United States has reached the point in its financial empire where numbers are moral.

Every choice — every tariff, every stimulus, every Treasury auction — is no longer just a matter of economics; it is a declaration about what kind of power the nation intends to be.

For eighty years, America's might has rested on the quiet arithmetic of imbalance. The world exported goods, the U.S. exported dollars, and everyone prospered. Now, that equilibrium is eroding from both sides. Abroad, nations want independence from the dollar. At home, voters demand protection from it. The same system that bound the world together has begun to divide it politically.

1. When the World Stops Lending

The first shock of de-globalization is always invisible: it begins not with empty store shelves but with thinner bond books.

As supply chains localize and trade flows narrow, the recycling of dollars through the Treasury market slows. Central banks that once absorbed U.S. debt as reserves now keep more of their earnings in local currencies or gold. The invisible buyer of last resort — the foreign saver — starts to fade.

When that happens, the U.S. faces the most un-American of predicaments: it must learn to finance itself.

For decades, the country's savings deficit was a privilege disguised as laziness. Foreign capital filled the gap between what Americans consumed and what they produced. That inflow kept interest rates low even as deficits exploded. But in a world of shrinking trade surpluses, those easy inflows dry up. Domestic savings must rise to compensate, which means households, corporations, or the government itself must consume less.

The empire of trust, in other words, must finally learn thrift.

2. The Politics of Paying Our Own Rent

A higher *r* does more than increase the cost of borrowing; it rewires politics.

Cheap money breeds complacency; expensive money breeds accountability. When every new policy carries a visible price tag in rising yields, ideology begins to meet arithmetic.

A trillion-dollar infrastructure plan looks different when the 10-year Treasury yields five percent instead of two. The national appetite for slogans shrinks when every slogan has a yield curve attached.

This is the hidden virtue of the Golden Guardrail. The market, not the ballot box, becomes the final editor of political fantasy. In that sense, tariffs and rising *r* perform the same civic function as interest itself: they remind democracy that choices have costs.

Yet this virtue turns punitive when politics refuses to adapt. If Washington continues to treat borrowing as infinite while trade flows tighten, the arithmetic will correct itself brutally — through inflation, austerity, or currency depreciation. The guardrail always enforces discipline; it is only a question of timing and pain.

3. Tariffs as a Strategic Tax

When understood correctly, tariffs are not economic medicine; they are geopolitical taxation.

Each percentage point on an import is a levy on efficiency — a deliberate slowing of the dollar's circulatory system to buy national insurance. The question is whether that insurance pays out.

If reshoring succeeds, the U.S. trades financial privilege for productive resilience: a smaller but stronger loop of domestic prosperity. If it fails, the country ends up poorer and less trusted — a debtor without a market, a consumer without supply.

The choice to tax trade is therefore the most consequential fiscal decision of the century. It decides whether the dollar remains a global public good or retreats into a national instrument.

4. The Geography of the Dollar

The paradox also has a map.

The dollar's strength depends not just on economic policy but on geography itself — the global lattice of allies, bases, and trade routes that guarantee open sea lanes and contract enforcement. Every tariff that isolates the U.S. commercially must be offset by a diplomatic expansion that keeps its currency embedded abroad.

History is instructive: the pound sterling's fall began not with default but with retreat — Britain's shrinking trade empire severed the very channels that recycled its currency. The dollar's empire of trust spans supply chains instead of colonies, but the logic is the same. When the goods stop moving, the money follows.

A durable American strategy must therefore pair selective protectionism with aggressive trade diplomacy. The goal is not autarky but *curated interdependence*: a network of allied markets that continue to trade in dollars even as global trade fragments.

Tariffs that secure independence must be matched by treaties that secure demand. Without that symmetry, the financial architecture buckles.

5. The Rise of the "Resilience Premium"

A new concept is emerging in global finance: the *resilience premium.* Investors are beginning to assign value not just to yield or liquidity, but to political reliability — to the ability of a country to withstand supply shocks without social breakdown.

In this calculus, a reshored America — with redundant energy grids, secure chip plants, and a healthier middle class — could ultimately command *lower* yields despite higher nominal debt. Credibility would migrate from financial orthodoxy to physical capacity. The safe asset would be safe because its issuer can produce, not merely promise.

This is the ultimate ambition of the tariff strategy: to convert short-term fiscal pain into long-term geopolitical credit. The U.S.

would no longer be trusted merely because it prints the world's money, but because it still makes the world's essentials.

If that transformation succeeds, the paradox evolves rather than ends. The trade deficit would narrow, but the trust premium — the willingness of investors to lend cheaply to a resilient America — could keep r low enough to sustain $g > r$.

6. The Danger of Weaponized Nostalgia

Every populist movement that promises to "bring manufacturing back" risks falling into the trap of weaponized nostalgia — the belief that the past can be rebuilt rather than reinvented.
The industrial base of the 1950s cannot be resurrected; its carbon footprint alone would bankrupt the planet. What must return is not the factory, but the capacity to innovate.

A nation's productivity is no longer measured in tons of steel but in terabytes of code, patents filed, and intellectual property exported. The challenge is not to rebuild the old assembly line but to own the algorithm that designs it.

If tariffs devolve into cultural symbolism — protection for industries that no longer matter — they will fail twice: economically and morally. The goal of protectionism should be future dominance, not past restoration.

7. The Credibility of Pain

All systems survive on stories. The story of the dollar has always been one of disciplined pain — the willingness to expose the nation's finances to the judgment of the market.

Tariffs, deficits, and debt all test that discipline. When the United States accepts higher short-term costs for long-term stability, it demonstrates seriousness. When it hides costs through accounting tricks or denial, it signals decay.

The paradox, once again, demands visibility: the pain must be public. That visibility is what convinces the world that the U.S. still plays by its own rules — that it will suffer interest payments, deficits, and political backlash rather than quietly default through inflation or devaluation.

The rent of power is not meant to be comfortable. It is meant to remind the tenant who owns the house.

8. Toward a Balanced Imbalance

In the end, the U.S. will not eliminate the trade deficit — and it shouldn't.

The goal is to balance the imbalance: to ensure that every dollar exported through consumption returns through investment in future capacity. If America buys the world's goods, it must sell the world its future — its innovation, its governance, its credibility.

A deficit that funds dependence is weakness; a deficit that funds invention is empire.

The next iteration of the Dollar Paradox may look less like Wall Street's spreadsheet and more like a map of industrial ecosystems — energy corridors, semiconductor hubs, digital trade routes. The bond traders of tomorrow will price risk not only in basis points but in bandwidth and rare-earth output.

The nation that controls those inputs will control the cost of capital. And as long as the dollar remains the settlement language of those markets, the paradox survives.

9. The Final Equation

The story now comes full circle. The U.S. can sustain its supremacy only by choosing, again and again, between comfort and credibility.

- If it insists on balanced trade, the world loses its dollars, rates rise, and the empire of trust contracts.
- If it tolerates endless deficits without reinvestment, growth stagnates and the trust premium erodes.

- The path forward is dynamic equilibrium — a system that keeps dollars circulating globally while using the proceeds to build domestic capacity fast enough to offset the cost.

The paradox thus resolves into a new national equation:

Resilience = (g – r) × Trust

Growth must exceed the cost of capital, and credibility must amplify both. Lose trust, and even high growth collapses under higher rates. Keep it, and even vast debt becomes strength.

10. The Choice Before the Republic

The world's reserve currency is not a trophy; it is a responsibility. Every Treasury bill is a social contract between America and the planet — a promise that the issuer of the dollar remains the custodian of order.

The coming decades will test that promise as no era since Bretton Woods. Technology, fragmentation, and domestic polarization will all tempt the U.S. to retreat from openness. The nation must resist that temptation or risk surrendering the quiet empire it built without conquest.

The next chapter of American power will be written not in wars or summits but in the mundane rituals of fiscal discipline: auctions, budgets, interest payments made on time.

The world does not need America to be perfect; it needs America to keep its receipts.

That is the essence of the Dollar Paradox — and the price of the privilege that endures.

EPILOGUE

The Rent Paid for Global Power

We began this journey with a question that defies common sense: **Why does the wealthiest nation on Earth borrow money it can print?**

The answer is the **Dollar Paradox**. The United States borrows not because it is poor, but because it is powerful. The entire ritual—the auctions, the debt ceiling debates, the yield curve, the interest payments—is not a weakness to be corrected but the price of *credibility*. That credibility is what makes the dollar the world's reserve currency and the United States the steward of the global financial system.

The Golden Guardrail and the Iron Law

The national debt is not a time bomb; it is the **Golden Guardrail**. It was forged in the historical fires that destroyed every nation that printed without restraint—from Weimar Germany to modern Zimbabwe.

The guardrail is held in place by the **Iron Law of Separation** (Chapter 3): the unbreakable barrier between the **Spender** (the Treasury) and the **Printer** (the Federal Reserve). The Treasury must borrow in the open market; it cannot demand financing from the central bank. That law forces the United States to endure the pain of accountability—to earn every dollar of credit from the global investor community.

Because of that separation, the *Mountain of Debt* is not a liability but an asset:

- It is the safest and most liquid collateral in existence.

- It anchors global inflation expectations.
- It fuels every transaction in the world's financial engine.

The paradox holds because the United States never lets convenience override credibility.

The Rent of Power

The interest payment on this debt—the trillions of dollars in annual coupons paid to bondholders—is the **rent America pays for global power**. It is the membership fee for the most exclusive franchise on Earth: issuing the currency that the world trusts most.

What does the United States receive in return for this rent?

1. **The Exorbitant Privilege — Structurally Favorable Financing.** Dollar-centered trade, deep U.S. capital markets, and the recycling of global surpluses—including petrodollar surpluses—support persistent demand for dollar assets. That broad demand can reduce U.S. borrowing costs relative to what they would otherwise be, helping America finance its budget, innovation, and military on unusually favorable terms.
2. **The Stealth Tax — Seigniorage.**
   Every dollar circulating abroad is an interest-free loan to the U.S. government. The Federal Reserve effectively taxes the world without legislation, collecting rent through trust alone. It is the quiet miracle of modern empire: global liquidity that pays dividends to its issuer.
3. **Geopolitical Leverage.**
   Control over the dollar-based clearing system grants the United States extraordinary diplomatic power. Sanctions, asset freezes, and access to the SWIFT network are all expressions of financial sovereignty—tools that can pressure nations without firing a shot.

The cost is visible on the Treasury's balance sheet; the benefits are invisible everywhere else. The rent is steep, but the return—global order—is priceless.

The Policy Choice Ahead

The future of the Dollar Paradox depends entirely on political will. The United States stands at a fork between two paths.

1. The Policy Trap — The Path of Opportunism

This is the path of short-term politics and long-term decay.
It is defined by the twin temptations of **austerity** and **monetization**: one seeks to destroy the guardrail by starving it, the other by dissolving it.

- **Internal Sabotage.** Every manufactured debt-ceiling crisis, every attempt to pressure the Fed into political service, chips away at the Iron Law. When Washington toys with default for partisan gain, it performs institutional vandalism before a global audience.
- **External Acceleration.** If credibility erodes, rivals will not wait. Central Bank Digital Currencies (Chapter 12) and de-dollarization campaigns (Chapter 11) will migrate liquidity to new systems. What now trickles will soon flood. The safe asset will lose its sanctuary.

2. The True Policy Path — The Path of Endurance

The second path is endurance—the discipline to accept pain in exchange for permanence.
It recognizes that debt is not to be eliminated but managed through the golden rule of sustainability:

g > r — the growth rate of the economy must exceed the real interest rate on the debt.

As long as productivity and innovation expand faster than the cost of borrowing, the burden shrinks in relative terms. The Mountain of Debt becomes a hill of prosperity.

This requires what Chapter 15 called the **Growth Agenda**: targeted public investment in infrastructure, technology, and human capital that raises the denominator (*g*) instead of merely inflating the numerator (*r*). Fiscal responsibility is not austerity; it is intelligent expansion.

The Final Condition

Dollar supremacy is not a birthright; it is a renewable contract built on four conditions of trust.

1. **Honesty — The Transparency of the Borrowing Ritual.** Every public auction is a confession of accountability: the world can see what America pays for its privilege.
2. **Safety — The Independence of the Federal Reserve.** The Printer must never become the Spender's servant. The firewall between monetary and fiscal power is sacred.
3. **Liquidity — The Depth of the Treasury Market.** The world must always be able to convert faith into cash instantly. Liquidity is credibility made visible.
4. **Growth — The Nation's Capacity to Earn Its Future.** Without productivity, even the safest promise decays. Growth is the solvent that keeps the debt from hardening into burden.

Lose any one of these four, and the paradox collapses. Preserve them, and the rent remains affordable forever.

The Price of Endurance

The Dollar Paradox is not a flaw to be fixed; it is the architecture of the modern world.
Its survival demands that the United States continue to pay for what it built—not in tribute, but in transparency.

Every interest check mailed to a pension fund in Tokyo or a central bank in Riyadh is proof that the system still works. Every debt auction completed without coercion reaffirms the unwritten promise that power in America remains *earned*, not decreed.

To default—politically, morally, or financially—would be to end the only empire in history sustained entirely by trust.

The Rent and the Republic

The rent of global power is not measured in dollars; it is measured in restraint.
It is the discipline to borrow visibly rather than print invisibly, to endure scrutiny rather than command obedience.

The question that will define the next century is not whether America can afford its debt.
It is whether America can still afford its *discipline.*

If it can—if it remembers that pain is the price of permanence—the Dollar Paradox will endure, and the United States will continue to rule the invisible empire of credit it built from faith, law, and the courage to pay its own rent

BIBLIOGRAPHY

This bibliography includes foundational works and official sources consulted in the research, fact-checking, and preparation of *The Dollar Paradox*. Sources are limited to materials published or publicly available by November 18, 2025, the book's original publication date.

I. Foundational Economic and Monetary Theory

Bagehot, Walter. *Lombard Street: A Description of the Money Market.* Henry S. King & Co., 1873.

Blanchard, Olivier. "Public Debt and Low Interest Rates." *American Economic Review* 109, no. 4 (April 2019): 1197–1229.

Domar, Evsey D. "The 'Burden of the Debt' and the National Income." *American Economic Review* 34, no. 4 (December 1944): 798–827.

Ferguson, Niall. *The Ascent of Money: A Financial History of the World.* Penguin Press, 2008.

Fisher, Irving. *The Purchasing Power of Money: Its Determination and Relation to Credit, Interest and Crises.* Macmillan, 1911.

Friedman, Milton, and Anna J. Schwartz. *A Monetary History of the United States, 1867–1960.* Princeton University Press, 1963.

Keynes, John Maynard. *The General Theory of Employment, Interest and Money.* Macmillan, 1936.

Kindleberger, Charles P., and Robert Z. Aliber. *Manias, Panics, and Crashes: A History of Financial Crises.* 6th ed. Palgrave Macmillan, 2011.

Minsky, Hyman P. *Stabilizing an Unstable Economy.* Yale University Press, 1986.

II. Central Banking, Treasury Operations, and Fiscal Governance

Bernanke, Ben S. *21st Century Monetary Policy: The Federal Reserve from the Great Inflation to COVID-19.* W. W. Norton, 2022.

Blinder, Alan S. *Central Banking in Theory and Practice.* MIT Press, 1998.

Board of Governors of the Federal Reserve System. *The Fed Explained: What the Central Bank Does.* 11th ed. Board of Governors of the Federal Reserve System, 2021.

Board of Governors of the Federal Reserve System. "Interest on Reserve Balances (IORB) Frequently Asked Questions." September 23, 2025.

Board of Governors of the Federal Reserve System. "Section 14. Open-Market Operations." *Federal Reserve Act*, as amended.

Congressional Budget Office. *The Budget and Economic Outlook: 2025 to 2035.* January 2025.

Congressional Budget Office. *The Long-Term Budget Outlook: 2025 to 2055.* March 27, 2025.

Federal Reserve Bank of New York. "Joint Announcement by the Secretary of the Treasury and the Chairman of the Board of Governors, and of the Federal Open Market Committee, of the Federal Reserve System." Circular 3665, March 4, 1951.

Federal Reserve Bank of New York. "Primary Dealers." Markets & Policy Implementation.

Federal Reserve Bank of New York, Markets Group. *Open Market Operations During 2024.* June 3, 2025.

Garbade, Kenneth D. "Direct Purchases of U.S. Treasury Securities by Federal Reserve Banks." Federal Reserve Bank of New York Staff Report No. 684, August 2014.

Garbade, Kenneth D. "The Institutionalization of Treasury Note and Bond Auctions, 1970–75." *Federal Reserve Bank of New York Economic Policy Review* 10, no. 1 (May 2004).

Goodhart, Charles A. E. *The Evolution of Central Banks.* MIT Press, 1988.

Hetzel, Robert L., and Ralph F. Leach. "The Treasury-Federal Reserve Accord: A New Narrative Account." *Federal Reserve Bank of Richmond Economic Quarterly* 87, no. 1 (Winter 2001): 33–55.

U.S. Department of the Treasury. "Quarterly Refunding Statement of Deputy Assistant Secretary for Federal Finance Brian Smith." November 5, 2025.

U.S. Department of the Treasury, Bureau of the Fiscal Service. *Debt to the Penny.* Fiscal Data.

U.S. Department of the Treasury, Bureau of the Fiscal Service. *Treasury Auction Regulations (31 CFR Part 356): Uniform Offering Circular.* TreasuryDirect.

U.S. Government Accountability Office. *Debt Limit: Statutory Changes Could Avert the Risk of a Government Default and Its Potentially Severe Consequences.* GAO-25-107089. December 11, 2024.

U.S. Government Accountability Office. *The Nation's Fiscal Health: Strategy Needed as Debt Levels Accelerate.* GAO-25-107714. February 5, 2025.

III. Financial Architecture, Collateral, Repo, and Shadow Banking

Brunnermeier, Markus K., and Lasse Heje Pedersen. "Market Liquidity and Funding Liquidity." *Review of Financial Studies* 22, no. 6 (June 2009): 2201–2238.

Du, Wenxin, Alexander Tepper, and Adrien Verdelhan. "Deviations from Covered Interest Rate Parity." *Journal of Finance* 73, no. 3 (June 2018): 915–957.

Federal Reserve Bank of New York. "Statement Regarding Repurchase Operation." September 17, 2019.

Gorton, Gary B. *Slapped by the Invisible Hand: The Panic of 2007.* Oxford University Press, 2010.

Krishnamurthy, Arvind, and Annette Vissing-Jorgensen. "The Aggregate Demand for Treasury Debt." *Journal of Political Economy* 120, no. 2 (April 2012): 233–267.

McCulley, Paul. "The Shadow Banking System and Hyman Minsky's Economic Journey." In *Insights into the Global Financial Crisis*, edited by Laurence B. Siegel, 257–268. Research Foundation of CFA Institute, 2009.

Mehrling, Perry. *The New Lombard Street: How the Fed Became the Dealer of Last Resort.* Princeton University Press, 2011.

Pozsar, Zoltan. *Shadow Banking: The Money View.* Office of Financial Research Working Paper No. 14-04, July 2, 2014.

IV. Dollar Supremacy, Geopolitics, Sanctions, and Digital Money

Bank for International Settlements Innovation Hub. "Project mBridge Reached Minimum Viable Product Stage." Updated November 11, 2024.

BRICS. *Rio de Janeiro Declaration: Strengthening Global South Cooperation for a More Inclusive and Sustainable Governance.* July 6, 2025.

Cross-Border Interbank Payment System. "CIPS Participants Announcement No. 114." October 31, 2025.

Eichengreen, Barry. *Exorbitant Privilege: The Rise and Fall of the Dollar and the Future of the International Monetary System.* Oxford University Press, 2011.

European Commission. *The EU in 2024: General Report on the Activities of the European Union.* Chapter 1, "The EU's Support for Ukraine." 2025.

Federal Reserve Bank of Boston. "Boston Fed, MIT Complete Research Project into Feasibility of a Central Bank Digital Currency." December 22, 2022.

Board of Governors of the Federal Reserve System. *Money and Payments: The U.S. Dollar in the Age of Digital Transformation.* January 2022.

Helleiner, Eric. *States and the Reemergence of Global Finance: From Bretton Woods to the 1990s.* Cornell University Press, 1994.

International Monetary Fund. "IMF Data Brief: Currency Composition of Official Foreign Exchange Reserves." October 2, 2025.

National Archives and Records Administration. Executive Order 12170, "Blocking Iranian Government Property." November 14, 1979.

Office of Foreign Assets Control, U.S. Department of the Treasury. "Libya EO; Libyan Sanctions Designations; General License No. 1." February 25, 2011.

People's Bank of China, Working Group on E-CNY Research and Development. *Progress of Research & Development of E-CNY in China.* July 2021.

Prasad, Eswar S. *The Dollar Trap: How the U.S. Dollar Tightened Its Grip on Global Finance.* Princeton University Press, 2014.

Subacchi, Paola. *The People's Money: How China Is Building a Global Currency.* Columbia University Press, 2016.

SWIFT. "FIN." Global Financial Messaging.

The White House. Executive Order 14178, "Strengthening American Leadership in Digital Financial Technology." January 23, 2025.

United States. *Guiding and Establishing National Innovation for U.S. Stablecoins Act (GENIUS Act).* Pub. L. 119-27, 139 Stat. 419. July 18, 2025.

U.S. Department of the Treasury. "Treasury Prohibits Transactions with Central Bank of Russia and Imposes Sanctions on Key Sources of Russia's Wealth." February 28, 2022.

U.S. Department of the Treasury. "Russian Elites, Proxies, and Oligarchs Task Force Joint Statement." June 29, 2022.

U.S. Government Accountability Office. *The U.S.-Saudi Arabian Joint Commission on Economic Cooperation.* ID-79-7. March 22, 1979.

Tooze, Adam. *Crashed: How a Decade of Financial Crises Changed the World.* Viking, 2018.

Index

Use the subentries to follow the book's major arguments, institutions, countries, and policy mechanisms. Page references identify principal discussions rather than every passing mention.

D

E

About the Author

Bosco Mutarambirwa is a researcher, analyst, and author whose work explores the intersection of geopolitics, money, and power.

Drawing on a background in global finance and political economy, he dissects how nations construct credibility, how institutions manufacture trust, and how the modern world's prosperity depends on invisible systems few ever question.

Mutarambirwa's books—including *Africa's New Scramble: Lobito vs. Belt and Road in the Superpower Showdown* and *The Dollar Paradox*—combine investigative clarity with narrative drive, revealing the economic logic behind political decisions that shape the century.

He writes and publishes under **Sterling Analytics Media**, where his work continues to bridge scholarship and storytelling for a global audience.

Disclaimer

This book is a work of nonfiction. It is based on factual research, publicly available data, and the author's original analysis and interpretation.
Every effort has been made to ensure the accuracy of the information contained herein; however, the publisher and author make no representations or warranties with respect to the completeness or accuracy of the contents and assume no responsibility for errors or omissions.

The material is provided for informational and educational purposes only and should not be construed as financial, legal, or investment advice. Readers are encouraged to perform their own research and consult qualified professionals before making any financial or policy decisions.

All opinions expressed are those of the author and do not necessarily reflect the views of any institution, organization, or government referenced in this work.

www.ingramcontent.com/pod-product-compliance
Lightning Source LLC
LaVergne TN
LVHW052033200926
848481LV00005B/1665